TRADING FULL CIRCLE

The Complete UndergroundTrader System
For Timing & Profiting in All Financial Markets

Jea Yu

MARKETPLACE BOOKS®
GLENELG, MARYLAND

Publisher: Chris Myers

VP/General Manager: John Boyer

Senior Editor: Courtney Jenkins

Art Director: Larry Strauss

Graphic Designer: Jennifer Marin

Graphic Design Intern: Jessica Weedlun

This publication is designed to provide accurate and authoritative information in regard to the subject matter covered. It is sold with the understanding that neither the author nor the publisher is engaged in rendering legal, accounting, or other professional service. If legal advice or other expert assistance is required, the services of a competent professional person should be sought.

From a Declaration of Principles jointly adopted by a Committee of the American Bar Association and a Committee of Publishers.

This book, along with other books, is available at discounts that make it realistic to provide them as gifts to your customers, clients, and staff. For more information on these long lasting, cost effective premiums, please call us at 800-272-2855 or e-mail us at sales@traderslibrary.com.

RealTick graphics used with permission of Townsend Analytics, Ltd.©1986-2007 Townsend Analytics, Ltd. All rights reserved. RealTick is a registered trademark of Townsend Analytics, Ltd.
Printed in the United States of America.

Library of Congress Cataloging-in-Publication Data

Yu, Jea.
  Trading Full Circle : The Complete Undergroundtrader System for Timing & Profiting in All Financial Markets / Jea Yu.
      p. cm.
  Includes bibliographical references and index.
   ISBN-13: 978-1-59280-390-3 (hardcover : alk. paper)
   ISBN-10: 1-59280-390-3 (hardcover : alk. paper) 1. Investment analysis. 2. Portfolio management. 3. Investments. I. Title.
  HG4529.Y8 2010
  332.6–dc22
                                      2010002746

"Jea Yu's latest book is a breath of fresh air, chock full of tape reading gems and time-tested trading strategies that actually make money. His razor-sharp focus on mastering today's tough markets will help traders at all experience levels."

Alan Farley, Editor & Publisher, Hard Right Edge
www.hardrightedge.com

"In an early part of *Trading Full Circle: The Complete UndergroundTrader System for Timing and Profiting in All Financial Markets*, Yu makes reference to 'Acquiring the Edge,' and this book certainly gives you the edge. I am reminded of a Japanese proverb, 'He whose ranks are united in purpose will be victorious.' By bringing together the specific trading strategies with his playbook section, detailed chapters on how to prepare psychologically and emotionally for trading, and Yu's focus on risk control, *Trading Full Circle* will be a resource you will use over and over again. In addition, it is fun to read!

Steve Nison, President, www.candlecharts.com
The very first to reveal candlesticks to the Western world
Author of *Japanese Candlestick Charting Techniques*

"What a great book—one thing that Jea emphasized was the fact we need to have that failure and pain, get to know what it feels like to lose, to have a beat down from the market both mentally and financially. Those that learn to lose and feel the pain will be better prepared for success. I have said for years, your success will be based on your ability to learn to be a good loser and accept pain as your friend. What great insight from Jea, what a great read!"

Christopher Terry
LBRGroup.com

"In his latest book, Jea has managed to discuss the potential pitfalls of passionate trading by sharing the experience he has gained via trial and error over the years. His plain speak and witty anecdotes set this trading guide apart as both an educational and entertaining read. Every trader who reads this book will feel that Jea is speaking directly to them at some point or another."

Chadd Hessing, Owner and President
Cobra Trading, Inc.
www.cobratrading.com

THIS BOOK IS DEDICATED TO:

*My princess, **KATANA LUCIA YU**,*
who brought vibrancy, bliss, warmth, and salvation to my life,

*My queenbee, **BENITA**,*
for her unshakeable resolve, love, and faith,

*My brother, **KEVIN**,*
who showed me the essence of brotherhood,
loyalty, and compassion

*My mom, **DUCK**,*
the strongest, most loving, and persistent
mother on the planet, imho

*My other mom, **MRS. VILLARI**,*
for believing in me from the beginning,

*My sister, **JULIAY** and her beautiful family,*
for their loving support and care

*My brother and sister-in-law, **BILL** AND **LINDA**,*
for being a warm and supportive sanctuary,

*My friend, **JOHN BOYER**,*
for the gift of redemption,

*… and last, but not least, my good buddy **PAIN**,*
for giving me clarity and enough material to
complete the legacy… and always sticking around… doh!

CONTENTS

INTRODUCTION

This book was ten years (and ten thousand tears) in the making. Ten years, thousands of hours in the market, thousands of traders coming and going worldwide. Extreme highs and stank lows. Fast women, fast cars… oops. Wrong movie.

I've been in the crevice and corn hole of every market paradigm shift almost every single day since January 1, 1999, when UndergroundTrader.com officially opened its doors. The reception was overwhelming and ground shaking. The markets were recovering from the Pacific Rim crisis as Greenspan went on a monster rate cut campaign that fueled the Nasdaq to 5,000 and sent the Internet companies parabolic. Those were great times. Stocks were trading in fractions, usually with only eight price increments between the dollars, instead of the 100 levels in pennies now. Broadcom (BRCM) was trading in the $200s, JDS Uniphase (JDSU) in the $200s, Cisco (CSCO) in the $90s, EBAY in the $300s, and YHOO ramped up through $300, driving up the Internet and IPO mania. It was common to see stocks move up $50 in a day. NetBank (NTBK) popped $100 one day. EntreMed (ENMD) single digit stock gapped to $70

"The purpose of life is to find happiness in the misery of living…"

after a halt, and Emulex (ELX) tanked from the $120s to $20s in 15 minutes before halting in the high $30s to re-open $100 higher due to a false press release. It was the wild, wild, and wilder west. Heck, there were still ax market makers back in the day. My first book, *The Undergroundtrader.com Guide to Electronic Trading: Day Trading Techniques of a Master Guerrilla Trader*, debuted well in the Amazon.com top 100 list. Day trading was white hot. The money came fast and heavy. Life was good—too good—to last.

As many rate cuts as Greenspan implemented to stir up the economy, he hiked them back up just as much—I believe he made 11 rate hikes—while cryptically spouting "irrational exuberance" to send the markets cratering. That's like the boy who led everyone into the movie theatre only to light a match and yell fire.

Imagine watching a show in a crowded movie theater on a Saturday night. Also imagine that you are wanted by the FBI, who has just surrounded both exits out of the theatre, waiting for you to come out, as there is no other escape route. What would you do in this situation to escape? Light your popcorn and yell fire! This would cause a hysteric panic situation that would overwhelm the FBI agents as they get trampled by the mob trying to escape alive. That's exactly what happened to the markets—a panic situation.

Nasdaq lost over 80% off its highs. YHOO, which traded in the $300s, tanked as low as $8. IPO paper billionaires who exercised some cheap options, anticipating their stocks' recovery, were rudely awakened when the IRS came knocking, looking for their cut despite the stocks losing 90% of their value. The bear market hit with devastating force. People who thought they were day traders were exposed for bagholders. Big traders who stacked the bids with $50,000 blocks to squeeze out the shorts started getting filled and subsequently massacred. I knew a kid who turned $30,000 to $2 million during the Internet mania, only to blow out in less than two months after the start of the bear market.

The bear market wasn't too shabby for the traders who actually used charts. It was just as lucrative on the downside on the backs of the hobbyists. What killed the traders and market makers was decimalization. The stupid penny increments added 100 price intervals in between dollar price levels. Market makers were being squeezed out on margins, and day traders were making much less. The penny increments were the stupidest idea ever. Who cares if mom and pop can read a price quote without having to figure out the fractions? What good is the "liquidity" when their stocks are losing over 70% of their value? The exchanges were the only ones to benefit, with their volume based fees.

Ever the undecipherable, monotone, laggard tool that he was, Greenspan cut rates in a fury, spawning a housing bubble, and in effect, taking us out of the frying pan and into the mouth of the volcano. We know what happened with that bubble. How many Fed chairmen can claim two massive economic bubbles during their reign?

With the double whammy of the bear claws and decimalization, day traders disappeared like the dinosaurs, as did numerous market making firms. The ECNs took reign, notably ARCA, ISLD, and INCA. Then 9/11 happened when markets were already weak. The war in Afghanistan kicked off a market rally that nearly doubled the Dow. Hedge funds became the hottest worst kept secret, making the rich richer, especially the big brokers catering to these leviathans through their prime broker services. Program trading volumes skyrocketed as black box, gray box, and algorithm trading grabbed chunks of liquidity. Dark pools have gotten larger, dealing only with institutional clientele. Goldman Sachs is making billions with their black box programs capturing spreads, liquidity, and flash quotes. What about the balanced playing field and transparency? Never.

The game is to find transparency before it becomes too transparent. Limit exposing your flaws while trying to exploit the market's.

Everything in this book is first-hand knowledge, revealed as a result of thousands of hours of market participation. If anything, it will save you the ten years I spent to complete the trading system. I have found that rarity in and of itself determines value. Demand usually follows. Build it—and hold out long enough—and they will come. Every thought and word in this book has been meticulously handcrafted through blood, sweat, tears, and broken keyboards.

It is the culmination of a journey and all its lessons. As much as this book is about the markets, it goes much deeper. It started with the markets and manifested into life epiphanies. You mean the markets are correlated with life? Believe me, it's true, it's true! That is what the journey is about; finding the truth, tasting the essence, and bathing in the enlightenment.

So let's get started.

PART 1

ACQUIRING THE EDGE BY STARTING AT THE END

CHAPTER 1

STARTING WITH FAILURE

We've all failed. No one is excluded.

The journey is about coming to terms with the truth. The vast majority of traders ultimately blow out. You have most likely blown out once, twice, or more. The reality is that trading is getting ever more difficult as markets get more so-called efficient.

So with the odds against you, why do you keep coming back?

The fact that you are still coming back is the key testament to your willingness to be in the 1% of traders who are consistently profitable. The mere fact that you have purchased this book is the litmus test. Congrats, you passed.

The journey of achieving "full circle" requires failure. It is only through these failures that we can learn. Learning in its purest form is error driven. The greater the magnitude of failure, the more quickly we learn.

"Full circle" means failing and coming back to evolve. Failure gives you a different perspective, if you pay attention. A full circle is a revolution; a completion without gaps, starting from one point and ending back at that point. The start and the end is the same; however, the significance lies in the journey undertaken to arrive at the destination.

The human component is imperfect. Humans can not compete against the efficiency of a machine. However, humans can adapt and out think, as long as they protect their flaws from being exposed. The purpose of the markets is to exploit inefficiencies and flaws. As a trader, you have to prevent your own inefficiencies from being exposed. This is the constant cat and mouse game that defines the market action. As much as this may sound psychological, the remedies come in physical form.

The theme is the achievement of "full circle," which means the completion of a journey. A circle is void of gaps. It characterizes clarity, completion, and most importantly, closure. The end point is identical to the starting point, ironically. Once a trader exhausts his efforts to find the "holy grail," and often blows out his account in the process, that is when the full circle effect materializes. The trader comes to the understanding that the reason for his failure was the execution of the game plan, not the game plan itself. Once a trader understands and embraces this thinking, he is ready to move forward.

So much as has been focused on various methods, patterns, and setups to the point of total exhaustion. A void has materialized in the market education space. The underlying theme has always been to find transparency before it becomes too transparent. The market is not only a zero sum ponzi game, but indiscriminative when it punishes—generous at times, and merciless at its worst. Everyone understands the markets are dynamic, yet most management systems are static, thereby causing the distortion in the results.

Why is it when a trader follows methods to a tee, he tends to make nice profits during one week and then gets splattered the following week? When this happens, the trader will conclude that the methods need further tweaking and will search out other models and setups. He may be profitable for another week or two, and then get slammed the following week. Once again, the trader comes to the conclusion that the methods are at fault and he again tries to tweak. He will also spend time back-testing the setups and methods. The trader may continue this process relentlessly for months on end, only to end up with further losses. Every time the trader goes through a winning phase, he is relieved into thinking he has finally found the right combination, only to have the rug pulled when he goes into a losing period again. This is an endless cycle that eventually concludes with the trader voluntarily quitting, or blowing out his account.

This is the standard evolutionary cycle of a trader. Having catered to over 10,000 traders worldwide over the past decade, I have been in a privileged position to intimately witness this phenomenon unfold for a vast majority of traders. I too have questioned why the methods can be so effective, with pinpoint accuracy at times, while being ambiguous and blurry at other times. The one factor that all too many traders tend to leave out when developing methods and backtesting is the very fact that markets are dynamic, not static. Most people tend to naively believe that markets are consistent; that they will repeat themselves in a predictable manner, and will follow time-tested static patterns. Or, they will apply dynamic methods while unconsciously assuming a static market in the background.

> Markets are dynamic, not static.

When a consistent method or system is discovered and applied successfully in real time, it is rarely the system that needs adjustment. The real adjustment lies in what environment that particular system can most effectively be implemented. In other words, the markets themselves play a larger role in the success of any method than the method itself. The new, "efficient," computer program-dominated markets prey upon the less efficient participants. This cannibalism is the same paradigm on a new scale. If you have flaws, the market will exploit them. In fact, the market will give you the rope to hang yourself. Therefore, traders need to start by galvanizing themselves before taking part in the game of trading.

USING FAILURE AS A GROWTH TOOL

Sun Tzu, the author of *The Art of War*, once advised a Chinese emperor during a war to pit his small army, outnumbered 10 to 1, directly into their path of destruction, guaranteeing absolutely no escape and even less chance for survival. His small army had no choice but to fight to the death. An amazing thing happened. When put with their backs against the wall, the men, having nothing to lose, fought with ferocity unseen and emerged victorious.

Strip a person of all inessentials and take him to the edge of the abyss, and you will find that that is when they learn the most about themselves. They say the brain feeds on failure. The more wrong you are, the quicker you learn. When you expect failure, that is when you are most prepared for it. When you have already tasted failure, it becomes familiar enough to prepare for it. In this preparation is how you avoid it.

When failure is anticipated, it immediately forces us to prepare. Learning from failure can only be accomplished when we fail more efficiently. There are two ways to accomplish this.

- **Soften the blow.** In trading, this means lower your downside risk by minimizing share size to a point where the maximum loss is insignificant. The key word here is to *minimize* the potential damage.

- **Scale down expectations preemptively.** It is human nature and a misnomer that once you succeed, you need to step it up and push harder. This is one of the key missteps in trading that can turn a small profit in the morning into a very large loss by the end of the day. It is very hard to scale down expectations in the heat of the battle, especially during a losing session. This is why it must be done preemptively. A key word that will be a cornerstone in your trading is *scale*. Scaling means to measure, adjust, and calibrate to attain the right balance. Scaling your risk. Scaling your shares. Scaling your allocation. Scaling your charts. Scaling your progress.

Failure triggers a pain reaction. Pain is avoided at all costs by human beings. This is why people shun failure. One has to reprogram the notion of failure to disassociate the pain trigger. I will defend my buddy Pain a little later. Poor little guy.

FAILING EFFICIENTLY FOR POST-TRAUMATIC GROWTH

Trauma is needed to stimulate growth. When failure is done efficiently, post-traumatic growth is triggered. It's not really that far fetched.

I'm sure you've heard the term muscle failure. To stimulate muscle growth, you need to exercise your muscles to failure through high intensity repetitions and sets. Bodybuilders constantly subject their muscles to trauma by breaking down muscle tissue to stimulate growth. Voila, post-traumatic growth. This is not an analogy, but a parallel. It is common practice in a physical fitness sense. It also applies psychologically.

As you see, trauma alone can't build muscle. Trauma is one of three key components. Trauma alone doesn't metabolize into growth. Proper rest and nutrition are essential components in addition to trauma for muscle growth. Proper resilience and enduring effort are essentials to psychological growth. Physical and psychological are correlated.

In bodybuilding, proper rest and nutrition also play a key role in triggering post-traumatic growth. The psychological parallel would be resilience and enduring effort.

The key to resilience is thinking more flexibly and learning to increase your array of options. Your mind is a courtroom where negative thoughts are put on trial. You need to rebut these with evidence to prove that the negative belief is flawed. The bad thought dies when doubt is cast upon it through evidence. This is an example of the counteract remedy for affliction. There are three remedies I will discuss further on in this book.

"Failure stripped away everything inessential. It taught me things about myself I could have learned no other way."

- J.K. Rowling

MY FRIEND PAIN

Pain doesn't suck. He is just misunderstood. It reminds me of a movie starring Brad Pitt called *Meet Joe Black*, based on the original movie, *Death Takes a Vacation*. Pitt plays Death in human form. What if Pain was a human being? Put yourself in his shoes. Everyone avoids pain. It's human nature. Pain is universally scorned and beaten. He's got to be the loneliest guy in the world. It's no wonder he's so angry.

FORGING A MEANINGFUL RELATIONSHIP WITH PAIN

Knowing that Pain is so widely hated, what would he do if someone accepted, respected, and embraced him? How touched would he be? How grateful would Pain be? How would Pain reciprocate the friendship? I know. Pain rewards his good buddies with strength and clarity. Strength is attained from the toughening of Pain thresholds. Hey, the more you hang out with Pain, the more acclimated you get. Clarity is gained from the natural filtering effect that Pain creates, as only the worthy ones are left when everyone else runs away. Nothing worth attaining ever came easy.

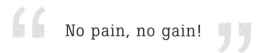

No pain, no gain!

PAIN'S GOT A BROTHER, PLEASURE

Here's a simple experiment: try stubbing your toe really hard in front of a mirror. Remember that look on your face. Go have an orgasm (how is up to you) and look in the mirror. Notice a similarity? Your facial expressions are identical. This is because the brain processes physical pain and pleasure in the same area. The physical outward reactions are identical.

"There is nothing good or bad, but thinking makes it so."

- Hamlet

GUILT VERSUS SHAME

These are two common emotions that are the product of repeated failure. We need to ascertain the differences between the two and nip something right in the bud from the get-go. Guilt results from something you've done. This can be fixed. Shame is something you are. This is a cancer. Feel guilty all you want, but never feel shame. Repeat after me: "There is no shame in my game." Shame is so debilitating because it invites all sorts of "nasties," including, but not limited to: depression, anxiety, panic attacks, low morale, fatigue, low self-esteem, and ultimately, surrender. Shame mutates the ability to metabolize failure positively. They haven't found a cure for cancer yet, so let's prevent this cancer before it has a chance to spread. All your feelings of shame should be moved and put into the guilt box. Don't even use the word. You should be ashamed to even use the word shame! Please erase the word from your vocabulary. Thank you. End of story.

Repeated failure can crush one's spirit. This is why one has to learn to fail more efficiently. Two steps forward and one step back is still making progress. In terms of trading, this is called a trend. No trend maintains constant momentum. Everything needs to follow a workable pace. Breakout, peak, exhaust, base, and breakout again. With each failure, one has to learn from it, recalibrate the emotions, and make efforts to try again. Failure, if anything, is another chance to try again.

COGNITIVE DISSONANCE THEORY

Your mind is constantly being bombarded with little bits of information known as cognitions. Each of these cognitions will carry a negative or a positive connotation. The magnitude of the dissonance between positive and negative cognitions will ultimately determine stress levels.

Developed by Leon Festinger in 1971, the cognitive dissonance theory explains that humans seek to alleviate stress by either changing beliefs or behaviors. This can be done consciously, and in most cases, is done sub-consciously. It is the mind's natural defense mechanism to prevent one from having a meltdown. However, this doesn't imply that the actions taken are efficient, or for the better. Cognitive dissonance theory explains how normal people, when placed in certain situations, can join paramilitary cults, or commit heinous crimes.

On the outside, it is easy to judge and decry the foolishness of these perpetrators. However, when placed in the eye of the storm, it is a different story, as anyone who has blown out their trading accounts can attest to. We have all committed heinous crimes to our trading accounts at one point or another. We can all plead guilty to that.

THE MENACE OF CONVENTIONAL WISDOM

Misery loves company. It is easier to convince 100 people in a hall than one person. Here's a dose of reality: the majority will always be wrong in the long run. Those who escaped the Nasdaq 5000 bubble got caught in the housing bubble. Conventional wisdom says stocks have out-performed every financial instrument, including real estate. Docs that sound familiar?

THE STOCK MARKET BAIT-N-SWITCH
You've heard it a million times from stock brokers and analysts. "The stock market has outperformed all financial instruments over time, in-cluding real estate."

By "stock market," we can assume they are talking about the Dow Jones Industrial Average. This is an index composed of 30 stocks that represent the leading companies in the strongest sectors of the economy. Even with the Dow at 9,000, it has climbed tremendously since the beginning, right? Wrong. The Dow Jones, like any other index, reserves the right to replace underperforming stocks. They get to cherry pick the best performers and swap out the duds.

It's not a static index and the components are not static, unlike real estate. The original Dow Jones index was composed of 100 stocks in the late 1800s. Do you know how many of them are still in the index? Only one, GE. It was kicked out once and they brought it back. The rest of the 99 original stocks either went out of business or merged and then probably went out of business. Smells like a bait-and-switch. Land, as in real estate, can't be swapped out if a patch underperforms. It's stuck and static, and if you dig real deep, you might uncover the carcasses of some of those original Dow stocks!

HUMAN THEORY

Bear with me—I created this theory, but stole (borrowed) many of the concepts.

Human beings seek comfort in two ways: being amongst others in the crowd, and offloading accountability.

George Foreman once said, "If I loan you one million dollars, and your cousin one thousand dollars, I will most likely be more concerned about that one grand because I can comprehend that. I can't really comprehend a million dollars." They say it's easier to convince one hundred persons than one person. It boils down to group theory. People have an innate need to be part of the crowd.

To accept whatever happens is an offloading of responsibility. The notion of fate is a great scam. You can't ever refute it, since it's only shown after the fact. Anything that happens is a result of fate. Fate takes all the credit. To believe in fate is a sign of complacency and pure laziness. It is just as bad as curve fitting an outcome and labeling it fate simply because the person didn't make the effort beforehand, when he could have narrowed the odds for a desired result.

Don't fall on your sword.

STARTING AT THE END

A full circle starts and ends at the same point, a full 360-degree revolution. A circle in and of itself is void of any gaps; it is continuous and complete. The analogy applies completely to the journey of the trader, from the booming, day trading, Internet-mania bull market days to the bust of the bear market and decimalization, and then the rebuilding period that brought in a more educated, technical, and capitalized crowd. The markets have evolved, but that is not always a good thing.

As any endeavor, sport, technology, or business evolves and becomes more efficient, it also diminishes the niche, and the edge. It is this type of thinking that makes me believe that there are no more Microsofts out there to be formed. That niche was found, filled, and saturated. The markets have so many more participants now than even two years ago. There is a capacity to evolution, bleak as that sounds.

As traders, we want to foster a condition once possessed as a child—the belief that anything is possible. Some call it naivety, some call it purity, some call it innocence. To believe once again, to reawaken what died, to reawaken the inner child. To take every situation as a learning experience and nothing more.

While we can't go back, we can place ourselves in an environment, as long as we identify it as such—as a sanctuary—where anything is possible and you earn the right to erase your past mistakes by paying through enduring effort accompanied by an open mind. As adults or pro wrestling fans, this condition is called suspension of disbelief.

Full circle—to start and end up in the same place with the experience of completing a journey. We all start off as children, and then something gets lost in the transition to adulthood and acclimating to society and relationships. To embrace the underlying essence of full circle means to work backwards to reawaken. Note that that something is not lost, just buried.

As Carlito Brigante beautifully stated in the movie *Carlito's Way*, "People don't change, they just get tired of running." This expression sums it all up. Something gets lost in the transition.

People get into situations, and conditions are forced upon them to the point of embedding the belief that the essence of their identity is dependent on these factors.

What worked back then has a very hard time working now. That's evolution in a nutshell. This is why people who have talk shows on certain financial channels claiming their success when they were running their hedge fund have no credibility with me. Those were the "good old days." With evolution comes the inevitable wall where there are just too many participants and not enough of an edge.

Technical indicators and trading methods come and go. And methods are theories at best, because they are never 100 percent. One must understand the nature of the beast. What is the market and who are the participants? Therein lies a clue to attaining the elusive edge.

Human beings, at least for now, are still in control. Program trading, black box trading, grey box trading, ECNs, and dark pools are all gaining in participation, but it is still humans that program the algorithms.

NO WIN AGAINST EGO

What is the stock market? The market is a cannibalistic man-made predator that preys on its weakest participants. It's that simple. What is the purpose of the game? The purpose is two-fold. To find transparency before it gets too transparent. You limit exposing your flaws while exploiting the flaws of the market. At the worst times, the purpose is to keep your profits and prevent exposure of flaws.

The psychological aspects of trading have been addressed and written about in countless books, seminars, and articles. I have seen and experienced the importance of a mental edge firsthand and through the eyes of over ten thousand traders that have used UndergroundTrader.com since its inception. This experience has given me a broader and deeper insight than most.

Let's get some simple premises established. In every battle, there are two sides, composed of the opponent and the victim. The victim is usually the one who thinks he is winning. This is because the opponent allows the victim to win a few battles. When the opponent finally makes his move and discloses transparency, the victim unravels. This is when the opponent goes in for the kill by simply allowing the victim to destroy himself.

Every man has an enemy within. He can never win against this enemy. This enemy is called ego. Ego sets the bar subconsciously. Once you fall under that bar, the ego goes to work. The lower you slip, the harder ego pushes, until your eventual demise. The cliché "cut off the nose to spite the face" is based on this very human phenomenon. The worst thing that can happen to anyone is to walk into a casino and win big. That sets the bar. It's the minefield theory as mentioned in my last book, *Secrets of the Underground Trader: Advanced Methods for Short-Term and Swing Trading Any Market*. Since the money was made easily, there is a dangerous precedent that is set going forward. Secondly, the person is more susceptible to losing multiples of his winnings because he tells himself that he is playing with house money when he tries to push his luck. This can happen on the second visit, or the tenth visit. Once a "mark" tastes a win, he is usually sucked back in. This is why casinos are so profitable. Throw in an element called "desperate money," and it turns into a catastrophe. Desperate money means the mark must win in order to pay the rent and put food on the table. This is a double whammy, as the ego is even stronger.

Watch a great movie called *Revolver*, starring Jason Stratham (who also appeared in the *Transporter* films). I recommend watching this movie to all traders, as it masterfully illustrates the embedded threat that every trader (and human being) must be aware of to prevent from unraveling.

TRADING ENVIRONMENTS

If one understands simple cause and effect, the goal is to avoid the cause. If you know that driving into a bad neighborhood at night will lead to getting car jacked, what do you do? You avoid going into that neighborhood at night. You keep going straight and don't take a detour. Sounds simple right? It should be, but it's not.

The market's trading environment is a primary element to success. This refutes the old beliefs that trading method and management alone are the keys to success. I have seen weak traders make more money in a fertile environment than strong traders in an infertile environment. When I refer to a fertile or infertile environment, I am not referring to an up or down market. I am referring to the trading environment.

A fertile environment has follow-through, liquidity, stock and sector synergy, momentum, and most importantly, an effective foreshadowing element. An infertile environment is the opposite. It is choppy, usually flat, and illiquid. A fertile environment can turn infertile in minutes. Luckily, when there is the most chaos and panic is when a fertile environment is created. This is usually found in the pre-market and the first hour of the market open. Once things settle down, the fertility is usually the first to go, as everyone is trying to leapfrog each other using every edge, resulting in coin-toss setups. Oscillation players may win for a while as the breakout players get chopped. Once the oscillation players let their guards down, they take the average ordinary looking wiggle and jam it into an extended squeeze, sucking in breakout players and squeezing out the oscillation players. Once the breakout players are comfortable, they pull a continuation to suck back in the oscillation players, and so forth. Understand that a 50/50 chance is called a gamble. Even 60/40 are gamblers' odds. Speculation usually requires 80/20 chances of success. This is what differentiates an infertile environment from a fertile environment—the inclusion of a foreshadowing setup (like a perfect storm, or dual mini pups, which will be addressed in the second part of this book).

> A fertile environment must include a foreshadowing element.

Trading is a physical game. This isn't referring to the punching of walls, smashing of keyboards, and kicking of monitors across the room. It means that just watching a choppy, flat market is enough to suck you back into the market. The only way to avoid going into that rough neighborhood is to physically cut the connection. That means to get up and walk away when the environment is infertile.

It is so important to understand that everything you see on the screens during the market day will affect your judgment and frame of reference. In fact, I believe your mindset has a sharpness gauge. The more you watch a market, the further you deplete your sharpness. Just as with a sword, the more you use it, the duller the blade becomes. It needs to be sharpened. The mindset is the same. People don't realize that making a trade is not using the weapon—the weapon is used every time a trader looks at the screen or listens to CNBC. Therefore, it is best to keep that focus only during fertile market environments, and replenish the gauge by taking physical breaks away from the screens during infertile environments. A deadzone break (from 12:00 p.m. to 2:00 p.m. EST) is implemented daily in the pit and has helped to prevent many unforced errors and blow-ups.

BIG FISH IN A LITTLE POND

This idea applies right back to the environment. Why be a tiny goldfish in an ocean when you can be a big fish in a little pond? In fact, this goes back to everything Sun Tzu wrote about in *The Art of War*. It's not about having a war of attrition and foolishly attacking a larger army; it's about neutralizing the odds so that the victory is all but sealed when the real battle engages. It's about environment and placing yourself in the most favorable position as it pertains to victory. I will discuss a lot about environment in this book, but this is a good underlying theme we need to establish and understand right from the get-go.

THE TRANSPARENCY PARADOX

The markets correlate with life. The principles are identical to life situations. Life is one big irony. The notion of "be careful what you want because you just might get it" is a farce. Most will never attain what they want; however, those who have the desire to keep striving and struggling will attain something even more desirable, and that is what true destiny is. Transparency is never truly transparent.

When someone strives so hard to attain a certain skill, believing that nothing less than the attainment of that skill is their destiny, they often end up harnessing another skill, which turns out to be their real destiny. When one reaches this point, it's an amazing, enlightening feeling. It's balanced.

Everyone doesn't attain this. In fact, very few people ever attain that level. Why? Simple—it's like chess; there are more pawns than any other piece. They are needed to take the fall. It's the structure of societies and life.

Much of what I am saying will sound shallow and cynical to the average reader. So be it. Everyone who has tried their hand at the trading game knows that it is not a compassionate playing field, but rather one that treats every participant as an equal and shows sympathy and respect. Welcome to life.

One earns their place in the trading world through truly tested desire. I have heard too many traders tell me how badly they want it, how they want nothing more in life than to be a successful top trader. This happens in the beginning. In the end, they fall into the abyss and don't make it back out. This is probably a good thing. Many traders have gone on to start businesses and other ventures where they found success. This is their destiny.

What does it take to become a professional, successful trader? The ability to endure pain, and still vigorously harbor the desire beyond the point of sanity.

Think you've got desire? Take that desire, throw it off the top of a hundred story building, have it run over by a steamroller after it hits the ground, let it get spit on, dragged through the mud, drowned, frozen, dragged through the desert, and tie it up on a flagpole to dangle in the wind through rain, sleet, snow, and heat for months—and then throw it in the gutter. If that desire is still there, then you have something worthy.

The point is that desire alone is not enough. It is common. Everyone has desire, but not everyone can survive having that desire thoroughly tested. Usually, reality kicks in after a few bumps. The key is enduring desire, as illustrated by the above example. The above was just a graphic analogy of how you discover enduring desire. The underlying theme is pain, and how much can be endured.

There are three forms of pain that one must endure and embrace in order to succeed, not only in trading, but to earn the gift of harnessing a skill or endeavor to uncover one's true destiny. They are:

1. Starvation

2. Deprivation

3. Isolation

Let these words resonate in your mind. Close your eyes and repeat each word, and think about what they mean to you. Very few people can endure those three forms of pain, and even fewer people can embrace those elements in their lives.

RECIPROCITY

The essence of harmony, symmetry, parallel, respect, karma, and balance all lie in one word... reciprocity.

Life is about balance. You've heard that said many times, I'm sure. This is a very common cliché. Most people would interpret that as balancing your work, home, and play.

Think more laterally.

I am referring to life on a macro level—nature and the universe. When a person loses a sense like his sight, what tends to happen naturally? His other senses improve to compensate for the loss and balance the remaining senses.

For every force there is an equal and opposing force. What goes around comes around—the idea of karma. The recurring theme here is balance. The markets are all about balance.

The law of attraction, as illustrated in the movie *The Secret*, basically underlines the cliché of "believe and you will achieve," or "if you wish for a result hard enough, the universe will grant it." This is one-sided and too easy. Nothing comes without sacrifice or effort.

ENDURANCE

Everyone can desire, but few can make the effort. Desires are like opinions, everyone has them. But test that desire through the three elements of pain, and you know that it is for real. That is what I call enduring desire.

Life is about balance, in that one force pushing in one direction will eventually result in the same force pushing back. Note the word *eventually*. This is why many people believe in the notion of karma—what goes around, comes around. Well, it does, just not immediately at times.

Therefore, the harder one struggles, strives, and pushes to attain a result. A result will eventually be attained; that effort never goes unnoticed. This also is why most people will only be pawns; they are set in their ways and only wish for something better. Everyone can wish. It's the ones who make the effort, and continue to make the effort who will be rewarded with their destiny.

ENDURING EFFORT

They say when a person loses one of their five senses, the other senses make up for it. Lose your hearing, and your sense of taste or sight gets stronger. This is the balance that we find in ourselves and nature. Everything balances out eventually. The magnitude is dependent on the effort that is put into it. Once again, that enduring effort.

Effort is the key.

Luck is when hard work meets preparation. Hard work is viewed as putting in the time and the hours to accomplish some goal. This is admirable when it comes to an office job or a business endeavor, but in trading, hard work is not the traditional definition.

ENDURING DESIRE

Those who struggle and endure, and still continue to desire are a very special breed of people. These are the kings and queens among us. This is my definition of royalty. A person may be born into money and power, but true value comes from how precious the essence of that person is.

DESTINY EARNED

So the question is, will you endure to earn your destiny? This destiny may come in the form of trading success, or it may come in the form of another skill that is uncovered during your efforts to reach trading success.

They say you can make your own destiny. This is a safe statement since destiny is only revealed after the fact. But I smell a bait-and-switch. Does the chicken or the egg come first? Believe that you can earn your destiny, but know that it will take great pain and sacrifice in the form of enduring effort and desire. The juice is worth the squeeze.

MEDIOCRITY LOVES CROWDS

It is easy to be mediocre. People find comfort in being part of the crowd. This is why bubbles happen—people like to stick with the majority, even when they know better. When Joey gets a foreclosure notice on his home, he feels down until he finds out that Sam, Timmy, and Tony (his neighbors) are all getting foreclosed on too. His justification is "well, I'm hurting just like everyone else, so it can't be that bad."

This is a weakness which is exploited every day, and not just in the markets. Most people spend their lives seeking comfort, and stave off insecurity. Statistically, the number one fear is public speaking. Being thrust into a crowd of 100 strangers to give a 15-minute impromptu speech scares most people. If we delve deeper into this fear, we find that the true fear of most people is abandonment, to be alone, to be left dangling in the wind. Most people absolutely fear being alone. This is not the same as being lonely. Being alone brings with it feelings of helplessness and insecurity, the reality of not being with the crowd—to stand out. They say, "A person who desires to be alone is either insane or has the makings of a God." This statement should give you an idea of how rare that type of person is.

> In life as in the markets, the rarer something is, the higher its value.

The rarer something is, the more inherent value it has. However, if the tree falls in the woods and no one hears it, did it make a sound? What is needed to attach a true value is demand. When people are told they can't have something, they demand it more, and will pay more for it. This is the forbidden fruit theory, that people want what they can't have. In Economics 101, professors speak of the elastic principle, composed of vices such as sex and drugs, which will always have demand regardless of price or economy.

Sigmund Freud said there are two urges in life, the sexual urge and the urge for recognition. The recognition urge can come in the form of money, power, position, prestige, or fame. Humility must always be an anchor in your trading and life. The loss of humility leaves the ego free to run rampant and take you along with it, straight into the abyss.

There is such a fine line between confidence and complacency that it's almost invisible. Confidence must be tempered with humility. This is why a drawdown day that is manageable is a good thing. The longer a trader's winning streak goes on, the greater the odds of the ego taking over to maintain the streak at any cost. It is not just the inevitable losing session that is the problem, although the eventual loss may be heavy. The problem is the series of losing days that accompanies many a long winning streak, empowering the ego to run rampant trying to reestablish the streak once again. This is why winning streaks are very often accompanied by losing streaks.

A TALE OF TWO SQUIRRELS

There were two squirrels that lived in a forest. Let's call the first squirrel Bob. Bob didn't spend much time gathering acorns, nor did he stress about it. Whenever Bob was hungry, he would intensely go hunt down his acorns in the forest and always eat until he was full. Bob always had a full stomach until he was hungry, and then he would fill it right back up until he was bursting. However, the rest of the time, he slept, played, surfed the Internet, and had a great time doing nothing. Bob didn't stress over having to go hungry because he always found food when he needed it. Life was good. He was confident in his abilities almost to a point of arrogance.

The other squirrel, Joe, was a paranoid worker squirrel. He was always stressed out in the summer to prepare for the winter, so he would spend every waking moment gathering acorns for the winter. He never ate until he was full for fear of running out of acorns, which explains why he was always hungry, and in a foul mood pretty much all the time. Joe never had a full stomach. His life was a grind and it sucked. However, he believed his sacrifice, hard work, and dedication would keep him alive and fed through the harsh winter. Deep inside, Joe resented Bob. It pissed him off to no end, working so hard gathering acorns in the summertime while Bob would lay out, all smug without a care in the world. He hoped one day Bob would learn his lesson. He secretly wished that one winter would come and there would be no more acorns left in the forest. Joe would be vindicated at that time. He had faith.

As much as these two squirrels contrast each other, their styles worked for them—until one winter, all the acorns in the forest finally dried up. Joe's secret wish had come true. Bob was out of luck and acorns. Joe felt his paranoia melt away, and for the first time, he was relieved that all his efforts were paying off. The good guys do win, he thought to himself. Joe couldn't wait for Bob to come knocking on his door with his tail between his legs, begging for a handout. He planned out exactly what he would do and how he would bask in his glory. He couldn't wait to rub it in Bob's face.

Not much later, Joe got a knock on his door and sure enough, it was Bob. At first glance, Joe sensed something was not quite right. Strangely, Bob didn't look stressed or even hungry. How could this be? He didn't seem to display any desperation, much less remorse. In fact, he seemed like the same arrogant Bob.

With the usual smug grin, Bob said, "Yo buddy, I can't find any acorns and I'm kinda hungry, give me some acorns, will ya?" Joe couldn't believe the audacity. He screamed at Bob, "Why you arrogant! How dare you come to me looking for a handout when you sat on your butt all summer while I busted my hump scrounging every acorn I could find! All those long days and sleepless nights, pushing myself and sacrificing my life to be prepared and ready for the worst—and now here we are. I win and you lose! There are no more acorns out there, I've got the last of them! Don't you get it? Are you stupid or what? Didn't you learn anything? You should be on your knees begging, at least pretend to make an effort! Ah, hell! It won't matter anyway now, because the answer is no! You don't get any of my hard–earned acorns, not now, not ever!" as he hyperventilated.

Bob just smiled at him, nodded, pulled out a machete, and in one smooth motion, lopped off Joe's head and proceeded to move into Joe's house stocked with acorns. Bob smirked as he gorged once again on acorns.

The End.

…Or is it?

THE MORAL OF THE STORY

Conventional wisdom would search for a moral to the story. That would be convenient. Instead, ask some questions to derive deeper meaning and parallels. This takes a little more effort, but opens up your mind in the process.

Why was Bob so confident? It wasn't because of his ability to hone in on acorns when he needed them. Bob truly understood his environment and worked it to his needs. Perhaps he knew that as long as Joe was stocking away the acorns, he would never go hungry. While Bob did not force Joe to stock acorns for him, he was in total control of Joe.

Bob needing Joe is obvious. What is not obvious is Joe needing Bob. Joe's need for vindication and redemption was what drove him fanatically to gather acorns, at any costs to his life. It was not to gather just enough acorns, but all the acorns. It was ego that drove Joe, not Bob.

As I mentioned, Freud said that the two urges in life are the sexual urge and the urge for recognition. That urge for recognition comes in many forms, but is most powerful when ego is thoroughly embedded into the equation. Bob probably liked Joe. Why wouldn't he? Perhaps, Joe hated Joe, not Bob. Joe wanted to be Bob and envied him.

Bob was the one in control, while allowing Joe to believe he was in control. Was Bob that much of a mastermind, or just lazy and lucky? Was Joe just delusional and filled with his own self-doubt and hatred? Was Bob simply a scapegoat?

Did Bob know that as long as Joe was stocking away the acorns, he would never starve?

The answers are based on your own interpretation. Instead of Bob and Joe, substitute different names or titles: master and servant, predator and prey, bank and depositor, government and taxpayer, hunter and gatherer, smart money and sheep, wealthy and poor, white collar and blue collar, upper management and employee, and so on. This reciprocal toxic relationship is everywhere.

THE FRUITS OF PERSEVERANCE

The more enduring effort one expends, the more he narrows himself amongst the playing field. This is perseverance. The more one perseveres in the face of adversity, the more he forces nature to offset and balance in the end. This is the will to survive and strive. A perfect analogy is the stonecutter. Imagine the poor stonecutter that hammers away at a boulder constantly. Each strike reverberates through his body as it aches with each blow. As he continues to strike, the rock shows absolutely no sign of breaking. After 300 strikes, his friends think he is wasting his time. After 600 strikes, his siblings think he has lost his mind. After 900 strikes, his own family has written him off as a lunatic. At 999 strikes, everyone has written him off as insane, and then, on the 1,000th strike, the boulder splits in half! Everything he has sacrificed has culminated in achieving his goal. He went from fool to genius, loser to winner, a lost cause to a hero. Anyone who happened to see him afterwards would swear that he was a pro, and talented as a stonecutter. The non-believers have been swayed by the results. He has succeeded. He has set himself above the rest of the crowd, the same crowd that wrote him off and was so sure he was wasting his time. This analogy applies to most personal and professional success stories. People like to simplify success and assume that the person was just talented or fell into it. Human beings tend to demonize failure and worship success, not realizing the difference can be narrowed down to that one extra blow that tilts the outcome. Of course, that one extra strike comes at the tail end of 999 prior strikes.

At any given point, you could be a single blow away from success. It's just a matter of your perseverance. The mere action of persevering narrows the field and statistically improves your chance of becoming the outlier and the exception to the rule. You have to earn that.

The stonecutter analogy is a very simplified example. The definition of ignorance is doing the same thing and expecting different results. In trading, perseverance must be tempered with conscious adjustment along the way. You must learn from each trade, each stop, each pattern that plays out, and each pattern that fails. The perseverance comes from constantly tweaking and improving how you hit that stone. In reality, one stone and 1,000 hits are not the end-all. Perseverance also requires improvement in the form of technique or tools so that the efforts are optimized. The goal is to progressively decrease the number of hits to break the stones. To work smarter, not harder, is where perseverance will take you.

> Constant refinement and improvement is the true result of perseverance—success is merely a by-product.

HOW IS YOUR FRIEND

They say it doesn't matter if you win or lose, it's "how you play the game." There is much truth to that in the latter part of how. How is such a considerate and compassionate word. It gives consideration to the history of an outcome. It respects the process undertaken to achieve the outcome. It acknowledges the guts behind the glory. The "how" is the true story of the journey. When someone asks "how," it implies the need to understand—it means they care—and while the sheep will focus on the outcome, the mavens will focus on the journey, the struggle, the components, the marination, the metabolizing, the refinement, the setbacks, and the passion that fueled the relentless drive forward in the face of adversity and doubt, to achieve success. True mavens of evolution focus on the "how," because they understand that improving the how is the reward.

While all this insight is making sense, you may be asking, how does this relate to trading? Thank you for your compassionate and respectful consideration.

PROFITS ARE A BY-PRODUCT

We know what the end goal with trading is. It is to consistently make and keep profits, right? Hmm. Well, I hope I've made it clear that profits (the achievement) are a by-product of the journey. The journey is continuous and dynamic, just as the markets are. Therefore, it boils down to the relentless effort involved to constantly refine and improve upon the process.

> By focusing on the process, the profits are a by-product.

By continuously striving to refine your performance, the profits are a by-product. By focusing on not just the methods, but also the filtering, the execution, the sizing allocation, the preparation, the environment, and the pacing, the profits become the by-product. Focus on perfecting the process of trading, and the profits become a by-product.

The bottom line is that everyone knows the outcome, but very few understand how that outcome was achieved, and even fewer set out to refine the process. Those who strive to understand the "how" are the ones who will take it to the next level. They are the courtesans of evolution. The reward is not profits, it is the enlightenment you earn.

And did I mention that the profits are simply a by-product? This is what "focus on the trade, not the money" means. The money must always be secondary, and that is the only way to make money in this game.

Lastly, just to drive the "how" concept into the ground, the price is not as important as how the price was achieved. Too many traders rely on a price level being triggered while overlooking how the price level was hit. This is why methods that rely on static price levels and targets tend to be no good. There is a big difference between RIMM spiking up to $65 from $64 in 3 minutes as opposed to taking 30 minutes to slowly grind from $64 to $65. While both may imply a breakout buy trigger, the reality is that the slower grind to achieve the price trigger likely results in a stronger breakout and follow-through. The impulse pop to $65 will likely stop out impulse buyers who chased the pop. These traders didn't take into consideration the "how;" they only focused on the achievement target, and lost because of it. More than likely, they will shift blame on the methods ("How dare they!") and continue on this path of ignorance right into the abyss. Let this not (or no longer) be you.

BRING IT FULL CIRCLE: TEST YOURSELF

PICK THE MOST CORRECT WORD FOR THE BLANK.

(1) Markets are _____.

    a) static
    b) dynamic

(2) _____ is needed to stimulate growth.

    a) Failure
    b) Attitude

(3) Pain's brother is _____.

    a) little Timmy
    b) guilt
    c) pleasure
    d) shame

(4) The three forms of pain one must not only endure but embrace in order to succeed are starvation, isolation and _____.

    a) depravation
    b) deprivation
    c) frostbite
    d) confusion
    e) stupidity

(5) Reciprocity is not _____.

    a) balanced
    b) karma
    c) respectful
    d) a one way street

For answers, please visit the
Traders' Library Education Corner at
www.traderslibrary.com/TLEcorner.

CHAPTER 2

WHAT IS THE "EDGE"?

A word that consistently gets thrown around by traders is the "edge," and the notion of traders possessing it. Once an edge is attained, it is assumed that vast riches accompany this acquisition.

The reality is much different. The very definition of an edge means that one has found an unpopulated niche. This is fleeting at best. The nature of the market is to discover, expose, and then populate every possible working niche until it is completely saturated. This idea lends itself to the notion of capacity, threshold, and most importantly....

In every endeavor, there is a boom, bust, rebirth, and saturation cycle. Day trading is no different. The 1998 to 2000 era of Internet mania was the day trading boom cycle, the good old days. Electronic trading had gone mainstream and every other person dreamed of being a day trader. Those were the days of the 30-point intraday ranges on AMZN, BRCM, JDSU, and so forth. It was absolutely an amazing time. Stocks made phenomenal moves in quarter- to half-point increments. The fraction based pricing made for a lot of fat profits for scalpers, brokers, and market makers alike.

The pattern day trading rule is a NASD and SEC regulation that requires any person who buys and sells a security in the same trading day four or more times in any five consecutive business trading days to have at least $25,000 in a margin account.

The bear market didn't kill day trading. It was the decimalization system that killed day trading, along with the pattern day trading rule, which is total BS. Granted, there was very little, if any chart reading involved or even necessary in the old days. Nasdaq Level II was all you needed.

THE MOST COMMON QUESTION

How long does it take to make it as a trader?

This is the question posed to me by newbies all the time. The answer is: between now and never. As much as I want to give a straight answer, I can't. There is no standard college course and exam that you can pass to be a trader. It boils down to the individual in every way, except for the quality of training he receives. How does one even determine when a trader has finally "made it"? If you want to be a trader, hit the buy button. Congrats—you made a trade, now you're a trader.

The markets are constantly shifting paradigms pertaining to tradability and environments. There were lots of people who made a living day trading in the years between 1999 and 2001, only to get snuffed out once the environments changed as decimalization kicked in, ECNs got bigger, and Nasdaq Level II transparency all but disappeared.

As mentioned earlier, enduring desire and effort—supported by another main income source to stave off desperation and risk capital—are the ingredients needed to support oneself in this endeavor. There is one very key paradigm shift in the day trading endeavor. Since there are so many participants in the markets, the windows of transparency are often in the pre-market and opening 45 minutes. It is possible to make a living or secondary income trading only one or two hours a day and then turning off the screens. In fact, the notion of full time trader is a misnomer. The less you trade, the better off you will be. The more you trade, the more opportunities you have to lose money against the ocean of better equipped, better informed, and better capitalized opponents. Until you start up your own billion-dollar hedge fund, your goal will be to pretty much pickpocket the market and run away before it figures out what you've done. The more

The less you trade, the better off you will be.

you keep going back and overtrading, the more likely it is that you will get slaughtered.

This boils down to your own motivation for pursuing trading. Is it for the money, or for the rush? This is a loaded question. If it's for the money, then the question of desperation comes into play. If it's for the rush, then ego comes into play.

In trading, the worst-case scenario is the typical scenario.

I believe that the best way to motivate someone is to show him worst-case scenarios so that he is aware of what not to do. Rather than try to build up and glamorize trading, I want to show you how most end up failing. The whole positive attitude mentality is that of sheep. You will find most of the things that human beings are taught to do in order to excel in other endeavors will lead you to fall right into the abyss when it comes to trading.

THE UPSIDE TO THE DOWNSIDE

Thanks to technology, books, DVDs, seminars, software, and simulators, one can become well-versed in trading much faster than ever before. The learning curve can be shortened at a cheaper cost these days. This is one benefit of trading today's markets.

 Making money is not the hard part, keeping it is!

That statement will resonate throughout this whole book constantly, so you may as well write it down on a sticky pad somewhere and read it every day.

Backtesting has never really appealed to me, since results can be curve fitted. There are many variables that are tough to factor in when backtesting, such as: market trading environment, fading, wiggle room for any particular stock, execution slippage, share allocation, and sector or futures convergence and divergence, to name a few.

The market is the worst loan shark. They make the credit card companies with their 30% interest rates look like humanitarian relief organizations.

The market loves to give you a quarter knowing you will eventually give back a dollar or more. Even more devious, the market will fool you into thinking you earned that quarter through skill and training. It's the same underlying theme mentioned earlier; in every battle, there is an opponent and a victim. The victim usually thinks he is winning because the opponent lets him think so.

THE IDEAL TRADING MINDSET

There was a posting on a trading message board, posted by a trader, that perfectly encapsulates the essence of the ideal trading mindset. He wrote:

> *"When I get up in the morning and start off the day, I shut off the computers as soon as I make my $400. That's it. It's that easy. The problem is most people don't or won't shut it down for the day. The market will give me a little bit of money every day and my job is to take it and not get greedy. I come from a place where I know how hard it is to make $150,000 a year. No one will give me the opportunity to make $400 in an hour and then give me the freedom to enjoy the rest of my day. This is how I have averaged 100k a year for the past 5 years. I am tickled at how nice it is…"*

This is the way to approach trading.

WARNING SIGNS OF IMPENDING BLOWOUT

Now that we have discussed all the ways you can fail as a trader, it's important to be able to spot when you are slowly falling victim to the market. Taking all of the examples we've discussed thus far, I have put together a checklist to consistently apply to your trading at the end of the day.

The changes happen in a slow and subtle manner; this is how the market operates. It creeps up on your psyche while slowly triggering your ego inch by inch, until you get to a point where you are completely trapped psychologically. No trade you make is ever good enough. You may follow the rules and scalp out +0.25 on 2000 shares into a 1-minute high band mini pup for a $500 gain, only to be pissed off that it ran 0.75 higher later (even though it retraced -0.50 from your exit point first). When you follow the rules of management, method, and allocation, and still get upset with the "shoulda, woulda, coulda" complex, this is a key sign that the market is taking hold of your psyche.

When you take a good stop as a 1-minute mini pup fails and you stop out -0.10 on 1,000 shares as it plunges -0.75, only to bounce off a 13-minute 5-period moving average and climb back up +1 above your stop level, and you get pissed off once again with the shoulda, woulda, coulda complex, the market is taking hold of your psyche.

Before we even go into the checklist, the first sign of trouble is when you start to believe your shoulda, woulda, coulda statements. Everyone will look at a trade they got out too early on, either for a profit or stop, and at some point say to themselves, "I shoulda held on a little longer." This is normal. However, when you start to really believe this, and get to a point where you are getting frustrated with profitable trades, that's when the warning lights need to come on.

I have seen excellent traders get so pissed off with their scalps that they try to hold on to the scalp size trades for the "bigger" move, only to have it backfire and keep adding size until they end up stopping out with big losses. The irony is that these traders usually play by the rules, but their ego overwhelms them slowly as they interject these shoulda, woulda, coulda statements throughout the day. When the best scalp you make following the underlying simple understanding—that is, heavier shares for a short period of time to profit into a climactic move—illustrated by a 1-minute stochastics mini pup peak above the 80 band, or a mini inverse pup lean through the 20 band, you are doomed, because it only goes downhill from there.

Here's the checklist to avoid falling into the "bystander" mode, where you know and see what you are doing, but don't react.

  ✓ Your bottom hurts from sitting too long.

  ✓ Your bladder hurts from putting off the bathroom break for two hours.

  ✓ You constantly quote "shoulda, woulda, coulda" on every trade that you make a profit. (Doom is near at this point.)

✓ You are still upset on winning trades because you "sold too early."

✓ You loosen your stop losses too far until panic sets in, and you stop out too late.

✓ You compare your measly gains or losses to how the markets are doing (i.e., the Dow is up 250 points, but you are down $500).

✓ You start to play the opposite direction on every trade with rising share size as losses mount.

✓ You start playing the cheap stocks as home runs. For example, taking 10,000 shares of a $3 stock looking for a move to make back losses.

✓ Desperation kicks in.

✓ You are playing the post-market with regular market scalp size out of desperation to get your account back to even.

As much a trader will try to deny it, there comes a time when he secretly desires to blow out the account and be forced to stop trading. Being forced to stop trading takes away the self-inflicted tension and stress that a beaten trader places on himself. This pressure mounts with each trade. Even the winning trades are not good enough, while the losing trades are devastating. Like an addict, he is out of control. He needs to be controlled by another entity—namely, the broker.

WHY TRADERS SECRETLY WANT TO BLOW OUT

We have to understand that the ego is a trader's worst enemy. When a trader starts to lose apathy, the ego starts to make its way back into the psyche. No one is immune to ego. It is human nature to succumb to ego. When a trader starts to get upset with his profit performance even though he is following the rules, this is when the ego gets a foothold and starts to make its way in.

The constant shoulda, woulda, coulda statements he will say to himself or to his friends becomes a self-fulfilling prophecy. The mind is a very sensitive listener and negative self-talk pretty much instructs it to expect disaster. Humans are so sensitive to everything around them. The conscious is not the problem, it's the subconscious that makes up the fiber of our being.

In Chapter One, we discussed cognitive dissonance theory, which helps to explain why people do irrational things. It basically states that it is human nature is to avoid stress by either changing one's behavior or beliefs. The greater the magnitude of the stress, the more drastic the measures necessary to relieve the stress.

Cognitions are little pieces of knowledge that are constantly flowing through your conscious and subconscious. (For example: I smoke cigarettes. Trading is fun. I like my house.) Dissonance is when opposing cognitions collide, resulting in stress. The volume or magnitude of the dissonance will determine the amount of stress. As the stress gets heavier and more unbearable, humans will resort to a change in beliefs or behavior to combat this. Ultimately, the goal is to minimize the stress.

With this understanding, it is easy to see why a trader constantly berates herself for taking money too soon off the table, or taking stops too late. The cognition dissonance creates such enormous stress that the trader realizes that she actually hates trading, yet, she grinds away against better judgment. The berating of herself is embedded at this point. The tension is so great that the only way she will relieve the stress is to stop trading. Her ego won't let her quit. Therefore, the only other option is to be forced to quit by blowing out her account.

Ironically, after the blowout, the trader will feel a sense of relief. This illustrates the magnitude of self-inflicted pressure and tension caused. This period of being out of the market, being forced to only watch is usually when the trader will make the most growth.

ANATOMY OF BLOWOUT #2

Blowing out an account is not only painful financially, but also emotionally. However, an interesting dynamic can trigger as the trader is forced to quit cold turkey. This will happen many weeks or months later.

A sense of clarity starts to seep in as the trader feels the tension being lifted. When the responsibility is taken away, the stress goes away. As this happens, the trader will start to see clarity of setups again. It is quite an irony and a tragedy that the most constructive period for a trader is during the hiatus after blowing out his account. It is during this period that the light bulb goes off and he sees the error of his ways. He realizes the mistakes that he made not only with the setups, but with the poor management of overleveraging, and the pathetic desperation and size overload that resulted. In this period as an outsider to the markets, he gains his clarity and confidence. This results in his eventual comeback many months later, after he has "perfected" his craft.

Now the trader is back, confident and aware of his prior mistakes, and sworn not to repeat them. At this point, it should be a storybook ending as the trader moves on to conquer the markets onward and upward until the end of time…

Unfortunately, this is not the case. The trader will usually start off on a nice winning streak, which confirms his newfound confidence in his ability. He feels good about himself and the new clean slate that he is starting.

GROUNDHOG DAY

Ideally, the time off from being forced to stop trading should allow one to gain extraordinary clarity (through contrast), which usually builds up confidence in being able to manage and filter trades better the next time around.

There is a nasty phenomenon that triggers once the trader gets back into the game. Yes, the trader has gained insight to his prior errors. Yes, the trader is more confident because he has been exposed to contrast in his forced hiatus. Yes, the trader will hit the ground running and usually rack up a series of carefully managed winning trades, or entire winning days. He feels it is different this time.

> Ego is a trader's worst enemy.

Then something unexpected happens—unexpected unless you have blown out more than once. Once losses come back into the picture, the trader may initially stave off the urge and the old habit of overleveraging and overtrading, but as losses and desperation mount, he completely falls into a conscious relapse. The ego appears to once again take over, as he can't believe that all that time he has spent healing has gone to waste. Yes, he can identify when he is screwing up, but he just can't seem to stop. That voice of discipline yells quietly during the day and gets loud after the destruction. In essence, he has become a smarter and wiser third person trader, but the first person in the eye of the storm has reemerged. The anguish that accompanies this nasty discovery is twice as bad as the pain felt from the initial blowout. The trader starts to feel incontrovertibly worthless, useless, weak, and unable to administer any discipline. All the demons come back at his worst periods.

When you make money, the cognitions are still not very positive, as it is never "enough." Cognitions like: You are still in the hole. You left too much money on the table. Why didn't you hold the trade longer? You need to make more money.

When you lose money, your cognitions run wild. Cognitions like: You are so weak. You have no discipline. You are a loser. You have now lost even more money than before. All you think you are is an illusion. You have let your family and yourself down. You are a fraud. This puts you right back on track to overleverage, overtrade, underfilter, and push until you blow out again.

WHY BLOWN OUT TRADERS BLOW OUT AGAIN

It is a kind of ignorance to continue doing the same thing each time but expect different results. This defines the losing trader. It's not to say that his methods haven't changed or improved, they may have. The trader may have actively trained to refine his methods and learn new patterns and setups.

However, what tends to remain the same is the force that pulls the strings—the mindset. Feeling better from the tension relief of not being able to trade is not a training method, nor does it change the corrupted programming that went into the trader's mindset, which will inevitably re-trigger another blowout. It's just a matter of when. This is an affliction that gets more deeply rooted with each progressive blowout. It is as if the trader gets further programmed to blow out and subconsciously expects it to happen, even if he is capable of being profitable, as he demonstrated in the first week or so back from his hiatus. In order to do something different the next time around, the trader has to focus his efforts on addressing the affliction that ultimately controls him.

THREE REMEDIES FOR AFFLICTION

I have discovered that there are three distinct remedies to fight any affliction. Afflictions can be physical, psychological, emotional, or spiritual, but they all contain two core factors: a trigger and an outcome. An affliction triggers suffering, that's the outcome. That's half the battle!

Note that these remedies are linear to all afflictions, not just trading. Why a person does something is not the issue. What makes them tick is of no interest. The issue is determining the trigger that produces the outcome. It is simple cause and effect. By trigger, I mean a stimuli, condition, event, or situation which causes the trader to act irrationally. The root of the affliction doesn't concern me. If we can prevent the trigger, then the outcome simply doesn't happen. If we neutralize the cause, then there is no effect. It is simple enough.

The person who best knows the trigger is the trader himself. He knows it intimately, but may be so deep in the eye of the storm that he has blocked it out. That's when he has to make an honest assessment. It doesn't take a forensic scientist to figure out the triggers once you know the effect. It's just a process of elimination. However, when it comes to trading, the fingerprints are right there on the trade activity reports.

Define the outcome and root out the trigger. The trigger is the key. Without a detonator, a bomb is harmless. So the focus is on combating the trigger. This is where the three remedies come into play.

1. **Roadblock.** To roadblock means to preset a detour ahead so that the trigger is avoided or can't be accessed. It takes the power away from the victim, and in essence, saves them in the process. The more seamless, fluid, and undetectable a roadblock is, the more effective it becomes. It's the difference between placing rubber cones on a highway exit ramp versus extending the freeway wall to seal the exit. This is a preplanned move. This takes foresight.

2. **Counteract.** This remedy means to reciprocate with an equal opposing force to neutralize the trigger. This is a reactive move set forth by the trigger.

3. **Dilute.** Diluting will diffuse, minimize, and dissolve the significance of the trigger to a point where it no longer remains a trigger. This is can be either preplanned or reactive.

Let's apply the three remedies to a situation. Timmy tends to panic when his losses go beyond the -$500 mark. This triggers Timmy to desperately overtrade in deadzone, which backfires, leaving him with losses around the -$1500 mark by close.

Timmy's outcome is taking big losses. Timmy's trigger is losing more than $500. The three remedies can be applied.

1. **Roadblock:** Timmy could have his broker set a maximum daily loss provision at $450 in the software, which would immediately cancel his buying power if he surpasses that mark. He would have no control over that.

2. **Counteract:** Timmy could immediately take the opposite position on his trade— wait, that's what he has been doing constantly, which is what elevated his losses to -$1500. That's not a counteraction. Timmy could rip the computer plug from the wall. Now *there's* an effective way to counteract the trigger to prevent the damaging outcome.

3. **Dilute:** Timmy could sell $500 worth of longer-term holdings to bring his net loss back to zero on the day (at least in his mind). This minimizes the significance of the -$500 loss trigger, which should help him regain his sanity to trade effectively again.

CONFIDENCE VS. COMPLACENCY AND ARROGANCE

While confidence is good, it can also backfire by opening the door for ego to raid the house. When the ego gets involved, confidence can easily manifest itself into complacency. When the degree of confidence gets extreme and the ego finds a home, it manifests itself into arrogance. In trading, nothing is ever attained and held permanently—not profits, not confidence, not methods, and especially not transparency. Everything is fleeting. Perception is the only reality.

TRADING IS A PHYSICAL ACTIVITY

I mentioned this earlier, and it bears repeating. With the understanding of the cognitive dissonance theory, a trader has to know that everything he says to himself or exposes himself to will produce cognitions. It's not the conscious cognitions that will be trouble, it's the subconscious cognitions. This also goes back to the premise of environment. Environment breaks down simply to what outside factors and forces you expose yourself to. Whether you are active in the environment or not, the environment will have an effect on you.

Suffice to say that most environments are physical. The physical affects the psychological. When a trader sticks around during the deadzone period of the market, which is usually chock full of wiggles, consolidations, and headfakes on light volume, she is still physically connected to the markets. Whether the trader knows it or not—it doesn't matter—she will be affected by placing herself physically into the oncoming traffic of the deadzone chop market. As she takes in the market moves, wiggles, and chop, she may say that she is just watching, but that's how the market grabs its victims.

THREE RELAXATION METHODS TO REDUCE AND COUNTERACT STRESS

Relaxation is incompatible with tension. You are either in a state of one or the other, never both. When I refer to stress, it includes tension and anxiety. A relaxation state is the most ideal zone for trading. It allows you to be resilient, objective, focused, and in control. This is easier to attain when you are profitable, at least for me. However, getting into this state even before you start your trading day will make for a smoother session.

Counteracting is one of the three remedies for affliction.

Self-inflicted wounds are a nasty byproduct of stress, anxiety, and tension. Despite conventional thinking, self-inflicted wounds are not accidents. Trading is 90% between the ears. To be effective, one has to neutralize stress. The mental state and physical state are correlated. In times of high stress, the heart rate jumps, breath shortens, muscles tighten up as the mind panics. By counteracting these physical symptoms, we can help to neutralize the mental symptoms. Below are relaxation exercises that you can practice before trading and throughout the day, as you prefer. The diaphragm breathing is recommended pre-market, before every trading session. The progressive relaxation technique is a good exercise during deadzone to replenish the sharpness gauge. Autogenic training should be used when you are really stressed and feel control slipping, on the brink of the abyss.

Diaphragm Breathing

There are two types of breathing. When you start to feel tense, breath shortens as shallow chest breathing takes over. In fact, you may be chest breathing now. We want to refill the brain with oxygen and induce a relaxed state through proper diaphragm breathing. Here's the method:

1. Lie down on the floor and place your right hand on your stomach around the waistline and left hand on our chest.

2. Forcefully exhale all the air out of your lungs to create a vacuum as you push your stomach down.

3. Take in a deep breath through your nose as the fresh air hits the back of your throat, flows through your lungs, all the way into your stomach.

4. Exhale slowly through your mouth, pucker your lips like you are exhaling through a straw. Feel the air flowing out of your stomach, back through your lungs, out your pucker, and through the straw. Your stomach should be flattened out, almost flexing your abs.

5. Repeat steps 3 through 5 for five to ten minutes.

Get in the habit of practicing the diaphragm breathing at least twice a day—make it part of your pre-market routine—and especially when you are feeling heavy tension during the trading day, or in anticipation of a stress inducing event, such as an earnings report. Controlled breathing is a key element of stress reduction, not to mention more air to your tiny brain is good.

Progressive Relaxation Tensing Method

This method was created by Dr. Edmund Jacobson and refined by Joseph Wolpe. Dr. Jacobson believed that the body responds to anxiety with muscle tension. Get rid of the muscle tension and you get rid of the anxiety. Deep muscle relaxation reduces physical tension, thereby reducing anxiety. The habit of responding with one blocks the habit of responding with the other.

Try lying down on the floor. Breathe from the diaphragm as described above. Each muscle group will progressively be tensed for 7 seconds (don't injure yourself), and then relaxed for 21 seconds. Release instantly, not gradually, so muscles go limp. Actively pay attention to the contrast between tension and relaxation when muscles go limp.

1. Curl up both fists, tighten forearms, and flex biceps for 7 seconds (bodybuilder pose), release, and take deep breaths from diaphragm for 21 seconds.

2. Roll your head around your neck clockwise for a complete circle, then the other way, then breathe for 21 seconds.

3. Wrinkle up your face like a raisin, with squinted eyes, wrinkled forehead, shoulders hunched and mouth open for 7 seconds. Release, relax for 21 seconds while taking deep breaths.

4. Arch your shoulders back as you inhale a deep breath, puffing out your chest, and hold for 7 seconds. Release, exhale, relax, and breathe for 21 seconds.

5. Take a deep breath and stick out your stomach, hold for 7 seconds, release, exhale, relax, and breathe for 21 seconds.

6. Straighten your legs while pointing your toes back towards your face, tighten your shins, stretch the calves. Hold for 7 seconds. Relax, release, and breathe for 21 seconds.

7. Straighten your legs, curl toes forward, tighten your calves, thighs, and buttocks at the same time, hold for 7 seconds. Relax, release, and breathe for 21 seconds.

Autogenic Relaxation Method

Developed by Oskar Vogt at the Berlin Institute and refined by Johannes Schultz, this method induces a hypnotic, trance-like state by thinking of heaviness and warmth in the limbs through verbal suggestions. Warmth and heaviness are feelings commonly associated with relaxation. The verbal formulas fall under six themes aimed at reversing the natural fight-or-flight response that is triggered when under stress. The six themes are as follows.

1. Heaviness promotes the relaxation of voluntary muscles like arms, legs, buttocks, etc. "My right arm is heavy."

2. Warmth induces blood flow throughout the body, which reverses the concentration of blood flow to the head, a characteristic of flight-or-flight stress state. "My right hand is warm."

3. Normalizing cardiac activity. "My heartbeat is calm and regular."

4. Regulate breathing. "It breathes me."

5. Relax and warm the abdominal area. "My stomach is warm."

6. Flow of blood to the head. "My forehead is cool."

Lie down in a quiet, warm, comfortable, dimly lit room. Close your eyes. Repeat each formula slowly, taking five seconds to say it, then pause for three seconds. For example, "My right arm is heavy… my right arm is heavy… my right arm is heavy… my right arm is heavy… my right arm is heavy…" This should take about 30 seconds. Passively concentrate on the limb you are mentioning. Do one set for the body and then the mind.

Here's a set of autogenic formulas for the body.

1. My right arm is heavy and warm (say slowly for five seconds, pause for three seconds, and repeat five times).

2. My arms and legs are heavy and warm.

3. It breathes me.

4. My heartbeat is calm and regular.

5. My forehead is cool.

This is for the calming the mind:

1. I am calm and relaxed.

2. I feel quiet.

3. My whole body feels quiet, heavy, comfortable, and relaxed.

4. My mind is quiet.

5. I withdraw my thoughts from the surroundings and I feel serene and still.

6. My thoughts are turned inward and I am at ease.

7. Deep within my mind, I can visualize and experience myself as relaxed, comfortable, and still.

8. I feel an inward quietness.

This will take time and practice (and memorization), so be patient. The suggestions are supposed to passively induce relaxation. Keep at it. Try to practice this technique several times a week, as time permits. This is highly recommended when you are on the verge of falling into the abyss.

HIGH INTENSITY FORCED TENSION

I know what you are thinking. Punch yourself in the head? Wrong. Although you can't feel two pains at the same time, that's not the best remedy. Better yet, go to the gym. But don't just go there to limp through the exercises, watching television and the clock to pass time. That's what most of the sheep do. Not you, my friend. Not this time. We need to exorcise—err, exercise the stress demons out of you.

You need to taste the burn and lactic acid as every fiber of muscle is screaming at you to cut this out, but you keep going until you hit that absolute moment of clarity where the pain is no longer a focus. Pain is spotting you. Where you give the absolute hardest effort to failure and keep going. All it takes is one set, after an initial warm up. I do this every workout. It's the ultimate stress relief, not to mention the side effect of having 19.5 inch arms. Here's what I do:

How to Enter the High Intensity Zone via Preacher Curl Machine, or "Tasting Nirvana Method"

1. Do a light warm up set for 12 reps to get the blood flowing.

2. Set the highest weight you can do for six reps and slowly squeeze out six grueling reps to exhaustion.

3. Release, still holding the bar, rest for seven seconds, then squeeze out two more reps with seven second rests in between. Do one more rep until you can no longer even lift the bar halfway.

4. Drop the weight by one-third and proceed to squeeze out more reps until failure, meaning you can't even get the bar halfway up. Take a seven second breather and squeeze out two more. By now, you should be glistening with sweat.

5. Drop the weight by half and squeeze out more reps to failure, but make sure to use good form. Grunting is permitted, just no crying. You should be shaking by the failure rep. Rest for seven seconds, and then squeeze out two more. At this point, people will be thinking you are out of your mind.

6. Drop the weight by half and rep out until failure. At this point, your head should feel like it shrunk to the size of a peanut, and your hearing is nil, as all your focus and concentration is on squeezing out the final reps. The sweat should be streaking down the preacher bench pad like streaks of blood, and pouring down your face as well. During those last two impossible reps is when it happens—nirvana. You will be in a zone of such pain, burn, and focus that it's enlightening. When you finally release the bar, take some deep breaths. Your arms should be absolutely blown up as if someone pumped water into them to twice the capacity, feeling as if they will explode. They should be so inflamed and gorged with blood that you can barely bend them. Get up and walk around, and remember to breathe and stretch.

The pump from this set will be one of, if not the greatest pumps and feelings of empowerment you will ever physically feel. You have gone where very few have gone, or will ever go. You hit the high intensity zone.

Feel free to go puke afterwards,
you earned it, soldier!

If gyms required people to train like this, there would be no such thing as gyms. Congrats. You have tasted nirvana for a few seconds. I guarantee that you won't be thinking about your losses or the trading day when mustering every ounce of willpower to complete the final reps of this high intensity drop set. If you aren't relaxed after this drop set, then punch yourself in the head! But you probably won't be able to reach since your arms will be so pumped up—ha!

NAVY SEALS METHOD

Borrowing from the Navy Seals training, they combine four methods to reach a cumulative effect of reducing stress. Each method alone may or may not be effective, but combining all four exercises triggers a synergistic effect.

1. **Goal Setting.** Think of the finish line ahead of time.

2. **Mental Rehearsal.** Visualize the best trading setup and its outcome. Think through the worst-case scenario and how you will react. Then factor in the first clues of the cause that will trigger the effect. Rehearse what to do for both the profitable and stop loss outcome.

3. **Self Talk in Third Person.** The mind talks 100-300 words a minute subconsciously; you can affect that by vocally speaking positively. Not so much positive, motivational mumbo jumbo, just rebutting the negative part. Rebut and replace words like "loser," and most importantly, "shoulda woudla coulda." Replace with "good stop," "could have been worse," "that was a good call anyway," and "that was good enough."

   Third-person speak reinforces a detached state to remain (or at least sound) objective. It is self-coaching. In another sense, it subconsciously offsets the burden of failure on oneself. Replace "I" with your name, or "he" or "she." By actively keeping a separation, it will allow for sharper analysis of what went right or wrong. The key here is to take yourself out of the eye of the storm so that you can objectively measure your sharpness levels, performance, and management. This is a key component in creating a true trading journal. Be clinical.

Replace words like "loser" with solutions like "next time, wait for a confirmation," "next time, wait for a better entry," or "next time, wait for confirmation." Don't forget to add your name—think third person. Speak to yourself out loud. Reinforce good habits. Dissect the error and prioritize not repeating it.

4. **Arousal Control.** Deep breathing through the nose helps to bring in oxygen to the brain and control the heartbeat, which is involuntary, but physical activity can affect that. Try to purposefully feel and slow down your heart rate even in the most stressful of situations. Breathe in deep through the nostrils and exhale with your diaphragm deep through the mouth. Breathe in energy and exhale tension.

Take a five minute break after every stop loss; try these four techniques to help you reduce stress throughout your trading day to improve your results.

A SUREFIRE STRESS RELIEVER: REMOVE YOUR BLOTTER

The majority of all stress related to trading comes when money is the main focus. Telling yourself not to think about the money is easier said than done. During the training phase, you must absolutely not be exposed to the money factor, even when you are trading 100 share minimum lots. By removing this money component, you will relieve a significant portion of stress.

The action here is to physically remove visual access to your profit/loss balance. Do it cold turkey. The only thing you want to have open is the actual trade confirmations and open positions. If the blotter is part of the open positions, then try to reshape the window to not display the profit/loss balance portion. This simple action allows you to focus solely on the art of the trade.

In fact, if you look back at your prior blowouts, most of the time, the stress came from constantly watching your profit/loss balance blotter throughout the day. This damaging measure of performance brings about tremendous unnecessary tension throughout the day, especially during losses from the top and drawdowns. Constantly watching a negative profit/loss balance throughout the day subconsciously creates the feeling of regression and falling behind. By physically removing access to your blotter (and consciously preventing yourself from peeking), you create a more viable stress-free environment.

WRITE IT, DON'T BITE IT: KEEPING A JOURNAL

At the end of the day, you should keep your journal as if you were a psychiatrist with a patient, or a boxing coach with an athlete, and objectively analyze and document his progress.

A journal should be a third party analysis of the "client." Unlike traditional journals, we are not keeping track of every single trade and the premises and results. You already have a record of that in your trading software and blotter. Through the years, I have realized there is no point in keeping records of every single trade in a journal. It is redundant, time consuming, and serves no utility down the road. Your blotter will show that anyway, which we don't even want to really address during the day.

There's been a lot of material written about the proper way of keeping a trade journal. Keeping a journal can be a tedious task, but anyone who has ever kept a diary knows how memories tend to come back. As much conjecture as there is about the capacity of the human brain and its ability to store infinite amounts of data in the form of experiences, those who have ever kept a diary understand one key reality—the brain can recall even the most minute details, as long as those details have been documented. The mechanics of posting the data is not the important part. A solid trade journal should actually be documented in the form of a diary. There are specific keywords that apply.

Here's a quick checklist of things to consider mentioning in your journal.

✓ How do you feel about your stock selection today?

✓ Are you happy with your entries and exits?

✓ How did you fare relative to your daily trading model?

✓ How was your focus?

✓ How were your stress levels? If you had the shakes, what caused it? Leverage?

✓ Did you pace well with the market?

✓ Did you overtrade or impulse trade? Were you able to stop yourself?

✓ How was your filtering today?

✓ Were you relaxed throughout the day?

✓ Rate your mood from one to five stars. [★ ★ ★ ★ ★]

✓ From one to five stars, rate your timing on entries and exits. [★ ★ ★ ★ ★]

✓ Rate your performance from one to five stars. [★ ★ ★ ★ ★]

✓ What do you feel you could have improved on today?

EVOLUTION

Embrace that word—evolution. Evolution is constant, but it is not a passive activity if you want to be part of it. Evolution is growth. Growth needs to be nurtured, just like a plant. It needs to be fed and protected. You must be consciously active in order to enable and foster growth to participate in the evolution as a trader.

As the methods of trading have gone through the evolutionary process, you will only benefit by going through the same process. Luckily, the precedent has already been set. You have to be fed piece meal until you are starving for more knowledge to fill in the gaps. This hunger and controlled deprivation is how you will methodically evolve as a trader. Hunger is the most basic human need. Physically, humans need to be fed to live. Psychologically, humans start off hungering for knowledge until they get jaded.

The voracious need to fill a void is the essence of hunger. In order to fill that void, you need to discover firsthand what that void is. Once you can identify that void, then the deprivation kicks in and re-triggers the hunger component.

For example, Chapter 8, entitled Basic Training, is meant for you to stick to the provided components only so that you can get familiar with the tools. You should try to dispute them and derive the flaw. This is how you discover what the void is. We are purposefully holding out on other components and tools of the methods so that you will discover the void and desire to fill it. Be flexible, yet critical. Lateral thinking is something you want to practice.

Hungry people appreciate food more than those who are force-fed. People tend to learn much more quickly when they have a true hunger to learn. This is what we want to foster. We want to re-trigger that innate attribute that we were born with as children but lost in the process of becoming adults.

MINDSET

Understand these simple premises. Stress can cause rational people, with rational intent, to do irrational things. Stress causes fear, anxiety, paranoia, and desperation. Stress triggers tension, which in turn causes more stress, resulting in a snowball effect. Stress causes blowouts as the human mind subconsciously strives desperately to diminish that stress. For traders, the only way to relieve the stress is to be forced out of the market, to cut off the source of that stress, which is trading.

Therefore, in order to maximize the foundation-building and learning process, one needs to absolutely eradicate any presence of stress in our "gym." Stress-free is the key component. This "gym" should be your sanctuary free of stress and tension.

We want to foster that detached state of apathy so that you can connect with the true nature of trading.

LETTING GO

Make no mistake. Making money had better not be concern at this stage. I can not stress this enough. You must not be concerned with making money right now. The money will come in time, but it absolutely can't be a factor in any sense, shape, or form. You have to let go of that stress. Let go of the concerns about having to make money to pay the bills.

Only by truly letting go will you be able to gain. Traders typically blow out their accounts and go through a period of clarity when things make sense. They are in that stress-free zone, but not by conscious choice (this is a very important detail). The problem is when they return to the trading game without properly building the foundation. They fall right back into the stress tension trap and blow out again. Déjà vu occurs. This is why it is imperative during that downtime to properly build the foundation and go through the proper training.

Just like the conventional wisdom of going to law school or medical school, students are there to learn their craft and build a foundation with the understanding that success will lead to wealth down the road, after they have achieved the required credentials in due time. Do you see medical students sweating the income factor every day as they go to classes? In fact, don't expect to make any money in the beginning. No expectations.

> **Repeat this mantra:** I have no expectations to make money during this learning process which may last six months to a year. It will eventually come. I will only concern myself with learning the art of trading and conditioning myself to improve on a daily basis.

In reality, there are two ways to make sure that you aren't desperate for the money. It's pretty much that simple. This means that you either have an income source or have enough money put away (at least six months) to not worry about paying bills. If this is not the case, then step back and get a second job. You must have the reserves to pay for at least six months of expenses in order to give yourself the proper opportunity.

Eventually, you will find that money is just a way of keeping track of your progress, a scoring system. Often during the training period, there appears to be no quantifiable measure of one's progress; therefore, it is essential to shift the paradigm and have measurable targets to assess your progress during this period.

BRING IT FULL CIRCLE: TEST YOURSELF

1. Cognitive dissonance theory shows that humans will either change their beliefs or behavior to avoid the stress caused by conflicting cognitions, pieces of knowledge, conscious or subconscious. Which of the statements is false relative to cognitive dissonance theory?

    a) Timmy hated Madonna on the radio so much, he went out one day and bought her CD.

    b) Timmy's best friend smokes cigarettes. Timmy knows smoking is bad. Timmy ends up becoming a smoker.

    c) Timmy couldn't care less about oranges. Timmy eats an orange for lunch on Monday.

    d) Timmy can't stand Loraine. Timmy's best friend has a crush on Loraine. Timmy asks Loraine to the prom.

2. The opposite of love is _____.

    a) hate
    b) like
    c) loose
    d) apathy
    e) lust

3. The three remedies for affliction are roadblock, counteract, and _____.

    a) pray
    b) kill
    c) dilute
    d) blame

For answers, please visit the
Traders' Library Education Corner at
www.traderslibrary.com/TLEcorner.

CHAPTER ③

MARKETS OVER METHODS

A VARIANT PERSPECTIVE OF THE MARKETS

Trading is simply a matter of trying to profit off of price fluctuations. Sounds pretty simple. A stock price can go up or down. How hard can it be to step in for the ride when it goes up, and sell before it goes down? How tough could it be to short a stock on the way down before it bounces back up? This sounds simple enough. If a stock can only go from point B to point C, or point A, then you just need to enter a position when it starts to make its way. It seems so simple.

*"Potential means
you ain't done it yet."*

- Darrell Royal

Let's add some more factors to this simple phenomenon. We can assume that a stock will eventually go from point B to point C or point A. However, it may start off going to point C initially, only to reverse quickly back through point B and end up at point A. In between point B and point C, there are ten mini stops in between, and five of those stops branch off towards other points in between. While it would be nice to get a straight move in either direction, in most cases, the stock will take many detours and look to change directions along the way before it eventually arrives at a specific point. In fact, when the stock looks the most likely to arrive at point C, it will often completely reverse back to point A in a panic, or vice versa. This is not to say that sometimes the movement from point B to point C can't be fluid and steady—in fact, that is when you want to be along for the ride. So the question is, how can you distinguish the steady ride from one point to another as opposed to a choppy, rough ride with no real clarity?

The word here is transparency. How does one attain transparency and pick the right moment to take a position in a stock that will fluidly move from one point to another without inducing nausea?

You will need some tools, my friend. Aren't stocks just random trades? How can you measure the buying or selling that comes into a stock? How can you know when John is placing an order to buy stock and Mary is placing an order to sell stock? Isn't it just a guessing game? These are all valid questions, and good starting points to understanding the way the market works.

First things first. John, Mary, and the rest of the neighborhood are insignificant. They don't make any impact on the market. These "little" guys don't matter. The "big boys," or "dinosaurs," are the mutual funds, hedge funds, market makers, and institutions. These are the only participants who make a lasting impact in any stock, and they don't randomly place orders. Remember—dinosaurs don't walk in the sand without leaving footprints.

> The greater the volume and trend, the more fertile the market is for trading.

Dinosaurs will place their large orders with traders or market makers and have them "work" the order. This means they will scale into or out of positions while trying to minimize market impact. In other words, they are trying to muddle transparency. This can come in the form of all kinds of games. If it were just one or two dinosaurs getting in and out of large positions, that would make transparency more difficult. However, one has to remember that there are numerous dinosaurs all trying to leap frog each other without getting screwed. When the majority of the dinosaurs are herded in the same direction is when the transparency gets clearer. This presents itself in the form of trend and volume. The greater the volume and trend, the more fertile the market is for trading.

The objective of trading is not to predict price action, but to track the footprints of the strongest dinosaur herds and ride their tails like a flea for profits before they shake you off or slaughter you.

When playing stocks, we like to use a lead indicator that dinosaurs tend to follow like the north star. These include the S&P 500 and the Nasdaq 100 futures. When the futures rise, program trading tends to come in to capture premiums multiplied by thousands of participants, which tends to pull equities markets higher— and vice versa when futures fall. The futures impact the leader stocks, which impact the rest of the sector stocks in a totem pole fashion. The strength of the futures flows down from the leaders of the various sectors to the lower tiers. In extremely strong markets, the strength can flow down to the lowliest stocks within the sectors. The dinosaurs will usually play within the framework of the futures by scaling out large sell orders in an orderly manner into rising futures, and vice versa. They want to avoid showing their transparency, so they will usually follow the flow. However, if an order is too large or is urgent, then it will create a divergence against the futures, which tends to stick out like a sore thumb. This type of divergence is called a fade. The fading can tip off other participants of a large seller, which then invites shorts to take advantage of the wounded dinosaur and sell down the stock when the futures slip. It's like the animal kingdom, chock full of carnivores and cannibals. Of course, when a fade becomes too transparent is when it may simply be a bear trap to lure in shorts to squeeze them out by triggering a buying explosion. This too can be foreshadowed and exploited with the right tools.

BE THE COCKROACH

Dinosaurs aren't the brightest creatures. Like people, some are stupider than others. The main thing to remember is that you can maneuver around these big beasts, so don't feel too small. Be the cockroach. Cockroaches outlasted the dinosaurs due to their ability to adapt and maneuver. Cockroaches can live a month without food.

If a nuclear war broke out, cockroaches would be the only survivors. They can live for up to three weeks without a head! They prefer warm, humid, protected, and dark environments. This is where they thrive, although they can survive in the desert or the arctic.

Of course cockroaches can get squished easily, if they stray into the wrong environment. We want to avoid this messy outcome, and avoid the decapitation part too! This is why we want to be most acutely aware of the environment.

The market climate will be a big determining factor in your ability to survive and thrive, like a cockroach. In so many cases, a newer trader learning the methods will see them play out beautifully on a Tuesday and fail miserably on Wednesday. What changed? The methods remained the same—it was the market, notably the trading environment. Market trading environments can make a system look like a hero, and then a zero the very next day. Therefore, it's imperative that you can identify when the environment is fertile enough to play and infertile enough to stay out.

IDENTIFYING MARKET TRADING ENVIRONMENTS

A trading environment has nothing to do with how much the Dow Jones is up or down. Don't even try to identify a fertile environment. The key is recognizing the characteristics of an infertile environment. Utilize the process of elimination to be left with fertile environments.

I can't stress enough how much environment plays a major factor in your trading results. If you can make a 0.20 scalp in an infertile environment, you will make triple that in a fertile environment because of the follow-through produced by volume, trend, and foreshadowing indicators.

Trading environments, like markets, can be broken down into macro and micro periods. The macro takes into account how tight and range bound a market is based on the daily and weekly charts. The micro breaks it down into the intraday and how effectively stocks are trending and following through. The micro focuses on the time periods where you can get the best and widest window of opportunities.

FERTILE ENVIRONMENTS
A fertile environment is also referred to as a trader's market. Characteristics of a fertile environment include:

- Minimal amount of chop

- Volume

- Liquidity

- Trend

- Good oscillation ranges

- Forgiveness for sloppy or late entries and exits

- Allowance for reversal trades with follow-through

A fertile environment is forgiving in the sense that you can take a stop and reverse the trade to make back losses and add gains on top. It has enough liquidity for you to max out size. Stocks will trend and barely touch, much less wiggle, on the respective 5-period moving averages when trending. One-minute stochastics oscillations are sharp and tag the upper and lower Bollinger bands effectively 80% of the time. Fertile environments allow for late entries and even chasing entries, because there is plenty of liquidity to sell into. Just make sure that you are scalping out into the same leg.

INFERTILE ENVIRONMENTS

Characteristics of an infertile environment include:

- No trend

- Tight Bollinger bands and moving averages

- Chop and headfakes resulting in constant failed breakout or break-down attempts

- Decapitation of late and sloppy entries and exits

- Cannibalistic, paranoid, panicking idiots (including you and I)

- Very small window of opportunity to capture a move

- Tendency to give you a little profit early just to suck you into the abyss

An infertile environment is prone to constant panics at extended stochastics levels to screw oscillation players and then ultimately stop out trend players who chase. Infertile environments absolutely punish chasing and late entries. Infertile environments tend to constantly overshoot and chop the respective 5-period moving averages, resulting in flat moving averages and failed breaks. In these environments, a morning loss can be virtually impossible to recover from as liquidity thins out and everyone is paranoid on break attempts in either direction. There are very few effective foreshadowing elements because of the lack of volume. The lack of sustained volume makes it very tough for mini pups and even perfect storms to play out.

Infertile environments suck you in by giving you an early gain and then ruining you in the end. Breakouts will fade to stop out the breakout players and suck in breakdown shorts only to coil back up and stop out the breakdown players. While the oscillation players get a piece of this action, the market will eventually revert to squeezing higher and leaning lower at exhaustion levels through the Bollinger bands, almost randomly. In the end, break players lose, oscillation players lose, and momentum players get slaughtered.

 The brokers are the only ones who win—while you get broke-er

Although the rule of not going to the well too many times applies in all markets, infertile markets only allow one trip before you fall into the (empty) well.

A sloppy trader who only trades fertile environments has a much greater chance of outperforming a skilled trader who only trades infertile environments. These are two theoretical ends of the spectrum. This is very similar to amateur poker players who rack up the chips when dealt great hands. The only problem is these "fish" tend to keep playing the same way when the hands turn weak. It is easier in theory to stay out of bad markets and trade the good markets. The shortfalls come from lack of discipline, inexperience, ego, desperation, and unwillingness to quit.

The word "quit" has such a negative implication in our vocabulary. It implies weakness, failure, lack of motivation, and defeat. This is why stop losses are so hard for people to take. Replace the word "quit" with "pause." That is really all you are doing when you take a stop on a trade or a session. Markets will continue to exist. Whether your account will continue to exist will hinge on the decision to stay in or take a "pause."

You wouldn't walk across a busy intersection when cars are zipping by, would you? You would wait until the coast was clear of danger before crossing. This is the same thinking when trading. Avoid being roadkill by pausing your trading activity through infertile market environments and periods intraday. Just wait on the street corner until the light says walk.

CLOSURE

Here is a great word—closure. Allow me to use it in proper context. Closure, as in close-ur trade, close-ur platform, close-ur account screen, close-ur connection, close-ur eyes.

Closure lets you sleep well at night and allows you to replenish your sharpness gauge and rejuvenate your mind. Closure is a physical act that you have to take so that you can mentally relax. Too much screen time will wear you out and have you seeing things (that aren't usually there). Break that physical connection. There is nothing more detrimental than staring at screens during an infertile market period. All it does is tempt you into making impulsive, dumb trades as the mind tries to curve fit setups, like trying to jam a square peg into a round hole. God forbid you turn your green profits into red losses—that is when the market's voodoo goes into effect and takes control of your mind and emotions.

> Break that physical connection.

Closure is a work in progress that gets easier the more often you practice it. Get in the physical habit of walking away from the screens during deadzone periods every day. Once you make closure a habit, it builds upon itself.

GRUMPY (NOT GREED) IS GOOD: GET P.I.S.S.-ED!

You might notice there is more mention here about infertile market environments than fertile. That's because the bad markets far outnumber the trader's markets. Consolidations and chop outnumber trends and breakouts. Sad but true. You can pretty much assume every market is an infertile market until proven otherwise. Sounds paranoid, gloomy, and pessimistic, no? This type of mentality in a social setting is referred to as being grumpy. In terms of trading the markets, I consider it "Preemptive Instinctual Sensory Sifting," or P.I.S.S. for short.

When you assume that the market is no good, it becomes pleasantly obvious when it is good. This is like focusing on not making red trades, and amazingly the green ones take care of themselves. It's like finding a lit candle in a dark house. It becomes more and more obvious. So wipe that smile off your face, cockroach! Be grumpy, get P.I.S.S.–ed, and remember to wipe the slate clean, with closure. You are on your way, my friend.

"My friend, you are not my friend."

- New York City cab driver

MISTAKING MARKET PERFORMANCE FOR MARKET TRADING ENVIRONMENT

Investors tend to think of the stock markets in terms of being in a bull or bear market. Traders, on the other hand, have to think of the markets in terms of fertile and infertile trading environments. There is very little correlation between a market's trading environment and the performance of the Dow. How many triple-digit Dow gain days have you felt the trading opportunities were no good at all? On the flipside, how many days where the Dow is down triple digits have you found many opportunities on the long side? A market's performance and trading environment are two completely different things. Not only does a trader have to understand this, he has to absolutely accept this. Why? When you fall into the thinking that a +200 point Dow day means you should be making big profits, what do you tend to do? You tend to overtrade, even in low probability setups, because your ego has taken over. The Dow may be up based on a large unplayable gap, or the trend moves are so tight that scalpers find it virtually impossible to scalp gains. Please remember this very key point: The market trading environment has no correlation to market performance. Once you accept this core belief, you will alleviate much unnecessary tension about your own performance.

The market trading environment has no correlation to market performance.

The market trading environment affects traders and is defined as a fertile or infertile market trading environment. Determining fertility is based upon the magnitude of:

- High probability trading opportunities

- Length of window of opportunities

- Consistent pattern follow-through

- Foreshadowing effect

- Playable trends

- Playable ranges

- Heavy volume

- Heavy momentum

- Liquidity

- Sector and stock synergy

Market performance affects investors and is based upon the percentage or point gain or loss on the Dow Jones Industrial Average, Nasdaq, S&P 500 Index, and Russell 2000.

MACRO MARKET PERIODS

The overall market goes through its own peak and valley cycles, where the trading environment gets fertile with news-driven activity, and then infertile as news flows shrink. These are concentrated around the four quarterly earnings reporting seasons throughout the year. General market fertility perks up about two weeks prior to earnings season and then wanes about three quarters of the way through, and falls into a valley period of infertility during the periods preceding the next earnings season. I liken this to peaks and valleys, as the peak periods tend to be more forgiving with sloppy traders due to the abundance of news and momentum.

Unfortunately, the sloppy traders tend to maintain this style as the peaks turn into valleys as market fertility goes through a drought period. Even the sharp, experienced traders have a hard time reaping large gains, so what do you think happens to sloppy traders? Sloppy traders get all chopped up, slaughtering their trading accounts in the process. This likens to the poker analogy of what separates the pros from the "fish." Everyone eventually gets the same cards. Amateurs will score nice profits when they go through their period of peak cards and flops. The difference lies in the fact that the pros adjust their play during the inevitable valley period where the cards are no good. Amateurs will try to overcompensate for poor hands by playing just as aggressively, only to get blown out. Their egos take over as they go full tilt out of control and get blown out. This is what traders tend to do as well. The moral of the story is to play aggressive offense in the peak periods and play defensively in the valley periods. This is easier said than done, of course.

> Play aggressive offense in the peak periods and play defensively in the valley periods.

MICRO MARKET PERIODS

Every trading day for the U.S. equities market is composed of six trading periods. Think of these periods like pieces of a horseracing track. The competitors will start off fast out of the starting gates, but then pace themselves, depending on the particular style of the horse. Frontrunners will start off fast and furious out of the gates to amass a big lead before pacing into the finish. Last-spurt horses will stay behind to conserve stamina for the final stretch explosion into the finish. Stretch runners are a combination of both. None of these types of horses go full steam all the way throughout the race. It's not possible, as there is a limited capacity of stamina. It's reckless and suicidal to even consider going full steam all the way. As logical as that sounds, so many traders tend to hit the gas and never slow down during the market day, or they will pace incorrectly, starting off slow and burning out during the middle of the track, only to collapse before the finish line.

The markets are very similar. Markets don't start off with the heaviest relative volume and maintain that pace all day. It's not possible because the field isn't set up that way. Those who fail to identify the six periods and pace accordingly usually find themselves deep in the hole at the end of the day. You have to align your activity with the market in order to maximize opportunities and minimize risk. Too many traders have it the other way around and don't even know it!

Each of these periods has distinct characteristics and nuances. Some of these periods will provide better and more opportunities than others. It is crucial that you are intimately familiar with these trading landscapes. I will go through each trading period in detail below. The methods of playing these periods are in Chapter 11, The Playbook.

THE SIX TRADING PERIODS OF THE MARKET DAY

Pre-Market: 8:00 a.m.-9:29 a.m. EST

Most brokers allow ECN access starting at 8:00 a.m., and that is usually when the flurry of buying and selling kicks off. Always take a reading of the futures trends patterns on the daily, 60-, 13-, and 8-minute charts. Make special note of any mini pup formations with trend channels in place. This is the period to play earnings reports that were released the prior evening. The reaction, conference call, stock halt, and analyst comments are usually out of the way by this point.

ARCA (an ECN) can be accessed as early as 6:00 a.m., but that will be contingent on your broker platform. The pre-market gives the first crack at a stock move before the tourists show up. Trading in this period is similar to combing the sands of Miami Beach at the crack of dawn with a metal detector to uncover jewelry before the tourists wake up. Most traders shy away from the pre-market due to liquidity concerns, which is a viable concern if there are no gaps or volume. The key here is to get first crack at gapper and dumper stocks that are trending with volume utilizing the awesome 5- and 1-minute pre-market data charts. Due to the lack of automated trading programs, the movements are much more orderly when trends do form. Not every morning will reap rewards, but you should make an effort to start watching the gapper and dumper stocks pre-market from 8:30 a.m. onward.

As of 2009, ARCA is the world's second largest electronic communication network (ECN) in terms of shares traded. Much like other ECNs, ARCA implements a liquidity fee/rebate program to improve overall market liquidity. (investopedia.com)

This is also a good time to get your stock candidate list together for potential trades. Start off with small shares if you find setups here. Windows off opportunity and market fertility improve from here into the opening hour, so pace with the market.

Opening Hour: 9:30 a.m.-10:30 a.m. EST

And they're off! Volume is consistently at its highest off the first 15 minutes. Stocks can make some very large ranges at a frenetic pace. The heavy volume tends to over-exaggerate panic moves, allowing an experienced trader to chase 1-minute mini pups above the 80 band

and 1-minute mini inverse pups below the 20 band. Well-prepared traders can make their daily nut in these first 15 minutes. The key is preparation and reaction. When the action is hot and heavy, pace fast with the market action, but limit share size.

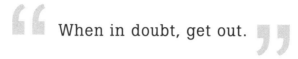 When in doubt, get out.

After the initial 15 minutes, the volume starts to wane as traders get more acclimated to the ranges. Trend moves will usually set up near the top of the hour as the 8- and 13-minute charts start to come into play. This is where you should be trading your best setups with the heavier allocation, especially when you spot perfect storm setups. Pace with the market.

These setups will usually get some follow-through up to the 11:00 a.m. hour. Slow down your activity and tighten filters for setups past the 10:30 a.m. mark. The action and liquidity tends to thin out past 11:00 a.m., as the market starts to enter the deadzone period because traders get hungry and go to lunch. The futures 8- and 13-minute channels tend to flatten out, along with stocks in general.

Deadzone: 11:00 a.m.-1:00 p.m. EST

Ranges are usually tight, moving averages are flat, and volume is the lightest. This period is when traders who don't slow down with the market end up overtrading themselves into a hole. What worked off the open, like chasing 1-minute high band mini pups, will fail miserably in deadzone due to the lack of volume. This is the importance of adjusting your pace with the market as it slows down. Undisciplined traders who made profits off the opening hour tend to slowly give it back in the deadzone. They can't believe how slow the market is but won't quit, so they do what? Keep trading. The automated programs make absolute mincemeat out of these guys. This is where the market can suck you in if you let it. The only remedy for avoiding this trap is to simply stand up and walk away from your screens. I can't stress this enough. Nothing good comes from staring at a flat market. It only wears out your mental sharpness and patience. All it takes is a few small stops and a small win to lure a trader into overtrading hell. Closure is key here.

Witching Hour: 1:00 p.m.-2:00 p.m. EST

This is a strange time period, because nutty things tend to happen. Trends seem to form but are short lived due to the light volume. A trader that got chopped in deadzone will find the final nail in his coffin during the witching hour. Follow-through is elusive, as a 5-candle trend move can evaporate with a single heavy volume candle resetting the price right back to where it started. This is another time frame when it pays to be extra careful. Even perfect storms can be dangerous due to the lack of volume. However, make note of any stocks that form perfect storms in this trading period. Often, I have seen the same perfect storms reform going into the last hour with volume that finally forms the momentum move with follow-through. I know this first-hand, having been chopped on no-volume perfect storm setups, only to see the mirror pattern play out perfectly as volume returns into the last hour.

Last Hour: 3:00 p.m.-4:00 p.m. EST

This is where volume will resume for the final stretch of the market day. It's actually best to watch from the 2:30 p.m. mark going into the last hour. I have noted some interesting time inflection points based on the 13-minute count. The last 20 minutes is where the most volume will start to climb into the market close, as institutional orders and market close orders are placed. The final 5 minutes is like the opening 5 minutes, when heavy volume can make for overextended moves. Once again, chop is what you want to avoid. If there is a trend in place, then watch for possible opportunities. It is very important to make sure you keep an eye on the clock and get out of positions before the 4:00 p.m. closing bell! There's nothing worse than playing a liquid stock during market hours and suddenly have the spreads widen from 0.02 to 0.75! Market makers and specialists are immediately shut down the moment that 4:00 p.m. closing bell rings. This is a rude awakening for anyone that unknowingly holds shares too long. Listed stocks are the worst by far. Even widely held stocks like IBM can suddenly widen to 0.80 spreads between the nearest bid and ask.

Post-Market: 4:00 p.m.-8:00 p.m. EST

Don't spend much time playing post-market unless it is during a significant event like earnings. The spreads tend to get very wide with thin liquidity most of the time. Even with an event and volume, you should rarely ever trade past 5:00 p.m. EST, 6:00 p.m. at the very latest. It's simple. Traders leave for the day. What you have left is far too few participants, resulting in wide spreads and thin to no liquidity. Who needs that?

Traders who fail to realize this find out the hard way that the games in the post-market are tailored to screw traders on the spread with hidden, iceberg, peg, and flash orders. Many stocks have peg orders in place going into the post-market. Just for fun, sometimes you can throw in a bid and a peg order will step in front of you, just to show you they can screw you even when they aren't there. Exploiting this is like trying to find a needle in the haystack, though, so don't even waste your time.

DUPLICITY INFLECTION TIME POINTS

Through the years, I have found that patterns are not only linear, but they tend to repeat in an almost sophomoric manner. When sell programs kick in on Monday and Tuesday one week, setting up a paradigm shift until Wednesday which throws it off, this is usually tossed away as no big deal. However, when significant patterns are faded and disrupted, this is something very key. For years I have noticed this phenomenon, but have not been able to completely capture a solid tracking method because it is so elusive. When perfect storms fade, this is a very significant phenomenon. When perfect storms fade two days in a row, look to spot the time inflection points.

What I have discovered are the critical fade times based on 13-minute normal time frame candle closes, provided there is a trend in place capped by a perfect storm fade.

Once again, if there is a general trend in place, then these time inflection points will either accelerate, or fade and reverse. If they fade and reverse a perfect storm on Monday, pay attention to the exact inflection times on Tuesday (the trend may be opposite). The goal is to get a foothold on the inflection time point or action more so than the exact trend. As long as we know the program trading will kick in, that is all we need to know.

AN EXAMPLE

- 2:05/2:18 p.m. EST – first clue
  These times will either accelerate or reverse an existing obvious trend.

- 3:23 p.m. EST – institutional buy or sell orders

- 3:36 p.m. EST – institutional buy or sell orders

- 3:49 p.m. EST– reversal or further leans

Once again, there is nothing concrete and perfect here. The only evidence of a trend's existence is the proverbial litmus test of the best possible setup that gets faded. When a perfect storm composed of five or more time frames gets faded away on Monday, focus solely on those inflection times, as they may very well repeat on Tuesday.

Here are the criteria for recognizing such a situation.

1. There is a strong trend in place with four to five lane perfect storms.

2. They fade literally out of the blue and completely reverse everything back down starting with the 2:05 p.m. 13-minute candle close (but get in earlier, about 2:01 p.m.). Usually these will sell off to a wider time frame, such as the daily 5-period moving average support level, especially if there is a daily mini pup in place.

3. The trend reverses until the 3:23 p.m. 13-minute candle close, when channel tightenings come in to fade potential perfect storms again. From 3:23 to 3:36 p.m. is where the strongest impact hits the market.

4. A follow-through or fade occurs at 3:49 p.m.

The key is to note any significant powerful trending patterns that fade exceptionally. Once these are set up, look for duplication the following day.

APPLYING PACING TO YOUR TRADING

Now that you have an understanding of the market landscape and how it is broken down, let's go over your own pacing. Through the years, I have learned first-hand the very real presence of support and resistance levels. This obviously applies to markets, but with pacing, I am referring to your own threshold levels, notably a trader's profit and loss thresholds. Markets are linear to human behavior because human beings make up the market. Just as a stock hits a resistance level, too many rejections there will cause it to reverse and collapse. Traders, too, can hit resistance levels and reverse into losses, even collapsing, or as far as blowing out completely. The markets are always in motion; the velocity and direction is what changes. This is why pacing is so important.

TRADING COMFORT ZONE

Everyone manages better when they are near the high end of their profits for the day. That is a nice scenario I wish we could all enjoy daily, but that is not the case. Some days will start off with small losses which won't necessarily throw us off initially. Every little victory helps. The toughest days are those when profits turn to losses. To have and give back more is a nasty thing for human beings to deal with. The ego takes control if those losses get worse, and it will drive you right into the abyss. For this reason, a roadmap of your trading profit and loss sustainability areas must be made.

Every trader has a comfort zone of profits they usually can attain, and more importantly, losses they can endure and still keep a steady heart rate. Exceeding these comfort zones is when the trader will fall apart. The trader will panic and often do irrational things. Poker players who start to sustain larger losses beyond their manageable levels will find themselves taking bigger and bigger risks to inevitably go on "tilt" and blow out.

GOING ON TILT: LOOK OUT BELOW!

Going on tilt when losing money is familiar to most traders. However, traders often go on tilt after making profits beyond their comfort zone too quickly. As they maintain an attitude of "striking while the iron is hot," they will overtrade too many tickets and too much size to have that profit slip back into losses. They can't deal with the idea of giving back all that profit, so they take bigger risks and bigger losses, eventually going on tilt. If we charted this, it would look like a lower Bollinger band rug pull panic. In fact, you can actually chart this, and as a trader, it makes even more sense.

A trader's performance is like a stock. I'm not referring to percentage gains tracked like the S&P 500, but the average gain and loss levels generated without stepping out of the mental and emotional comfort zone. Ideally, you want a steady uptrend of higher highs and higher lows with a relatively small trading channel. The threshold levels are the Bollinger bands. If these threshold levels get broken, the reaction can be dramatic. A solid trader may get a squeeze and pull up the trend on an upper Bollinger band break. A sloppy trader will exhaust back through and collapse the lower Bollinger bands when their ego can't take the losses. As a trader, you want the channels on these bands to be expanding upwardly during peak market periods, and you expect constriction during valley periods. This is why it is so important to be aware of your actual threshold levels and turn up the focus, and down the activity when you get near.

DETERMINING YOUR MONETARY CONTAINMENT ZONES

If you review your trading history, you will be able to determine accurate monetary containment zones for your profits and losses. Every trader has a very real and consistent profit resistance and loss support price range. Take an average dollar amount of the profits you can hit pretty easily early in the day before they start to slip away. Do the same thing with losses that you can bear early on and usually recover from without breaking too much of a sweat. Especially note that dollar amount level that you have usually been able to bounce off of to get back to green. These are like static pivot points that I call containment zones. As long as you are within these zones, you can still maintain control of your activity. When you exceed these initial containment zones, control starts to slip away, drawing you towards final threshold levels. If these threshold levels crack, that's when you are susceptible to going into full tilt mode.

DAILY TRADING MODEL

The daily trading model is the roadmap of your containment zones. Here, I have included an example of my own personal levels. I tend to get to the $300-500 area relatively early on. The $700 range of profits is where I notice a sticking point. I am usually able to work back losses up to the $400 range without much of a problem. However, when losses crack past the $600 range, I have personally started to overcompensate with riskier trades and poor leveraging. If I get beyond $1000 in losses, I find myself most susceptible to going on tilt. This is an honest assessment. The truth hurts, but it can set you free.

Bollinger bands are a device employed by technical analysts to measure the volatility of a market or security, and to determine levels of support and resistance. A moving average of prices is first plotted on a chart, then additional lines, or "bands," are plotted two standard deviations above and two standard deviations below that moving average. This defines a trading channel, which is wider when volatility is high and narrower when volatility falls. When current prices approach the upper band, the market or stock is assumed to be overbought, and when they near the lower band, they are said to be oversold.

(TradersLibrary.com/ glossary)

Figure 3.1

Sample Daily
Trading Model

For a closer
look, please visit
TradersLibrary.com/
TLECorner.

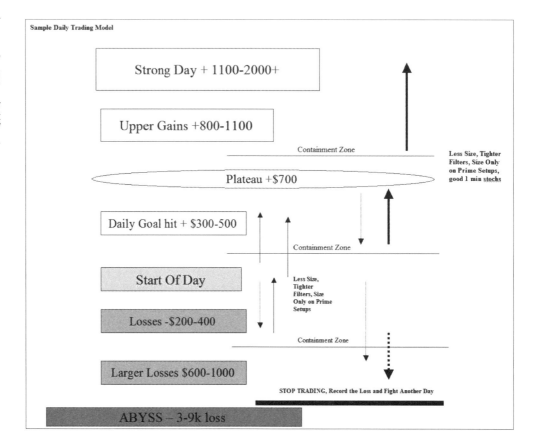

Sample Daily Trading Model

With the roadmap in Figure 3.1, I know that once I get up near that +$700 upper containment zone (usually during pre-market or opening hour) of profits, which I also refer to as the plateau, I have to slow it down. That means less shares and tighter filters to preserve profits. Placing a profit stop loss on the day at my +$300-500 containment support zone keeps me from risking the rest of the profits and falling back into the red. If I can slowly grind through that +$700 plateau area, it's because the market is very fertile that day and will usually propel me slowly through the +$1,000 level, using a break of the +$700 as a profit stop area.

Every trader has a very real and consistent profit resistance and loss support price range.

On the flipside, if I find myself approaching the -$400 loss area, I slow it down, pace and size wise, and pump the brakes to slowly scalp back more tightly filtered setups. If I fall lower past -$600, I will take a break and give it one more try post-deadzone or in the last hour. If I can't get back under -$400, then I call it a day. Never will I allow it to crack that -$1000 final containment zone. I know first-hand how bad it can turn into a -$5,000 loss (most of that comes from commissions alone). It's not fun sitting in front of your computer screen at 7:00 p.m., being the only idiot trying to find liquidity in a pretty much closed market. That is called the abyss. Try not to make too many trips there!

PUMP RELEASE PACING METHOD

I referred to pumping the brakes near containment zones. When traders make profits or losses too sharply, they can turn that trend into inconsistent chop. The key is to be steady and paced. Think about how a solid trend moves. It pumps up first, then pulls back to a higher support, then pumps up and pulls back to a higher support, slowly but surely. It's like pumping the brakes in icy weather to come to a steady stop rather than slamming on the brakes, which can result in skidding out of control right off the road. Pumping the brakes keeps you in control and avoids accidents. Pump and release is the pacing rhythm. This mindset should be applied to your trading activity utilizing the daily trading model (like the one in Figure 3.1) as a roadmap. On the next page is an actual slide from yours truly that best illustrates this method in its raw, unedited, misspelled glory.

Much like driving in icy conditions, consider the first containment zones like a red traffic light on losses. The second containment zone is a stop sign. With profits, the first containment zone is a yield sign. Remember to pump those brakes! When you find yourself in front of that stop sign, turn off the computer, get up and walk away. Trust me, it is the best alternative, unless you like driving off a cliff!

PUMP/RELEASE PACING METHOD

- Everyone has a Profit and Loss threshold they hit—and then…Pump Pacing Method is similar to pumping the brakes at each containment zone/threshold level—Turn off Platform and Take a Walk.

- First thing is to determine what is your basic profit range before you start giving back.

- Then determine what is the manageable intra day loss range you can comfortably hit and recover from AND what level do you slip into the ABYSS?

- Once you can determine this, you have to set in physical containment zones. I mean physical and conscious. Mental is b*llshit. Gotta get to PHYSICAL. Physically turn off broker and PHYSICALLY WALK AWAY. If you don't want to get mugged, you don't walk around in the ghetto at 2am on a Saturday morning, right?

- Once you pump up to $200-$400 in profits, turn off the platform and watch only

- Only once you spot a set up so irresistible you have to take it, then turn it back on and place the trade—this is how you pump up the profits incrementally, like pumping the brakes.

- Step away during dead zone, turn off platform and especially WITCHING HOUR 1-2pm est, trim share size LIGHT if you play anything from 12-2pm est.

- Where trader's lose is when their allocation goes haywire. Chasing high, scalping out and then adding higher and heavier in most cases takes green straight to RED. Impulse trading, desperation trading and heavy size trading on flat choppy light volume.

- If you go red into the threshold, first thing, trim size and look for small victories. Nurse it back to less than red then green on the day. If you hit the threshold loss, turn off system and just watch. Closure and Apathy. Remember your ABYSS day and how a -1k loss turned into -6k. It can always be worse. When you break the lower threshold, it means you are not clicking with the market, it's just not there, walk away.

- Also remember, a sucky chop day can result in a sold momentum volume action day tomorrow. Be ready for tomorrow. Pacing is KEY and BREAK it up, turn off broker platform through the day—this PHYSICALLY prevents impulse trading.

BRING IT FULL CIRCLE: TEST YOURSELF

1 A fertile environment has which of the following characteristics:

    a) volume
    b) follow-through
    c) momentum
    d) trends
    e) trading channels
    f) all of the above
    g) none of the above

2 Consolidations are great formations to trade during dead zone.

    a) True
    b) False

3 Proper pacing means to hit the gas during fertile trading periods and pump the brakes during the infertile trading periods.

    a) True
    b) False

4 When you hit your plateau on the daily trading model, you should trade heavier size and more often.

    a) True
    b) False

For answers, please visit the
Traders' Library Education Corner at
www.traderslibrary.com/TLEcorner.

CHAPTER ④

TAKING TIME OFF FROM TRADING

Not everyone is cut out to trade, and there is no shame in that. Anyone who feels too pressured to make money from trading needs to step back. As I mentioned earlier, having savings put away, alternative sources of income, and only using risk capital is the only way to approach this game. If any of the three are lost or depleted, then you need to take a voluntary break to realign those conditions. There is nothing more harmful than desperation in trading. Desperate money always loses in the end.

If you find yourself in a frustrating losing slump, make sure that you assess whether the cause is mostly you, or the market's trading environment. Well, actually, it's still your fault for trading in a poor market climate. You should be trading less in these environments. If you find that you are overtrading, playing deadzone, and sticking around post-market desperately looking for that one needle in the haystack to load up on…then it's definitely you. You can not control the markets. You can control yourself. If taking intraday and deadzone breaks doesn't help, then take a week off.

> Anyone who feels too pressured to make money from trading needs to step back, take a break, and reevaluate.

IT'S NOT YOU DEAR, IT'S ME

If you are feeling tension and/or desperation every time you place a trade, then it's likely you. Try finding different core stocks and trim your share size. If you find yourself chasing entries and waiting too long on exits, it's likely you. The market will always have a major role in your slump, but the question is if you are sabotaging yourself regardless of the market. If you find yourself not having the interest or energy to do morning research, then you need to take a break from the markets. Take a clean, cold-turkey week off to replenish your gauges. You can attain that same moment of clarity from blowing out your account, without actually doing it. Just take a week off. Voila!

THE REWARD FOR CALLING IT QUITS

Being in this business as an educator has been a heart breaker. I have seen most try and fail in this game. There are countless people that I have grown attached to and wanted so badly to see them succeed, only to have them quit the game. Last year, the reality of this game and life hit me square in the face… not all will make it. This only makes the juice even more worth the squeeze.

Of those who didn't succeed as traders, those who gave the most effort very likely uncovered another skill and went onto success elsewhere. The trading was a stepping stone to harness and uncover another strength— not an alternate destiny, but their true destiny. Remember balance; the more enduring effort you pay, the more worthwhile your reward will be.

Abraham Maslow was a humanist psychologist who believed that human beings have a hierarchy of five basic needs. Maslow's hierarchy is often illustrated by a pyramid, with basic, physiological needs at the base, building up through safety needs, needs of love, affection, and belongingness, to needs for esteem, and finally, needs for self-actualization.

To find one's calling is perhaps what Maslow was referring to in his hierarchy when he speaks of self-actualization. Maslow's hierarchy of needs pertains to the needs of human beings, from basic needs— food, shelter and clothing—at the bottom, on up to the tippy top, which is self-actualization. Self-actualization means what? Knowing who and what you are, what your destiny is, and finding the transparency within.

THE "EDGE" DEFINED

The common belief of attaining an edge is a misnomer. One can't possess an edge indefinitely. An edge is always fleeting. Inside information and order flow can give the trader a temporary edge (though not legally), however, even those will be applicable for a limited duration of time. Traders assume an edge is a static component that, once attained, can be routinely utilized at will. The reality is that the edge is an elusive, fleeting, and dynamic condition that forms upon the convergence of the right combination of the markets, methods, and management. The edge is a paradox, in that once it becomes too transparent, everyone will try to exploit it, thereby diluting it in the process. The edge is never completely owned. It is borrowed at best.

> The edge is an elusive, fleeting, and dynamic condition that forms upon the convergence of the right combination of the markets, methods, and management.

The goal of a trader is to identify and exploit the edge as it presents itself, with the understanding that it can only be borrowed. Therefore, a trader must maximize when he has the edge, and minimize exposure when it is relinquished. Embracing this understanding brings the trader that much closer to attaining the edge—temporarily, of course.

PART ❷

THE COMPLETE TRADING SYSTEM FULL CIRCLE

This part of the book will delve into the tools, indicators, methods, and how to apply them step by step. The goal is to educate on the complete method so that the reader can take what works best for them, whether it is the whole system or pieces of the system.

This system is the result of all the years and tears. Take the time to learn it slowly, one piece at a time. You saved ten years of trial and error.

CHAPTER ⑤

THE TOOLS

The tools implemented now are still very similar to the tools I have used for many years. They have just been tweaked a bit over time. Since these tools are dynamically form-fitting to the movement of the underlying movements, they don't need much modification. There is one new tool that I will introduce in this chapter that is perhaps the most significant addition to the arsenal. It took me over a year to begrudgingly add this tool to my arsenal, and as much as I minimized its utility, it kept proving me wrong. It also filled in a deep gap in my methods that had to do with pre- and post-market trading. Before this tool, I had to rely mostly on instinct and static price levels. However, this tool enlightened the murky waters and forced me to see the light. This new tool can be found on the CobraIQ platform at www.cobratrading.com. I highly recommend them as an online broker and charting platform.

STACKING

The concept of stacking has many connotations in the market. Most commonly you hear of stacking the bid or the ask. The basic underlying theme of stacking is to galvanize. When bids are stacked, it implies fortitude and solid support. Well, this is not the stacking I'll be referring to. The concept of stacking does still apply, though. The purpose of stacking is to galvanize and fortify.

When you are setting up a trade, you have to actively look for premises to support your trade. These premises and components need to be stacked to increase the probabilities that your trade will play out to fruition. Stack the components. Think in terms of stacking when assembling your trade. The more you stack, the stronger your trade will be, as well as your own confidence in the trade. In the nature of reciprocity, we have all heard the phrase "having the deck stacked against you." The job of every trader is to have the deck stacked for you.

For example, say that RIMM has an 8- and 13-minute dual mini pup with a 3-minute make-or-break and a 1-minute mini pup at the 40 band with upper Bollinger bands 0.70 higher, trading near a double overlapping support, and the NQs have an identical pattern. This is a stacked trade in your favor with a nice 1-minute mini pup trigger.

WHAT DO YOU NEED?

The "father of modern architecture," Louis Sullivan, coined the phrase, "form follows function." Another way to view this is to thoroughly work a tool until the missing element becomes apparent. By thoroughly working a tool, it means you utilize it and believe in it, but you may start to notice some inconsistencies. You try to downplay the inconsistencies (according to cognitive dissonance theory) until they become blaringly apparent, too apparent to write off. That void is what drives the hunger. It's a form of deprivation. This is how I developed the methods.

> Traders should also utilize deprivation
> with their own journey. Yes, deprivation,
> sound familiar?

The biggest drawback with the access to methods, tools, and indicators today is that it is handed over on the silver platter. The deprivation factor either doesn't come into play, or takes much longer to become a necessary factor.

Let's go over the basic tools. Much of this I have written about before, but if it works, then use it. I will also breakdown the nuances of the tools that I have personally come across through the thousands of hours.

NASDAQ LEVEL II SCREEN AND TIME OF SALES

This is used primarily for point-and-click execution. There are no more ax market makers like the good old days. The time of sales is significant because you can see the flow of trades, which are the actual footprints displayed on the charts. Make sure that you have two Nasdaq Level II screens with time of sales, with the point-and-click execution panels, on every trade you make. You want to have the same symbol on both screens whenever you make a trade. The primary screen will execute your entry and exits. The second screen will be for backup emergency stops.

It's always good to have two weapons available. I like to use the primary module for the main trading for a particular stock. I can work the scaling in and out, and adjust the shares. The second Level II screen will always have the total shares keyed up with a sweep order ready in case I have to exit quickly, preset to route to an ECN (I usually use ISLD). The backup Level II is such a life saver that I don't trade without it. In the few seconds it may take to adjust an order on the primary Level II, I would already be out on the second Level II. When panic kicks in, those precious few seconds are the difference between a paper cut and an amputation.

The difference may be seconds, but those seconds can be costly if you're not already lined up and ready to execute. This can be set up with the "link" option on most platforms. Link the primary Level II screen to a set of stochastics moving average charts for each time frame (1-, 3- , 8- , 13-, and 60-minute, daily regular data and 1- and 5-minute on pre- and post-market full time data).

Since the Level II will be the primary execution tool, I want to cover trade execution and its nuances.

ROUTING ORDERS
With professional direct access platforms like CobraIQ (www.cobratrading.com), you will have to choose where to route your order when placing trades. There are basically two types of entities to route orders to: market

makers (on Nasdaq) and specialists (on listed NYSE, AMEX, etc.), or ECNs (ARCA, ISLD, etc.). Market makers and specialists don't charge an extra liquidity fee, which cuts down on costs if you aren't in a rush to get in or out of a trade. This works out decently with thick, liquid stocks in slow markets. Keep in mind, they are usually getting order flow kickbacks from your broker, so don't think these clowns are being charitable. The lack of quality and speed of the fills will be most apparent in fast-moving markets and thinner stocks. ECNs, on the other hand, are much faster, but you pay for that speed and liquidity through additional fees. Market makers will pickpocket you on the back end, ECNs pretty much screw you to your face. However, they dangle the rebate carrot to entice more liquidity, which builds upon itself.

ECN FEES AND REBATES

ECN stands for Electronic Communication Network, which is an electronic marketplace that allows traders to trade with one another on an exchange. An ECN connects major brokerages and individual traders so that they can trade directly between themselves without having to go though a middleman. ARCA and ISLD are among the most popular ECNs. (www.investopedia.com)

The ECNs (electronic communication networks) have taken over the markets. ARCA (which is actually an exchange that owns NYSE) and ISLD are the two dominant players. There are smaller players such as BTRD, BRUT, and whoever offers bigger rebates to attract more liquidity—maybe one day they will make a dent.

As of this writing, ARCA charges $0.004 for taking liquidity and rebates $0.002 for providing liquidity. ISLD charges $0.003 for taking liquidity and rebates $0.002 for providing liquidity. Make sure to check with your broker on the current ECN fees. Providing liquidity means you buy on the inside bid or sell on the inside ask. Taking liquidity means you buy on the inside ask or sell on the inside bid.

For example, if your commission rate is $0.006 per share and you buy 1,000 shares of RIMM through ARCA on the ask and sell through ARCA on the bid, your commission cost will be $10 per ticket ($6 broker commission and $4 for ARCA fee), a $20 round trip. If you buy RIMM on the inside bid on the pullback for 1,000 shares and sell into the ask, your broker commission cost is $6, but you get rebated $2 for providing liquidity. That makes it a $4 total commission per ticket, for a $8 round trip cost versus $20. If you average 40,000 shares a day, you are looking at $400 in total commissions and fees costs (taking liquidity from ARCA) versus $160 for entering and exiting on the inside bid or ask through ARCA. That $240 savings every day for 20 trading days a month is $4,800 in monthly savings that could be going into your pocket.

 This ain't figurative thinking, this is a cold hard cash reality.

That money either goes into your pockets or to the ECNs. Of course, you won't be playing inside bid and ask all the time, but even trying to provide liquidity on the exits will amount to significant savings, which in turn go towards your profits. A penny saved is truly a penny earned when trading.

The other benefit of entering trades on the inside bid or ask is that it forces you to plan out the trade ahead of time. You obviously have to be aware of support and resistance levels to properly place these types of trades to fill. Getting filled on the inside for trade entries usually puts you into a profit zone right off the bat if timed right, which affects the bottom line immediately.

When you need to get in or out of a stock fast, there is no alternative to using ECNs. Market makers and specialists are not only pathetically slow, but will end up screwing you anyway if given the chance. Keep in mind that specialists through NYSE charge a $0.003 per share fee to route with no refunds. It's bad enough you screwed on the fill, but the additional fee is just pouring acid in the wound. AMEX specialists are the worst, charging $0.005 per share for trades. This is another reason to stay away from specialists.

It is best to use a market maker to route. Check with your broker for specific routing fees, as these tend to change. Pre- and post-market trading is only accessible through ECNs. Depending on your broker, ARCA opens at 6:00 a.m. EST, and ISLD opens at 7:00 a.m.

HIDDEN AND RESERVE ORDERS
ARCA and ISLD allow you to place hidden orders, as well as reserve orders that will only display a fixed share size until the complete order is taken out. While these may sound like powerful, sneaky tools, they are pretty obvious in lighter volume markets and stocks, and can backfire if misused. It's not a very covert tool when almost everyone has access.

These should only be used when volume is heavier. You must pull the order once it becomes too obvious so as not to stifle momentum, especially on exits!

When 15,000 shares go off on the ask in 100 share increments while you are sitting on the inside ask with a 100 size displaying, you are not only being obvious, but holding up traffic while risking a momentum reversal as other cockroaches will step in front of you and bids get pulled. Remember, greed is not good when you make it obvious. Infertile trading environments are especially sensitive to these orders.

> Keep your hand in the cookie jar too long
> and it will get lopped off.

The goal is to get in and get out without making a market impact and leaving footprints. These are most effective when entering a trade, as your hidden or reserve order can give the perception of a reversal.

Market makers and traders are extremely sensitive and resentful to hidden and reserve orders that are overused. Anyone who abuses them will likely get shaken out. The goal is to use them without leaving your footprints. Don't have too many shares set at one reserve price level. It's best to sprinkle them out, especially in pre- or post-market.

TYPES OF ORDERS

MARKET ORDERS

Never use these orders in a fast market. I stick to the adage of never using them, period. You basically put your trade in someone else's hand. It's not that every market order will get you slaughtered. The problem is that when you do get screwed hard on a fill during a panic or fast market, there is really no recourse. It's a license for the market makers or specialists to mug you in broad daylight. Just adding a limit price will protect you from these "rare" disasters.

LIMIT ORDERS

As the name implies, a limit order places your trade up to a specified price level. The only way to get ECN rebates is with limit orders. When exiting a position for profit, the limit order allows you to sell into the buyers or cover into sellers.

In emergency situations when panic sets in, the limit order placed well below the bid is a worst case safety net that prevents you from getting completely screwed. This order basically says fill me on the inside bid, down to this worst case price. Don't make your limit orders too tight on your stop or exit on the secondary Level II. The goal is to get filled quickly. Placing your order 0.10-0.20 below the bid (contingent on the stock spreads) is referred to as a sweep order. You are instructing to sweep all the bids down to your limit price to exit your position. Don't be too stringent on limit orders. The last thing you want to do is to have to constantly re-enter the limit price because the stock is slipping past your tight limit prices. This is precisely what you are trying to avoid with a sweep order.

PEG ORDERS

Peg orders will "peg" to the inside bid or ask until your order is completely executed up to your limit price, adjusted, or cancelled. Peg orders adjust automatically with the stock price. If the stock moves beyond your limit price, it will stay posted there until filled or cancelled. Peg orders are only available through ECNs.

There are three types of peg orders.

1. **Market peg orders** peg the price to the inside ask up to your limit price, and vice versa if selling.

   For example, say you place a market peg order for 500 shares of ABC, limit 19.10, currently trading at 19.05 x 19.08. Your order would try to fill at the inside ask at 19.08. If you fill 300 shares before ABC upticks to 19.07 x 19.09, your order will immediately try to fill the rest of the shares on the inside ask up to the 19.10 limit. If you only get 100 more shares at 19.09 before ABC jumps to 19.12 x 19.13, the rest of your order will sit at the 19.10 limit until filled, adjusted, or cancelled.

2. **Mid peg orders** will round to the nearest penny and try to split the spread if possible, by placing you on the inside bid when buying, or the inside ask when selling, up to your limit price. This type of order is designed to rack up ECN rebates. The nice thing here is that you may often be the only order on the inside due

to the spread splitting mechanism, which increases the odds of getting filled. Measuring the momentum is critical to successful peg orders.

For example, you might place a mid peg order for 500 shares of ABC, limit 19.10. ABC is currently trading at 19 x 19.05. The mid peg order will automatically split the spread and place you at 19.02, and adjust up to your limit price until executed. If ABC jumps to 19.12 x 19.15, your order will stay posted at the 19.10 limit price until filled, adjusted, or cancelled.

3. **Primary peg orders** place your order price completely to the inside bid when buying, and the inside ask when selling, up to your limit price. The order price will automatically adjust with the stock price until you are filled. This type of order is good for ECN rebates, but you will be competing with other orders on the inside, which will greatly limit your chances of getting filled if the market moves away from you.

Say you place a primary peg order for 500 shares of ABC, limit 19.10. ABC is currently trading at 19 x 19.05. Your order will post at the inside bid price of 19. If ABC upticks to 19.03 x 19.06, your order will automatically uptick to 19.03 on the inside bid. If ABC jumps to 19.12 x 19.15, your order will stay posted at 19.10 limit price until filled, adjusted, or cancelled.

STICKY 2.50 AND STICKY 5

These sticky levels are aptly titled, as they tend to be momentum sticking points. They are the equivalent of a speed bump that can turn into a wall. Stocks tend to exhaust ahead of these levels and stay contained within these levels once penetrated. The levels are a phenomenon that may be linked to options pricing increments, which are usually priced in 2.50 increments up to $50, and then in $5 increments. To calculate the sticky levels, just count in 2.50 increments from 5 on up—5, 7.50, 10, 12.50, 15, 17.50, and so on. Sticky 5s are the 5 increment points like 5, 10, 15, 20, 25, 30, etc.

We factor in a 0.10 overshoot by adding and subtracting 0.10 from the 2.50 level to derive 17.40 and 17.60 as the upper and lower range of the 17.50 sticky 2.50 levels. Overshoots are a result of panics and sweep orders.

With sticky 5 levels, take the respective 5 increment level and make it the midpoint, which means adding 0.50 to each side, as in 14.50 and 15.50, with 15 being the midpoint. Then add and subtract the normal 0.10 overshoots to each side of the upper and lower range, which gives 14.40 x 14.60 and 15.40 x 15.60. These make the lower and upper ranges of the sticky 5 levels.

The way this phenomenon tends to play out is when a stock is rising, especially on momentum; it will tend to hit a momentum exhaustion or peak at that 17.40 resistance level. It will take extra volume to crack that level, at which point the 17.50 is the next sticking point, on up to 17.60. It works the same way as support levels when stock prices fall. That 17.60 tends to hold pretty strong support off the bat and it takes a surge in volume to crack that level, then 17.50, and lastly 17.40. If the momentum is just enough to penetrate into that 2.40 x 2.60 (15 plus 2.50, plus or minus 0.10 overshoot) area without breaking the upper range, then stocks tend to get stuck in that range, until volume comes in and breaks it through.

The sticky 5 levels work in the same manner with the lower and upper range points. For example, if AMZN is trading at 69.20, then we know that 70 being the sticky 5 level means 69.40 x 69.50 is the lower range, and 70.40 x 70.60 is the upper sticky 5s range. If you are long AMZN from 68.95, you want to place your sell limit orders before that 69.40 resistance, like 69.37. When that 69.40 first ticks, it will tend to peak and exhaust back down, especially when 1-minute stochastics are trading above the 80 band.

STICKY 0.75 AND 0.30

Strangely, I have noticed other price sticking levels that have become apparent on the thicker liquidity stocks like AAPL and RIMM. The 0.30 and 0.75 areas for some reason tend to be very sticky. Watch AAPL when it cracks a round number on buying momentum; very rarely will it break through the 0.30 level. In fact, that is where exhaustion will most likely set in. The same applies to AAPL when it sells off through a round number; very rarely will it break through the 0.75 level on the first attempt. Knowing this, traders tend to place limit orders near those levels to catch panic sweep orders to buy or sell. These levels almost become a self-fulfilling prophecy once enough traders are watching. The SPY definitely follows these levels.

It sounds like voodoo until you actually see it play out consistently, day in and day out. These are default support and resistance price levels on every stock. Always remember that they are extra sticky if they overlap with other support and resistance levels (such as pivots, moving averages, or Bollinger bands). As with any support or resistance level, adjust your trade to utilize these levels for entries and exits.

The other very important function of knowing these levels is to prevent you from trading in that area when the market environment is infertile. Choppy, flat markets are the worst to get trapped into playing anywhere near these levels. Save your ammo and your sanity by avoiding these levels during such market periods.

BASIC EXECUTION RULES

1. Always use limit orders with two Level II execution modules in place.

    a. Be generous with your sweep stop prices to avoid having to adjust them while the stock is panicking (on the second Level II screen/order execution).

    b. Pre-plan exit levels with the sticky 2.50s and sticky 5s.

2. Try to provide liquidity when possible to collect ECN rebates—this is an absolute for oscillation scalpers.

    a. Sprinkle in buy and sell orders at various levels.

    b. Use peg orders if your broker allows them. These are orders that will automatically place you on the inside bid or ask as the stock moves.

    c. Map out overlapping support and resistance levels ahead of time.

    d. Use the hidden or reserve orders as you get filled; your order can work for you by stifling the momentum back into your favor.

3. If you are not in a rush to get into or out of a stock, it is best to route straight to a market maker or specialist directly, as they don't charge liquidity fees. But beware, you will get screwed in a fast market or illiquid stock.

4. Only use hidden or reserve orders during periods of heavy volume.

    a. If your size is under 1,000 shares, just break it up into pieces without using hidden or reserve orders. You will do more harm if misusing these orders, especially in the pre- or post-market.

5. Utilize the sticky 2.50, 5, 0.30, and 0.75 levels in a traders' market, and avoid those levels like the plague in choppy, flat markets. These levels are notorious for headfakes and the primary areas where traders get churned to death.

CHARTS

LINEARITY, CONVERGENCE, AND DIVERGENCE

Right off the mark, I will use these three words a lot throughout the book, as they are key factors in all markets. *Linearity* means that if a pattern consistently plays out in one time frame or market, then it should play out in all time frames or markets. All proven patterns are linear. Pup and mini pup patterns are linear throughout all time frames. *Convergence* refers to stocks, patterns, and indicators pointing in the same direction. Perfect storms are when three or more pups or mini pups converge. *Divergence* is when they conflict. For example, AAPL may be diverging with the Nasdaq futures, meaning it is selling off while futures are rising. Time frames will often have diverging trends.

Most of the charts will contain identical studies and indicators. The only difference will be the time frames (1-, 3-, 5-, 8-, 13-, and 60-minute, daily, weekly, monthly) and time range of data (market

A stock or any financial instrument can be in an uptrend and downtrend simultaneously at any given time. However, the transparency only reveals itself when the time frames all converge.

hours only and full 24 hour including pre- and post-market). Remember this rule: the longer a time frame is, the stronger the patterns and price levels are. This means a monthly 200-period moving average resistance is much stronger than a 3-minute 200-period moving average resistance. A weekly mini pup is stronger than an 8-minute mini inverse pup. The wider time frame price levels override intraday price levels.

The best scenario is when wider time frame levels overlap with the shorter time frame levels. This galvanizes the price levels and allows one to plan trades at those levels, like placing bid/asks (which provide liquidity) at those galvanized support and resistance levels. The best pattern scenarios are when the daily, weekly, or monthly time frames have converging pup or mini pup patterns.

> The longer a time frame is, the stronger the patterns and price levels are.

Implant another key rule into your brain. The wider time frame patterns will only provide the follow-through when the shorter time frames trigger in that direction. For example, a 60-minute pup or mini pup breakout doesn't trigger until the 8- and 13-minute charts turn back up. The strongest impact comes from the convergence of the time frames in the direction of the wider time frame charts. Got that?

CHART COMPONENTS AND STUDIES

Don't buy into the general criticism about the ineffectiveness of moving averages, stochastics, and Bollinger bands. People misunderstand how, and more important, when to apply these tools synergistically. Styrofoam cups are good to drink coffee out of, and gasoline is good to fuel your car. That's about it. That is the same conventional wisdom that believes moving averages, stochastics, and Bollinger bands are limited tools. MacGuyver would be very disappointed. These people don't realize that when you combine the two everyday items, Styrofoam and gasoline, it produces napalm.

 Boo-yah. The same principle can be applied with basic charting tools, MacGuyver style.

A tool is only effective if used correctly. Through the thousands and thousands of hours of use, I have found that an effective tool can be even more effective when combined with other tools. It's like taking basic household items and combining the right mix to create a powerful agent, just like Styrofoam and gasoline making napalm. One tool is not enough, but combining several tools together can produce something explosive. The standard tools can harness an outlier effect when used effectively with other tools.

Standard tools used in a non-standard way will produce this. My thousands of hours of trial and error have resulted in the right mix of tools used in a certain way to ultimately create a foreshadowing element in the right setting. This is as close as you get to a crystal ball in the stock market.

You will still need to put in the time to get acclimated, as well as to be convinced of their effectiveness. What good is making napalm if you end up burning yourself because you don't know how to use it?

 Don't try that at home, kids!

OVERLAPPING PRINCIPLE FOR SUPPORT AND RESISTANCE GALVANIZATION

If a single resistance level is good, then three or more is super. While a single resistance level's strength may be determined by the time frame, when that level is also a resistance level on other time frames, this causes an overlap effect that galvanizes the level. For example, ABC's daily 200-period moving average resistance sits at 19.60. However, that 19.60 level is also a sticky 5 resistance level, and may be a 60-minute upper Bollinger band resistance, and perhaps it is a weekly 5-period resistance on an existing downtrend. This overlaps three separate indicators at 19.60, thereby galvanizing the resistance. The rule of thumb is that three or more overlaps make for a solid, galvanized level. With this knowledge, you will be able to lock in profits ahead of time, before momentum peaks on spikes, or short near that level with a trail stop just above it in order to profit off a reversal.

> Three or more overlaps make for a solid, galvanized level.

CANDLESTICKS: PRICE TOOL

I still use candlesticks on my price charts. They are tried and true as long as you stick to the basic reversal patterns. I don't go much beyond hammers and stars. I like to keep it simple because I have found that the more complicated the candle formations, the more room for failures. A machine with a few parts is more reliable than one with a hundred moving parts, and easier to fix.

DON'T JUDGE A CANDLE BEFORE ITS CLOSE

Don't make the mistake of judging a candle before it actually closes. Due to the common knowledge of candle formations, traders may often try to paint a hammer or star mid-candle close, only to step off right before the close. When I refer to close, that means the final formation of the candle based on the incremental time frame of the chart. For example, on a 5-minute chart, a candle finalizes its formation every 5 minutes from the top of the hour (10:00 a.m., 10:05 a.m., 10:10 a.m., etc.). A candle may look like a hammer at 9:57 a.m., but at 9:59:21, the buyers may pull their bids and panic out more sellers, only to close as a solid continuation red candle at the 10:00 a.m. candle close. This happens numerous times during the trading day with numerous stocks. They are as common as wiggles. Always wait for the candle close (which updates the moving averages too) before judging the candle. Don't be too anxious.

> "Wiggles" refers to price movements that reverse quickly just as it appears that a trend may be forming. Wiggles, headfakes, and chop are all synonomous and found in consolidations, tight markets, and make-or-breaks.

SHOOTING STARS

Shooting stars are exhaustion candles that form at the peak of uptrends. Usually, they form on the final climactic pop on volume as the last of the buyers panic into the stock in a frenzy—only to look down and realize that they chased too high. The panic selling triggers earlier buyers to start taking profits. The shorts smell this and start shorting the stock in anticipation of further selling. This is illustrated with a small candle body with a long tail or shadow at least twice the size of the body, as in Figure 5.1.

> The more consecutive continuation candles prior to the shooting star, the stronger the reversal effect.

Shooting stars are only viable at the top of the range of an uptrend followed by at least three consecutive green continuation candles. The more green candles that precede the star, the stronger the reversal. Not only do you have to wait for the star to form upon the actual candle close, but the subsequent candle must close below the low price of the shooting star to make it viable. The low of the shooting star candle is the proverbial line in the sand and the trap door.

Don't make the mistake of taking a star candle out of context. Too many traders focus on the visual identification of the star with the small body and long tail, without noticing the context. If a star candle forms without prior consecutive trading candles, it's basically just a wiggle, similar to the pup that looks to form without a stochastics cross. These end up being nothing more than chop. Filtering is the key. Secondly, the star is not confirmed until

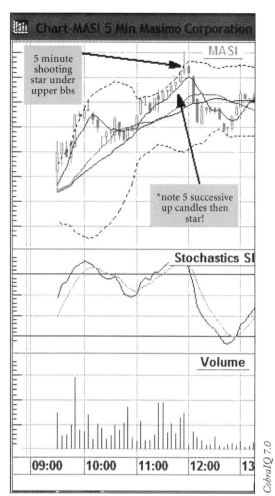

Figure 5.1
Shooting Star

For a closer look, please visit TradersLibrary.com/ TLECorner.

the second candle trades and closes under the low of the star. This is what sets off the selling process. The last of the breakout buyers panic into the stock, only to realize they chased it too high, and then they fall over each other to get out of the stock. When the low price of the shooting star is violated, this triggers earlier buyers to take profits, as well as invites shorts and oscillation players to short the stock back down.

GRAVESTONE DOJI CANDLE

This is a variation of the shooting star candle with no body. It signals a top and should come after successive up, green candles. It looks like a shooting star with no body due to the open and close being at or near the bottom.

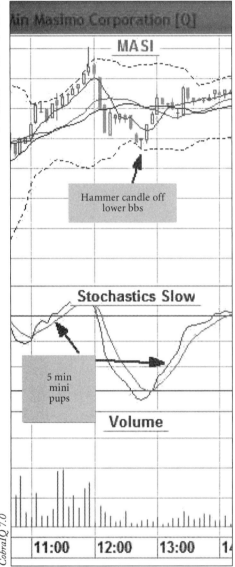

HAMMER CANDLE

Hammers are the inverse version of a shooting star, where the last of the sellers capitulate in a panic and shorts chase down entries before the buyers step in. The tail is at least twice the length of the body. Preferably, you want hammers to form off a lower Bollinger band, as seen in Figure 5.2. These need to form at the lowest price range of a downtrend, on volume, followed by at least three consecutive red candles. Always wait for the candle close to form. The next candle needs to close at or above the high of the hammer candle to trigger the squeeze effect, as late shorts will be the first to panic out, thereby sucking in bargain-hunting buyers off the fence. The high of the hammer candle is the line in the sand and the squeeze trigger. That is the level you want to enter when playing a hammer reversal tightening.

DRAGONFLY CANDLE

This is a variation of the hammer candle with no body because the open and close occur at or near the top of the candle. It is a reversal candle that signals a bottom and needs to have successive down, red candles preceding it.

The key to stars and hammers is filtering.
You want as many consecutive continuation candles before the reversal candle forms (and closes) for the most effective moves.

VOLUME BARS

When a stock price jumps on a very heavy volume bar that is five times or more than the prior volume bars, jot down that candle close price level. This will be a key support area on pullbacks and a breakdown area if it collapses. A heavy volume bar accompanied by price movement sets a line in the sand. At the end of a momentum move, a heavy volume bar signals a climax peak, especially if accompanied by a reversal candle (star or hammer).

FIB COUNTS

Call it superstition or voodoo, but whenever a momentum move takes place, I like to count the candles in anticipation of the inevitable exhaustion. I use the Fib counts 3, 5, 8, and 13 as key tests. If a momentum break continues on the 5-minute chart, I anticipate a test on the fifth candle. If it passes, then I will look for a continuation until the eighth consecutive candle, anticipating exhaustion. Obviously, this doesn't play out every time, but it does play out more times than not, and enough times to keep track.

STOCHASTICS:
THE ENGINE—MOMENTUM TOOL

Stochastics is the momentum tool standard on every chart we use. It is composed of two oscillators, a lead and a laggard. Depending on the trading or charting software, the values will be composed of 3 or 5 inputs. On CobraIQ, you want to select the %d slow with the components of 15, 3, and 5. On Realtick, choose 15, 5, and 2 for %d slow and 15 and 3 for %d. The standard use of buying 20-band crossovers and selling or shorting 80-band crossovers down still applies to some degree. However, the more significant use of the stochastics is with the mini pup patterns, which I will detail in great length later in this book.

5- AND 15-PERIOD
SIMPLE MOVING AVERAGES:
THE ROADMAP—TREND AND CHANNEL TOOL

These are the basic trend and channel indicators. The 5-period simple moving average is the lead and the 15-period simple moving average is the laggard. People tend to put down moving averages because they are laggard. But remember, we aren't trying to predict the future

Fibonacci numbers are pervasive in the universe and were originally derived by Leonardo Fibonacci. A Fibonacci sequence is a series of numbers where each number is the sum of the previous two numbers. The series of "Fib Numbers" begin as follows: 1, 1, 2, 3, 5, 8, 13, 21, 34, 55, 89, 144, 233, 317, 610, and so on. Many analysts use a series of numbers to derive Fibonacci ratios. For more on Fibonacci analysis, see Appendix A: Harmonic Pattern Trading.

with moving averages. The goal is to track the footprints to visually see the pattern of buying or selling. The 5-period moving average plays a key role in mini pup patterns because that is the main support area. This not only applies to breakouts and breakdowns, but also in channel tightening plays.

With the 5-period moving average, keep an eye on the sloping. Sloping refers to a curving of the 5-period simple moving average against the immediate trend. For uptrends, the 5-period moving average will gradually curve up against a falling 15-period. The opposite applies in downtrends, where the five-period will curve down against a rising 15-period moving average. Sloping signals that the "big boys" are getting anxious to reverse the trend as they methodically up their bids towards the 15-period moving average, in order to eventually set up the battle for trend. These happen in channel tightenings. In channel tightenings accompanied with a stochastics mini pup, the 5-period moving average will slope up—or down, depending on the immediate trend—by maintaining supports on all pullbacks there and coiling it back.

50- AND 200-PERIOD SIMPLE MOVING AVERAGES

These are powerful support and resistance levels that should be paid attention to when a stock price gets near them. The wider the time frame of the 50- or 200-period moving average, the stronger it acts as a support (if the stock is trading above) or resistance (if the stock is trading below). When a stock gaps beyond these levels, they will usually, at some point, reverse back to test those levels before resuming the direction of the gap. If these levels fail, then they become stronger as resistance.

PIVOT POINTS: STATIC SUPPORT AND RESISTANCE LEVELS

These levels were originally developed for futures, but also apply to stocks. They are composed for 5 price levels that act as support or resistance levels based on where the stock is trading. Most charting platforms carry them standard. These price levels are static and calculated based on the prior day's high, low, and close. The formula can be found at: **www.undergroundtrader.com/pivots**. As with any support or resistance levels, use these with the overlap principle to determine galvanized price levels to fade or play on breaks.

BOLLINGER BANDS: RANGE AND TARGET TOOL

Bollinger bands give an indication of the upper and lower range of a stock within the context of that time frame. They also show either a contraction where the range starts to tighten, or an expansion where range increases. Bollinger band prices become more significant as time frames get wider.

Since writing my last book, *Secrets of the Underground Trader: Advanced Methods for Short-Term and Swing Trading Any Market*, I have really grown a fondness for this wonderful tool. The Bollinger bands can significantly add to the napalm effect I mentioned earlier. The settings are 20 periods and 2 standard deviations. The results are 3 lines composed of an upper and lower envelope and a mid-range line, which is the 20-period moving average. The 20-period moving average is most significant on the 1-minute full data chart. If you can just add an upper and lower envelope without the 20-period moving average on the other charts, that works just as well since the 20-period is not needed outside of the 1-minute charts.

When a stock trades at or near its upper Bollinger band, it is considered overbought, and vice versa at the lower band. This is a common assumption, but not the end-all. There are nuances with certain time frames and instruments.

CONTRACTING AND EXPANDING BOLLINGER BANDS

Consolidations usually contract Bollinger bands until a breakout or breakdown triggers, which will tend to expand the bands. This isn't so much a setup but an indication that the longer the bands stay contracted, the more likely an expansion is around the corner in the form of a breakout or a breakdown. Oscillation players need to be aware of this danger and slow down the oscillation trading because they will eventually get caught in a hard short squeeze breakout or a panic selloff in a breakdown.

60-MINUTE BOLLINGER BAND NUANCES ON THE E-MINIS

We use the e-minis as a lead indicator on stocks, especially when they form perfect storms or 8- and 13-minute pups or mini pups, as these patterns resonate throughout the whole market. The biggest thing to be aware of is to make sure there is a trend channel in place.

This is one of those nuances that I discovered through trillions of hours of watching Bollinger bands. When the "noodles," the Nasdaq e-minis, are flat, the Bollinger bands tend to contract. In order for a trend to form and sustain, the futures have to hold at least two points above the upper Bollinger bands in order to pull up the 5-period moving average. This opens up a trading channel and lifts the 15-period moving average. Failing to hold at least 2 points beyond the Bollinger bands results in a headfake and wiggle back down and continues to keep the moving averages in a choppy consolidation.

Once the futures sustain at least 2 points above the upper Bollinger bands, that upper band becomes a momentum support in the uptrend (and vice versa for downtrends on the lower bands). Usually, futures will have to spike heavily above the upper Bollinger bands, and then will pullback to test and solidify that support and resume trending. This makes the Bollinger bands the first line of defense on futures trend failures or reversals.

Most upper or lower Bollinger band tests will result in an exhaustion and reversal. These are common areas for oscillation traders to fade. Because of this, an extended move beyond the Bollinger bands will trap oscillation players, resulting in an explosive trend breakout or breakdown. The more times the Bollinger bands get tested and fail, the stronger the breakout or breakdown will be when they finally explode. This is merely because the transparency of fading the Bollinger band levels makes oscillation players complacent, while it builds up frustration in the break and trend players. Use a Fib count of 3, 5, 8, 13 on the Bollinger band tests to be aware of the potential break.

DAILY, WEEKLY, AND MONTHLY
BOLLINGER BAND NUANCES

The wider time frame Bollinger bands naturally carry more weight. Always gauge to see where your stock is trading in relation to these levels and if there are any overlapping areas. The monthly Bollinger

"Noodles" is a slang term used by traders for the Nasdaq 100 e-minis futures, which are used as a lead indicator for tech stocks. These are usually correlated to the markets and spoos (the S&P 500 e-minis futures).

bands are the most powerful and carry the most weight where a stock is trading near them.

BOLLINGER BAND SLINGSHOT PLAYS

Stocks will usually revert back within the range of the Bollinger bands. The longer a stock stays beyond the Bollinger bands— above the upper bands or below the lower bands—the harder they will exhaust once they re-penetrate the "atmosphere." When you understand this phenomenon, you can look to play these types of exhaustions, which I call slingshots. When a stock gaps above or below the weekly or monthly Bollinger bands, there is a high probability they will revert back and retest unless the gap is just too strong.

> The more times the Bollinger bands get tested and fail, the stronger the breakout or breakdown will be when they finally explode.

Slingshot Short Scalps

For slingshot shorts, I like to see a shooting star candle close at or just below the upper Bollinger bands coupled with a 1-minute stochastics 80-band slip, or better yet, a mini inverse pup slip through the 80 bands.

Slingshot Long Scalps

For slingshot long plays, I like to see a hammer close at or above the lower Bollinger bands coupled with a 1-minute 20-band cross up, and even better is a mini pup through the 20 band.

BOLLINGER BAND FACTORS WITH GAPPERS AND DUMPERS

When a stock gaps up or down significantly, the 60-minute Bollinger bands will be critical support and resistance levels. The same type of slingshot play should be administered with such gaps that candle close back through the respective bands. Once the Bollinger bands are re-penetrated, they become barriers again, as support or resistance.

THE +0.20 SHORT SQUEEZE TRIGGER

This setup involves the 60-minute, daily, weekly, and monthly Bollinger band price levels. When a stock cracks through any of those upper band levels, the +0.20 mark is when the short squeeze triggers. It's a phenomenon that I have seen and played consistently. These setups usually require chasing a high band 1-minute entry, but they are the exceptions to the rule. The first ones to panic out are the oscillation traders, when they realize the oscillation is turning into a short squeeze, as in Figure 5.3.

For example, ABC stock has a daily upper Bollinger band resistance at 33.42. If ABC can break +0.20 above that daily upper Bollinger band price level to 33.62, then a short squeeze usually triggers. In fact, it takes just a tick above and you are off to the races. The trail stop on the initial entry will be just under the daily Bollinger band level, which is usually a -0.25 set stop. Once the stock gains traction, you can up your trail stop to a few ticks below that momentum support level, around 33.40. Don't stick around too long if they crack that short squeeze price level, because it can collapse very quickly. In fact, that break can set up a short entry for the more experienced traders.

Figure 5.3
+0.20
Short Squeeze
Trigger

For a closer
look, please visit
TradersLibrary.com/
TLECorner.

THE -0.20 TRAP DOOR

This setup is the opposite of the +0.20 short squeeze trigger; it also involves just the 60-minute, daily, weekly, and monthly Bollinger band price levels. If ABC has a daily lower Bollinger band at 33.42, a break of 33.22 will likely cause the stock to collapse in a panic, allowing one to profit with shorts. The first ones to panic out will be the oscillation players who were bidding the daily lower band support levels. The entry will likely be a short under the 1-minute 20 band as the bidders throw in the towel and panic out.

CATCHING PANIC BOTTOMS AND TOPS
WITH BOLLINGER BANDS

When a stock panics down abruptly, whether it's news or market driven, an opportunity to catch an exhaustion bounce will arrive. This is where the 5- and 1-minute full data charting will come into play. In addition to having galvanized support levels identified, the trigger will be when a candle closes above the 1-minute lower Bollinger bands, preferably with a hammer. This will usually coil the stock to the next resistance, likely the 5-minute lower Bollinger bands. A candle close above the 5-minute lower bands will push the stock to the next resistance, usually the 1-minute 20-period moving average, or the 5-minute 5-period moving average. Keep in mind that pivots, sticky 2.50s, and sticky 5 levels are defacto resistance levels at all times.

SLOPING OF THE BOLLINGER BAND

Like moving averages, Bollinger bands also slope in the form of contractions or expansions. It is important to be aware that even with an uptrend, sometimes the upper bands can be sloping down. This is a warning sign to be aware of possible peaks and prepare to exit at or just ahead of the down sloping band. The opposite applies in downtrends.

This sloping effect is very important on the 1-minute charts, where you may have taken a nice 80-band short entry on a 5-minute mini inverse pup to target the 5-minute lower Bollinger bands. However, if the 1-minute lower Bollinger bands are sloping up, you should look to lock in most, if not all profits at that area. On the flipside, more experienced traders may look to use the 1-minute, upward sloping Bollinger bands as a price area to consider bidding into a longside position. Like the 5-period moving average sloping, the Bollinger band sloping is an early sign that bidders are stepping up to the plate. If you get both a 5-period moving average slope and lower band slope up, that makes for an even stronger countertrend trade.

So remember, rising lower Bollinger band slopes when shorting is an early sign to take profits, because the price range is tightening against you. Inversely, slipping upper band slopes when long is a sign to take profits.

CHART TIME FRAMES

Anytime the price chart is too tight, either scale the chart to your screen or trim down the number of days of historical data. Stocks that have had a big range can end up looking too tight on the moving average charts. We usually want to have at least 200 periods total to accurately gauge the 200-period simple moving average level, but if the stock range is too large, the charts can be too tight to read. Use the scale to screen option (if applicable), or shrink the historical data.

INTRADAY TIME FRAMES

The Secret Tool Unveiled: The Rifle Charts

Every single trade I make or alert now goes through this new weapon, the 5- and 1-Minute Full Data (24-Hour) Rifle Charts. I give credit to CobraTrading.com and their CobraIQ platform for being instrumental in my development and testing of this weapon. I created a preformatted template of the UndergroundTrader Rifle Charts for the CobraIQ platform at CobraTrading.com specifically for my readers and their clients, so open up an account there if you are serious about pursuing the trading journey. The advantage of the full time frame data fills in many gaps and gives a more thorough picture of the setups. I also added the 5-period simple moving average to the 1-minute chart, which is invaluable when playing mini pups to determine to the penny where the dynamic support level is. Kudos to my friends John and Phyllis Hill for helping me add that critical mechanism.

Until I started using this tool, I didn't think the pre- or post-market was navigable due to the lack of data and charting. This new tool has not only opened up these pathways, but allows one to optimize and filter with such pinpoint accuracy that you can literally time a breakout to the minute ahead of time. This new tool has actually allowed me to take advantage of a less traveled landscape that has yet to be super saturated with program trading, black boxes, market makers and manipulation. It has become so essential that every single trade I make must first past mustard through this tool.

> You know the saying, "This is my rifle and this is my gun, this is for fighting and this is for fun...."? Well, this tool is my rifle.

These two charts are similar to the basic stochastics moving average charts, but with the inclusion of pre- and post-market data. Unfortunately, many systems don't allow for a full 24-hour stock data feed, or they have inconsistent data. The best trading platform for this is the CobraIQ platform (www.cobratrading.com), bar none. I have tried to utilize the pre-market charting on all the major platforms and for one reason or another, there were just some nutty irregularities.

The chart settings are as follows.

The 5-Minute Chart

- Candlesticks

- 5- and 15-period simple moving averages

- Stochastics (%d slow 15, 3 or 15, 3, 5 depending on provider)

- Bollinger bands (20-period, 2 standard deviations) which contain an upper or lower envelope and a 20-period moving average

- Volume bars

The 1-Minute Chart

- Candlesticks

- 5-period simple moving average

- 50- and 200-period simple moving averages

- Stochastics (% d slow 15, 3 or 15, 3, 5 depending on provider)

- Bollinger bands (20-period, 2 standard deviations) which contain an upper or lower envelope and a 20-period moving average

These charts give the best edge when it comes to pre-market trading on stocks with volume. The most applicable stocks are gappers and dumpers, or the higher volume leader stocks when the futures are gapping up or down strong. As long as there is some volume, these charts are great.

PRE-MARKET TREASURE HUNTING

My late, great mother-in-law, who used to live in Miami Beach, would hit the beach at 5:00 a.m. every morning to comb the "sea store" with her metal detector before the tourists showed up. It was amazing the tons of jewelry she would find in the sand. This was the result of two key factors—she got there early, and her metal detector worked beautifully.

This same concept can be effectively applied to pre-market trading, thanks to the 5- and 1-minute pre-market stochastics moving average charts. Getting to the beach before the tourists is half the battle. The other half is utilizing an effective tool to successfully comb the beach. While the lack of market participants tends to keep program trading and most individual traders away due to liquidity concerns, an effective tool turns this downfall into an amazing edge. Fewer participants means less chop, and the wider spreads can result in a larger profit margin, if played correctly.

PRE-MARKET OR POST-MARKET?

Many years ago, I would have said that the post-market and pre-market both offered identical opportunities. Now, there is nothing further from the truth. The post-market is a losing game after 5:00 p.m. most of the time (and by most, I mean 90%!). Liquidity dries up too quickly. The pre-market is the beginning of the day, so the liquidity increases along with transparency going into a fresh market day. Post-market is damaged goods. Most importantly, if you lose money in the pre-market, there is opportunity to make it back going into the opening. In the post-market, if you lose money, the liquidity only gets worse and the fact that the market closes at 8:00 p.m. for 11 hours can panic some traders into trying too hard to create opportunities where there are none, resulting in deeper losses and "hail mary" overnight holds out of desperation, not to mention the resulting sleepless night. Post-market is the equivalent of death valley. It

Please do not hold stocks past 4:00 p.m. unless you know there is liquidity. Many stocks, especially listed stocks, can evaporate spreads in mere minutes after the closing bell. This has happened way too many times to even joke about. Ultimately, the trader is forced to hold overnight, or sit there and pray for a bid to show up. Pay attention to the clock.

is only playable until 5:00 p.m. at the latest. Do not get into the habit of playing afterwards. Nothing is worse than taking 1000 shares of a stock on the ask as the bid evaporates 0.50 below the ask with only 200 shares of liquidity…ouch. It's happened to all of us.

THE ONLY TWO PATTERNS TO PLAY PRE-MARKET

There are really only two patterns that I look for with these charts pre-market. They are the pup and mini pup breakouts and breakdowns, and the 5-period moving average channel tightenings accompanied by a mini pup. The greatest feature of the 5-minute chart is the updating of the moving averages on a 5-minute incremental basis, which allows one to literally time the momentum thrusts that kick in around the fourth minute or within the first minute of the 5-minute interval. When a trend is present, the 5-minute chart is so pinpoint accurate that you can have your sweep stop orders set to trigger immediately upon violation. It is important that you don't sit around and let the 5-period moving averages wiggle and wait for a candle close in the pre-market or post-market, because the spreads tend to be wider, and liquidity can vanish in an instant.

THE NEW WAY TO PLAY GAPPER AND DUMPER STOCKS

In my other books, I wrote that the way to play stocks that form significant gaps up or down based on news is to wait out the first 10 to 15 minutes until the 3-minute moving average updates and "catches up" to the stock price. Once the 3-minute 5-period moving average forms, then we look to play either a continuation of the gap or a reversal of the gap via pups and mini pups. Prior to the 3-minute 5-period formation (as it needs at least 3 candles to assess the moving average value from the 9:30 a.m. market open), only the most experienced traders could play scalps based mostly on reversal candles, 1-minute stochastics, and a lot of intuition. The reality was the almost 9 minutes of the opening high volume action was avoided waiting for the 3-minute data to update and formulate a 5-period moving average. Not only were opportunities lost, but it was a significant blind spot. That first 10 minutes of the market open is consistently the most volatile and voluminous period of the

When there is an opportunity to make a day's gains in ten minutes, it's imperative to find a way to capitalize on it.

market day. When there is an opportunity to make a day's gains in 10 minutes, it's imperative to find a way to capitalize on it.

The 5- and 1-minute pre-market charts not only fill in the 9-minute blind spot on the 3-minute charts, but actually give full transparency going into the open. Instead of guessing how they will move a stock off the open, the 5- and 1-minute charts have the ability to pinpoint a heavy breakout squeeze or a rug pull. Since the data is continuous in the pre-market, there is no gap or guessing involved. This is not to say that every open is predictable, no way. Most are not. However, there are instances where the 5- and 1-minute pre-market charts line up a dual mini pup that triggers at the 9:30 a.m. candle close, which not-so-coincidentally happens to be the market open.

TIMING THE 5-MINUTE CANDLE CLOSE

Due to the perceived lack of liquidity in the pre-market, spreads can be pretty wide, even for such widely traded stocks like AAPL and RIMM. If a 5-minute pre-market chart has an uptrend (even better if supported by a 5-minute mini pup), there may be a lull in the action with a wide bid at or under the 5-minute 5-period moving average—until the actual candle close at the 5-minute mark starting at the top of the hour (i.e.; 8:00 a.m., 8:05 a.m., 8:10 a.m., etc).

The paradigms have shifted in the sense that the trading environment is at a saturation point and therefore one must seek out an "edge" where there are less participants. This is where being a big fish in a little pond applies.

The charts in this section are all on regular market time data from 9:30 a.m. to 4:00 p.m. EST.

The regular market charts have the same studies as the 5- and 1-minute charts, but also include pivot points. Stochastics settings depend on the broker or chart platform, but are usually 15, 3, 5 or 15, 3 or 15, 5 or 2, 15, 3 for the %d slow and %d.

1-MINUTE CHART

Use 3 days of historical data on these charts to derive a 200-period moving average. This chart is your trigger entry and exit chart. The 1-minute

5-period moving average line is where mini pups form as prices bounce off that level. Entries above the 80 band or below the 20 band are considered chasing, so be careful not to overplay there. The average trader will chase at these levels. The average trader blows out. Don't be average. Momentum markets tend to be more forgiving when chasing, provided

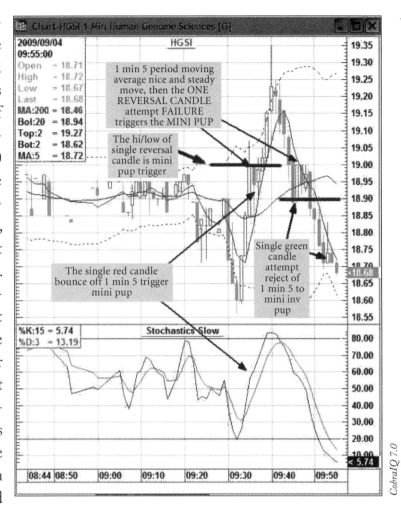

Figure 5.4
1-Minute Chart

For a closer look, please visit TradersLibrary.com/TLECorner.

there is high volume and a perfect storm to back you up. Don't get into a habit of chasing this stuff in an infertile chop market climate. You should be exiting into the latecomers, not entering with them. The 1-minute high band mini pups (above the 80 band) are primary exit areas on longs to sell into the climax tops. The 1-minute low band mini inverse pups (under the 20 band) are the primary exit areas to cover shorts into sellers. For the more skilled players, they can be ideal spots for short or long entries if they are near galvanized support or resistance levels. See Figure 5.4.

The 20 and 80 bands are very significant. Stocks that cross under the 80 band will likely pull back to the next support levels, usually a 3- or 5-minute 5-period moving average on uptrends. The same applies for stocks that cross back up through the 20 bands on downtrends to a 3- or 5-minute resistance level.

3-MINUTE CHART

Use 5 days of historical data on these charts. This is a primary short-term trading trend chart during market hours. Pup and mini pup patterns with the 1-minute trigger make for a good scalping tool. Be extra careful to step back and view the wider time frame charts if there isn't a trend and channel in place. It is too easy to get caught up in the chop on a 3-minute chart, ignoring the fact that there is no sustained trend in the wider time frames. It is often possible for a 3-minute chart to trend during an 8- and 13-minute consolidation, but these are usually short-lived and chock full of headfakes and wiggles.

WHEN 5- AND 3-MINUTE CHARTS DIVERGE

Sometimes, the 5-minute chart may actually diverge against the 3-minute chart. Usually, you want to avoid situations like this, but they do happen, especially on gapper or dumper stocks. In these situations, assume that the 5-minute chart will prevail and in doing so, you can time your trade to exit ahead of the 5-minute, 5-period moving average before it explodes against you.

For example, the 5-minute chart may have formed a mini pup in the pre-market with a rising 5-period moving average that has turned into an uptrend. The 3-minute chart may be in a mini inverse pup. Prior to the discovery of the 5- and 1-minute pre-market charting weapon, we would normally step into a classic 3-minute mini inverse pup continuation breakdown dumper play, unaware that the 5-minute chart is setting up a nasty surprise for the shorts. This is like jumping into the ocean unaware of the tiger shark that has been circling the boat underwater.

The 5- and 1-minute pre-market charts literally give you a view of the depth of the ocean to spot danger ahead of time. Together, they form an absolutely amazing tool—I can't stress that enough. Convergence of the charts makes for the safest trades, but divergence also makes you aware of impending danger if you overstay your position.

The 5-minute chart containing pre-
or post-market data will override a 3-minute
chart with market hours data when they
are about to collide.

FORESHADOWING: THE DOPPLER EFFECT

The advantage of wider time frame setups is the foreshadowing element, much like a Doppler radar used by your local weatherman. When wider time frames form pup and mini pup patterns, it's a sign to pay attention to the shorter time frames to eventually trigger for the trade.

8- AND 13-MINUTE CHARTS

Use 8 days of historical data on these charts. These are the intermediate time frames intraday. They are best used to determine consolidations and overall trend. As a rule of thumb, you don't want to trade against the 8- and 13-minute direction for more than an exhaustion or oscillation scalp. If you are playing a trend, you want to have those 8- and 13-minute charts on your side. When you find yourself getting chopped on trades, always step back and see if the 8- and 13-minute charts are flat. If so, then you are wasting your ammo trading a consolidation.

> You don't want to trade against the 8- and 13-minute direction for more than an exhaustion or oscillation scalp.

60-MINUTE CHART

Use 30 days of data to derive an accurate 200-period moving average if your platform doesn't have a "scale charts" function, or can't give a 200-period moving average reading without the data. Otherwise, 13 days of data is sufficient.

If the range is too wide, the chart may be ineffective, so make sure that you pick the scale option. This is the widest time frame chart for intraday. It's used primarily to observe underlying trends (if any) and the ranges. Being the largest time frame intraday also makes it the most powerful intraday chart when it comes to support and resistance levels, and underlying patterns. If the 60-minute chart has a mini pup, the goal is to align your trade in the direction of the mini pup and time entries with the shorter time frames.

WIDER TIME FRAMES

DAILY CHART

Use 250 days of data to get an effective 200-period moving average reading if your platform doesn't have a "scale charts" function or can't give a 200-period moving average reading without the data. This is the go-to chart when first looking at any stock. This chart can often set up the direction of the intraday trading if there is a trend in place. It will not only show you which direction to lean towards, but also make you aware of which direction to stay away from.

WEEKLY AND MONTHLY CHARTS

Use 220 weeks and 220 months of data to derive an accurate 200-period moving average reading if your platform doesn't have a "scale charts" function or can't give a 200-period moving average reading without the data.

These leviathans are the overriding trend, trading channel, and pattern tools. The ranges can be so big that they will only really be useful when a definitive pattern forms (like a pup, mini pup, or perfect storm), or when a stock is trading near the 5-, 15-, 50-, or 200-period moving averages and Bollinger bands. However, when either of the aforementioned applies, you want to take note and write down the pattern and the nearby significant price levels. These price levels will be extra useful when identifying galvanized support and resistance levels for your intraday trading. These levels should be checked during the weekend and evening research on your stocks. It is absolutely vital that you check these levels on any gapper or dumper stocks you consider playing, or swing trades. They only need to be gauged once a day to jot down applicable levels and patterns.

CHART PATTERNS

Now that you have the charts, you have to be able to use them effectively. Charts are a visual aid to track the footprints of order flow. This is not to say that the charts will tell you everything about a stock's direction. In fact, most of the time, the divergence will result in a lot of noise. This is expected. The noise will far outweigh the clarity.

The strongest patterns form when perfect storms set up on the daily, weekly, and monthly charts. This is also the strongest foreshadowing setup. This puts your trading plan on autopilot because you are aware of the direction in which the stock will eventually move. It's just a matter of timing the intraday entries upon the intraday charts convergence. Options can also be played on these types of plays because they foreshadow an explosive move in a relatively short period of time.

This is important, as I stated before. When a powerful pattern finally lines up, the move can be explosive, because clarity invites volume, momentum, and trend. All the suckers who got chopped are finally relieved and step in with a vengeance. It's all about filtering. Expect noise and be pleasantly surprised when clarity starts to form. Of course, the key is to find the transparency before it becomes too transparent. A wise man coined that phrase…

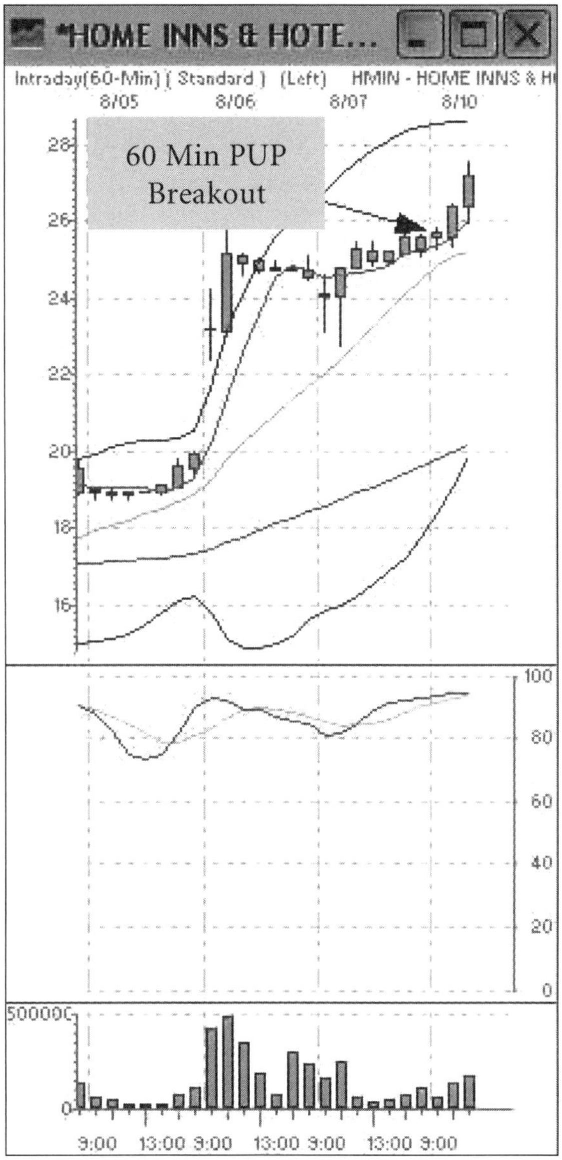

Figure 5.5
60-Minute Pup Breakout

For a closer look, please visit TradersLibrary.com/TLECorner.

RealTick by Townsend Analytics, Ltd.

PUPS

I have mentioned pups and mini pups many times already, assuming you know what they are. Let's get this out of the way and definitively explain these two key patterns, as they are the core ingredients in my methods. I want to go through pups and mini pups so thoroughly here that you will be seeing them in your sleep!

Pups are an acronym for PowerUPtik, because of the powerful uptick that triggers a breakout from this pattern. These patterns form on the 5- and 15-period moving averages on uptrends. They can form on any time frame. Figure 5.5 is an example of a pup breakout on a 60-minute time frame. The wider the time frame, the more weight it carries. The 5-period moving average being the lead will peak out once a breakout exhausts and the price pulls back. When the stock starts to chop around the 5-period moving average for an extended period of time, this causes it to move sideways while the laggard

Figure 5.6
5-Minute Pup
and Mini Pup

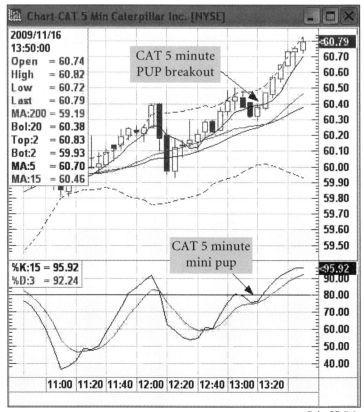

CAT 5 minute
PUP breakout

CAT 5 minute
mini pup

CobraIQ 7.0

Figure 5.7
1-Minute
5-Period
Moving Average
Mini Pups

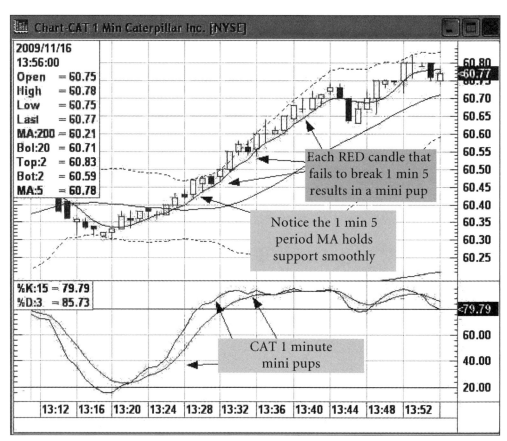

Each RED candle that
fails to break 1 min 5
results in a mini pup

Notice the 1 min 5
period MA holds
support smoothly

CAT 1 minute
mini pups

For a closer
look, please visit
TradersLibrary.com/
TLECorner.

CobraIQ 7.0

15-period moving average continues to climb. The stochastics will no longer be rising and will usually cross back down. The sellers keep a lid at the 5-period moving average, while the buyers are slowly lifting the 15-period moving average. As the trading channel (the range between the 5- and 15-period moving averages) gets tighter, steam is building. Eventually, the stock will have to break one way or the other. When the stochastics cross back up, this triggers the buyers, who push the stock back up through the 5-period moving average with a candle close. The steam explodes to the upside as shorts get squeezed in a panic and buyers come off the fence as the stock then resumes its uptrend momentum until the next peak and exhaustion.

> The stochastics must absolutely, definitively, and positively cross back up for a pup breakout.

Figure 5.6 shows both a pup and a mini pup on a 5-minute time frame. Figure 5.7 shows a mini pup on the 1-minute chart. Please note that the stochastics must cross back up! The common pitfall with newbies is only watching the moving averages without confirming a stochastics cross. This tends to result in getting chopped back out.

UndergroundTrader's Rules for Pup Breakouts

- Always confirm the pup with the stochastics cross first!

- Trail the 5-period moving average candle close.

- The wider the time frame, the stronger the pup.

- There must be a trend and trading channel in place.

- All pups and mini pups need volume. Flat moving averages on light volume are kryptonite!

Figure 5.8
Inverse Pups

For a closer
look, please visit
TradersLibrary.com/
TLECorner.

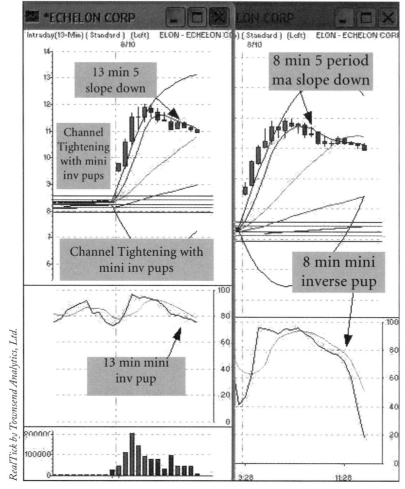

INVERSE PUPS

The inverse pup (Figure 5.8) is the same pattern, but for breakdowns.
The 5-period moving average will start to flatline once the downtrend
stalls out as buyers try to support the stock. The 15-period moving
average will continue sliding and tightening the channel. When the
stochastics cross back down, the sellers wipe out the 5-period moving
average with a candle close, thereby panicking the bidders and triggering more sellers to dump the stock. This resumes the downtrend
until the next bottom attempt and exhaustion.

MINI PUPS

Mini pups look like pups, but form with the stochastics. The %d (lead
oscillator) will stall out as the underlying stock peaks on the uptrend.
The %d slow (laggard oscillator) will continue to rise. The stock will
pull back to test the 5-period moving average. If the 5-period moving

Figure 5.9
5-Minute Chart
with Mini Inverse
Pup

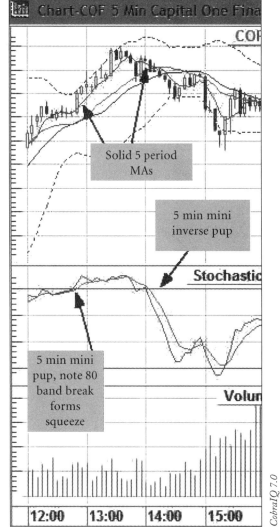

Figure 5.10
Inverse Pup and
Mini Inverse Pup

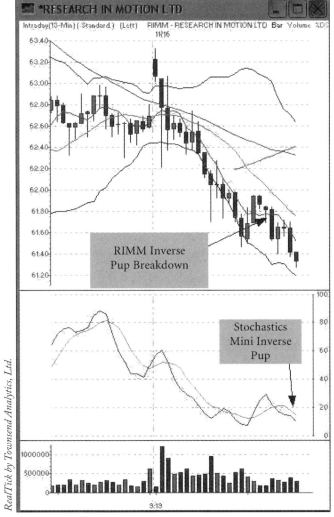

For a closer
look, please visit
TradersLibrary.com/
TLECorner.

average holds support, the shorts will get nervous and start to cover, which will slope the %d back up, triggering a short squeeze and buying frenzy on volume. The targets are the upper Bollinger bands on these moves, and the support is the 5-period moving averages.

Mini pups are not only excellent foreshadowing setups, they are great entry signals on existing trends, due to the fact that they result from market-tested supports (5-period moving averages) with accurate targets (Bollinger bands) pre-wired.

The beautiful thing about mini pups is that the sellers and the shorts already test the support and form the line in the sand. When the %d stochastic oscillation stalls out, the shorts are anticipating an oscillation move back down once the 5-period moving average can break. When the 5-period moving average holds firmly, this causes the %d to slope up instead of crossing down. The shorts panic out and buyers come off the fence as the stock explodes to the upside.

Mini inverse pups, like the ones in Figure 5.9 and Figure 5.10, are the same pattern, but upside down for breakdowns.

UndergroundTrader's Rules for Mini Pups

- The 5-period moving average is the line in the sand and trail stop on breaks.

- The Bollinger bands are the nominal targets.

- The wider the time frame, the stronger the mini pup.

- There must be a trend and trading channel in place.

- All pups and mini pups need volume. Flat moving averages on light volume are kryptonite!

FORESHADOWING WITH WIDER TIME FRAME PUPS AND MINI PUPS

Since patterns are linear across time frames, it only makes sense that a pup or mini pup on a wider time frame will eventually play out once the shorter time frames trigger. This how the pups and mini pups on a wider time frame foreshadow the impending move. When you spot these, it gives you an early opportunity to step into the shorter time frames to capture the move. This is the Doppler effect, identical to a weather forecast that says a thunderstorm is on its way to your neighborhood even though it is sunny outside. It makes you aware of what is looming and gives you the time to prepare to take action.

Speaking of storms, if a single time frame pup or mini pup is strong, imagine what happens when three or more time frames form these power pups and mini pups?

PERFECT STORMS: THE MOST POWERFUL PATTERN

As powerful as pups and mini pups are, they are even more powerful when linked simultaneously on multiple time frames. When three or more time frames have pups and mini pups, this is called a perfect storm pattern, like the one in Figure 5.11. The degree of the follow-through and strength rises when wider time frames are included in the perfect storm. These are the highest probability setups that I use. In most cases, you will have two intraday time frames with mini pups. The trigger of the third time frame, usually the shortest (1-, 3-, or 5-minute) is what will set off the explosive move, and the wider time frames give it more follow-through.

UndergroundTrader's Rule for Perfect Storms

- Link 3 or more pups or mini pups.

- Use the 1-, 3-, or 5-minute time frame as the trigger.

- Wider time frame perfect storms are strongest for foreshadowing and follow-through.

Figure 5.11
Perfect Storm
Breakdown

For a closer
look, please visit
TradersLibrary.com/
TLECorner.

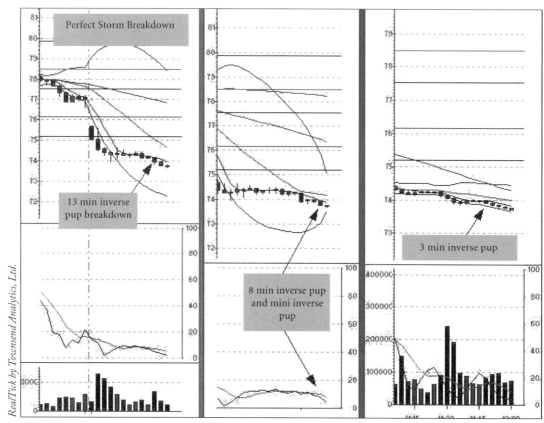

Failed Perfect Storms: Market Litmus Test and Opportunity

As with anything in the markets, nothing is 100%. Knowing that a perfect storm is the most powerful pattern, what does it mean when this pattern fails? If a perfect storm is strong, then a failed perfect storm is even stronger. This presents an opportunity to play the opposite side of the trade. Who knows better how weak a stock is than someone who is long? And vice versa.

Thinking in a wider context, if the strongest pattern setup can't break out, what does that say about the market climate? Likely it is an infertile market. Logically thinking, if your best weapon can't seem to hit any targets, why would you assume that a weaker weapon will do better? You wouldn't. Therefore, when perfect storms fail, it is a sign of a market reversal or a weak market.

PUP AND MINI PUP MAKE-OR-BREAKS: DANGER SIGNS

The reason why the stochastics cross is so important for pups is because of the many headfakes that usually occur prior to a breakout. The period prior to a pup breakout or failure is called a make-or-break. Usually, the moving averages will look like a pup trying to form, but the stochastics will look like a mini inverse pup. One side will play out. Always wait out the final outcome before playing.

This can also happen after the 5-period moving average fails and forms a channel tightening to the 15-period. When a stock completes its channel tightening by reaching the 15-period moving average, it will set up a final battle that will determine if the trend will reverse completely or resume. Make-or-breaks will eventually resolve into a trend. The problem is that it will take a lot of time and chop in most cases. Make-or-breaks are just as bad to trade as consolidations. In the same thinking, one should actually wait for the break to happen before playing. Make-or-breaks are a warning sign to stay out to let things marinate before eventually trending.

UndergroundTrader's Rules for Make-or-Breaks

- Stay out of make-or-breaks. They are just as bad as consolidations.

- Make-or-breaks are usually tight or flat moving average channels with light volume (the kryptonite to pups and mini pups).

- Only play make-or-breaks after the new trend is established and confirmed with both moving averages and stochastics crosses in the direction of the trend.

- The only time to step into a make-or-break is when the wider time frames are foreshadowing a breakout via a perfect storm.

CONSOLIDATIONS

When the 5- and 15-period moving averages are moving sideways, this indicates a consolidation. This doesn't mean the underlying stock price

Figure 5.12
Consolidation

For a closer look, please visit TradersLibrary.com/TLECorner.

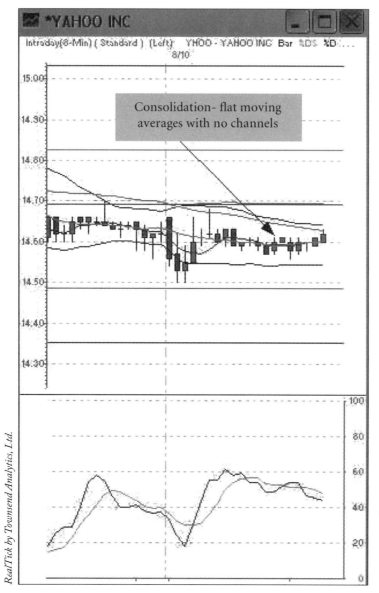

RealTick by Townsend Analytics, Ltd.

is static. Usually, the stock is gyrating and chopping, but can't sustain an extended move. Bollinger bands tend to be constricted in a tighter range on consolidations as well. Usually the chop will stay contained with tight Bollinger bands. Consolidations, as in Figure 5.12, indicate that neither buyers nor sellers are being aggressive. The big boys are on the fence, or more aptly, playing possum. The volume is relatively light. Ironically, it is these consolidation periods which tend to chop traders the most, because they try to get in early on a breakout only to get headfaked out. Oscillation traders who get a handle on the chop eventually get flushed out when a breakout actually does form and their shorts get squeezed, giving back all the little gains they collected.

Intraday consolidations are best determined with the 8- and 13-minute charts, because they give a bird's eye view away from the chop of the shorter time frames. The 3-minute charts are too short a time frame to get a handle on consolidations and they are prone to constant failed breakouts and breakdowns. In fact, using too short a time frame when stock is consolidating is how traders end up getting chopped in consolidations. When the action slows down, revert to the wider time frames to reassess the playing field. When the action picks up is when you want to focus more on the shorter time frames.

It's better to gauge the forest from the trees with wider time frames to determine consolidation.

BREAKOUTS AND UPTRENDS

When a price breaks the range on volume to the upside and sustains the move with rising 5- and 15-period moving average supports, this is called a breakout. Breakouts result in uptrends. Uptrends signify rising prices with higher highs and higher lows. These are illustrated on the charts with the 5- and 15-period moving averages rising higher. Trying to catch breakouts can be a frustrating game, as they are identical to wiggles until after the fact. It's actually best to let the breakout happen, then look to step in on a pullback with a mini pup formation. The exception is when the wider time frames actually foreshadow the breakout on the shorter time frame. For example, an 8- and 13-minute dual mini pup that foreshadows a consolidation breakout on the 3-minute chart is a good setup to go long once the 1- and 3-minute stochastics cross up.

BREAKDOWNS AND DOWNTRENDS

A breakdown forms when prices break the range to the downside on volume and sustain the move with falling 5- and 15-period moving average resistances. Breakdowns result in downtrends. Downtrends signify falling prices with lower highs and lower lows. These are illustrated on the charts with the 5- and 15-period moving averages falling lower. The same caution applies to trying too hard to catch breakdowns. Unless you get a foreshadowing setup on wider time frames, it's best to wait for the breakdown to form and enter via a mini inverse pup on the 5-period moving average rejections. Bottom line, let the train leave the station first, you can always get back on at the next stop.

When the action slows down, revert to the wider time frames to reassess the playing field.

CHANNEL TIGHTENINGS

Channel tightenings are the first sign that a trend is possibly reversing. In uptrends, higher highs and higher lows are replaced with lower highs and lower lows. This is illustrated with a 5-period moving average sloping downward into a rising 15-period moving average with a stochastics mini pup cross above the 20 bands.

In downtrends, lower highs and lower lows are replaced with higher lows and higher highs. This is illustrated with a 5-period moving average sloping upward into a falling 15-period moving average with a stochastics cross down with a mini inverse pup through the 80 band.

WIGGLES, CHOP, AND HEADFAKES:
THE SCOURGE OF THE MARKETS

Since stocks have to move, most of the time, they will chop in a range. Flat 5- and 15-period moving averages are consolidations and they are always going to chop. Observe the rule of thumb to stay out of flat moving average charts with light volume. Wait out the chop and the breakout, as they are identical in the beginning. The difference lies in the support on pullbacks. The trend will pull back to the 5-period moving average and bounce, whereas the wiggle will slip right back through the 5- and 15-period moving averages as if they weren't even there.

Stay out of flat moving average charts with light volume.

Having the tools and platform in place is one portion of the equation. I made the distinction earlier that the environment of a market takes precedence over the methods. In the example of a sloppy trader only being exposed to a fertile market versus an experienced trader being forced to trade only the infertile markets, most people would give the edge to the sloppy trader. The tricky part here is being able to determine what a fertile market environment is, as paradigms seem to constantly shift through the years.

The goal of a trader is to profit from timing price fluctuations.

The goal of a trader is to profit from timing price fluctuations. This can occur on intraday time frames or multi-day time frames. While the time frames may vary, the goal and the methods (yes, methods) are linear.

BRING IT FULL CIRCLE: TEST YOURSELF

(1) When you are providing liquidity and receiving ECN rebates, you are selling your long position on the _____ .

    a) ask
    b) bid

(2) A reserve order shows the full size of your order on Nasdaq Level II.

    a) True
    b) False

(3) Which of one of the following is not an ECN?

    a) ARCA
    b) ISLD
    c) BTRD
    d) DOHR
    e) INCA

(4) Which of the following is not within the sticky 2.50s and sticky 5s range?

    a) 42.42
    b) 123.32
    c) 9.52
    d) 32.58
    e) 74.45

(5) A shooting star is the opposite candlestick formation of a hammer.

    a) True
    b) False

6 A mini pup formation is a:

    a) breakout formation that triggers on the stochastics.

    b) breakdown formation that triggers on the moving averages.

    c) breakout formation that forms on the moving averages.

    d) breakdown formation that forms on the pivot points.

7 A mini pup and mini inverse pup inherently contain stop loss and targets within the setup. The support for a mini pup and mini inverse pup is:

    a) the 15-period moving average.

    b) the 5-period moving average.

    c) The 200-period moving average.

    d) the 50-period moving average.

For answers, please visit the
Traders' Library Education Corner at
www.traderslibrary.com/TLEcorner.

CHAPTER 6

PROPER ALLOCATION OF SHARES

I am devoting a whole chapter to share allocation because this is the single most misused, neglected, and damaging aspect of trading. Allocation and leverage are synonymous. Careless share size allocation is what kills off most traders and blows out accounts. Whether this results from filtered intraday scalping, swing trading, investing, or the desperate all-in, hail mary desperation trade—size kills.

A trader's job is to identify fertile market environments with solid setups and take advantage with the proper leverage and allocation. A week's profits can be made on a single trade if you filter properly. As you evolve as a trader, you will understand the term "squandered opportunity." Only at these levels can you understand what Sun Tzu meant when he said, "A skilled fighter puts himself in a situation where defeat is impossible, yet never misses the opportunity to defeat the enemy."

"A skilled fighter puts himself in a situation where defeat is impossible, yet never misses the opportunity to defeat the enemy."

-Sun Tzu

The problem with most traders is that they fail to discriminate the superfertile situations. "Fail" is giving too much credit—most are simply unable to identify these situations because they have not put in the effort. Misallocation comes from ignorance, complacency, laziness, and desperation. This also goes back to acknowledging the clear separation between learning and earning mode.

I've seen some traders get desperate enough (especially when falling under the pattern day trading rule) that they will just overleverage a cheap stock. There is no more familiar scenario than the trader who may have gained a net profit of 0.50 on ten trades (eight were profitable), but ended up losing $500. The problem is that he took small stops on the eight 200-share trades and bigger stops on the two 800-share trades.

When someone trades 100 shares of the QQQQs, and then trades 500 shares of AAPL, it makes no sense when you figure that AAPL moves at a 4 or 5-to-1 pace to the QQQQs. In fact, the size should be the other way around, as in 500 shares of the QQQQs for 100 shares of AAPL.

THE DANGER OF STATIC STOCK SIZING

Don't fall into the habit of just trading 200 shares on every stock you trade. This is just as bad as saying you will take a static 0.20 trail stop on every trade you make. This is utter stupidity. The same 200 shares you play on a slow, thick stock like CSCO will end up getting you whacked on a fast mover like IBM or AAPL.

THE DANGER OF COST BASED ALLOCATION

This is another popular, yet dangerous technique where a trader will allocate $30,000 to every stock trade. This becomes a big problem when the $30,000 you use to play 500 shares of a $60 stock is also applied to 6,000 shares of a $5 stock. If the $5 stock is very volatile or thinly traded, that can amount to a much nastier loss on the same $30,000 trade amount.

ALLOCATION METHOD

Group the volatility by sector. In most cases, the rhythm of the stocks within a sector indicates how thick or thin the stocks may actually move. Solar stocks are by nature thin, as are fertilizers. From there, you can take them down the tiers and recognize the movements. You can also use stock beta for a general idea. But your best bet will be watching to see how the stock moves. A thick float coupled with a low price will mean smaller moves compensated with larger shares, and vice versa.

To get a better feel for how thick or thin the stock is, you should dip your toes in with 100 share lots and feel around. Remember that your share allocation is highly contingent on your own comfort zone and progress.

Go with one-half to one-third scalp
shares if swing trading.

BRING IT FULL CIRCLE: TEST YOURSELF

1 A fertile trading market environment has:

A) consolidations, light volume, and chop.
B) trends, heavy volume, and follow-through.
C) make-or-breaks, light volume, and follow-through.
D) trends, light volume, and chop.

2 Which of the following choices are false?
A shooting star candlestick:

A) forms when a stock price peaks.
B) forms when stock price bottoms.
C) is a buy signal.

3 A reserve order is a trade execution order that:

A) shows the full size of the trade.
B) shows the partial size of the trade.
C) shows no size.
D) is a market order.

4 The rifle charts are composed of:

A) 5- and 1-minute stochastics moving average charts with pre/post-market data.
B) 13- and 8-minute stochastics moving average charts with regular market data.
C) 5- and 1-minute stochastics moving average charts with regular market data.
D) 60- and 13-minute stochastics moving average charts with pre- and post-market data.

5 A pup pattern is formed on:

A) the moving averages.
B) the stochastics.
C) the Bollinger bands.
D) the weather.

6 A mini pup pattern is formed on:

    A) the moving averages.

    B) the stochastics.

    C) the Bollinger bands.

    D) the weather.

7 A perfect storm pattern is composed of:

    A) two or less pups or mini pups

    B) three or more pups or mini pups.

    C) the weather channel.

    D) consolidations on light volume.

8 A mini pup pattern:

    A) has support at the 5-period moving average.

    B) has support at the 200-period moving average.

    C) has support at the 15-period moving average.

    D) has no support.

Take a close look at the 5- and 1-minute rifle charts of WFC below:

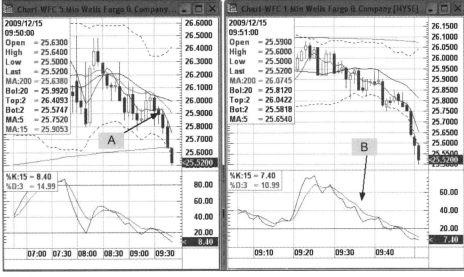

CobraIQ 7.0

9) On the 5-minute WFC chart (left chart), what is pattern is "A"?

A) Consolidation breakout
B) Mini pup breakout
C) Inverse pup breakdown
D) Make-or-break

10) On the 1-minute WFC chart (right chart), what pattern is "B"?

A) Make-or-break
B) Consolidation
C) Mini inverse pup
D) Short squeeze

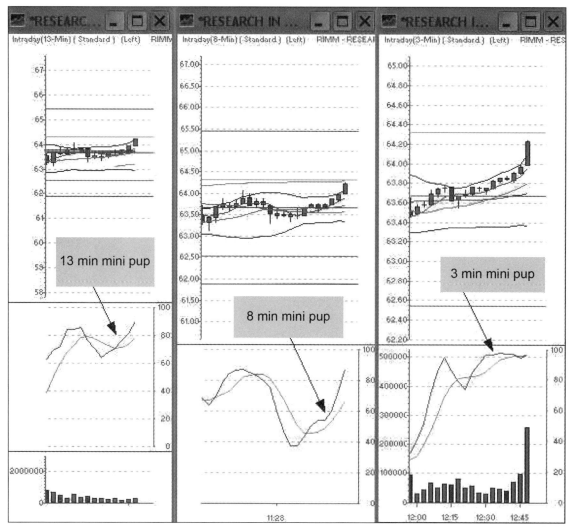

RealTick by Townsend Analytics, Ltd.

11 The previous chart pattern composed of 13-, 8-, and 3-minute mini pups is an example of:

A) a make-or-break.
B) flat consolidation.
C) perfect storm breakout.
D) perfect storm breakdown.

12 A perfect storm is the strongest chart pattern that forms when three or more different time frame charts form pups and or mini pups in the same direction. Which of the following is an example of a perfect storm?

A) 60-minute mini pup, 13-minute consolidation, 8-minute stochastics cross down
B) 13-minute mini pup, 8-minute pup, 5-minute mini pup
C) Daily mini pup, 60-minute mini inverse pup, 13-minute consolidation
D) 13-minute make-or-break, 8-minute mini pup, 1-minute mini pup

13 RIMM has a 60-minute mini pup, and 13- and 8-minute pups. The 5-minute rifle chart has a mini pup and the 3-minute is in an uptrend. What is the trigger to buy long?

A) 1-minute stochastics to cross up
B) 5-minute stochastics to cross down
C) 3-minute chart to breakdown
D) 1-minute stochastics to cross down

14 IBM's 1-minute stochastics just formed a mini pup through the 20 band on a 5-minute rifle chart mini pup on an uptrend. You should consider:

A) taking a long scalp.
B) taking a short scalp.

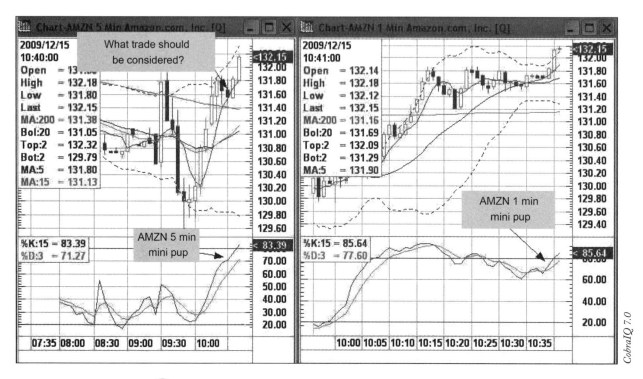

(15) On the above AMZN rifle charts, what trade should be considered based on the 5- and 1-minute dual mini pup patterns?

a) Short on the 5-minute 5-period moving average bounce

b) Long at the 5-minute 5-period moving average bounce

For answers, please visit the
Traders' Library Education Corner at
www.traderslibrary.com/TLEcorner.

CHAPTER 7

PREPARATION WILL SAVE YOUR (TRADING) LIFE

If you woke up in a pitch black house and was told there was a serial killer armed with a kitchen knife stalking you in the dark, you would likely feel anxiety and panic (to put it lightly). Take that same scenario, but this time you were briefed on the dimensions of the house and where the killer was hiding. That would certainly ease your anxiety a bit. What if you were suited in military armor, with night vision goggles, and had communication with "the base," who has GPS tracking of the killer's movements and is armed with a fully loaded semi-automatic weapon? The fear would likely dissipate. What if you were trained for this exact type of combat situation? At this point, you would feel confident in your abilities, and most important, the inherent advantage those abilities give you. The main difference between these scenarios is preparation.

In trading, preparation comes in the form of training and research. The training helps you to react almost instinctively to the situation. The research prepares you with the playing field and the targets ahead of time, allowing you to prepare an effective game plan. The training allows you to react on the fly to limit the damage you sustain if the situation turns against you. Fear will always be present. It is the degree of fear that will either work for you or paralyze and panic you into getting yourself slaughtered. Preparation helps you control fear to your advantage.

TRAINING

The goal of training is to properly bring together knowledge of methods with experience so that you are familiar with and able to react to situations. It is very important to instill good habits and then repeat them through constant, habitual reinforcement. Training doesn't mean practicing.

Training happens when you are continually exposed to situations and react accordingly. Training is a never-ending journey and a constant work in progress. I wish I could say that you can train for a few months trading and be off to battle, but the reality is that the markets are always shifting paradigms and the training is a constant. Training has to be considered in a different mindset. Once the methods are learned and ingrained, the training continues in the form of maintaining the discipline and effort to hold up the research and preparation. This is where most tend to fail, because it is easier to play on the fly—but that will only sustain you temporarily and will eventually backfire. Talent alone is not enough. Training turns into reinforcement.

Preparedness breeds confidence.

GOOD RESEARCH = NIRVANA

There is something to be said about good research. It can be a time-consuming endeavor, but when the research is thorough, a warm sense of confidence tends to blanket you. It is very hard to explain. Perhaps it has to do with knowing that you have bullets in the chamber, with distinct targets in place going into battle the next morning. Good preparation emanates confidence, knowing that you put your time in and have all bases covered. When you plan ahead, the fear is taken out. It is not that you can predict what will happen, but you are prepared to react when certain things do happen. Bottom line, preparedness breeds confidence.

Personally, a good 30 minutes during the weekdays and 2 hours on weekends is when the nirvana starts to kick in. Sector ETFs give you a good place to start, as you can work your way down the stock tiers if a particular sector is forming a strong setup. The only thing preventing that is laziness.

There, I said it. We've all been there, but preparation is what will prevent you from being a statistic. Put in the time and make the effort. The goal is to find just 3 to 5 candidates during the weekend research, and 2 to 3 from the daily research, added to a list of 3 to 5 core stocks. You may think that is not enough, but when you start to rack up more than 5, then you are spreading yourself too thin and the filters are too loose. The nice thing about finding just a handful of ideas is that they will tend to lead to other opportunities in the form of synergy or laggard plays.

MARKING YOUR CANDIDATES

With each candidate, you want to specifically jot down the setup, the overlapping support and resistance levels, and most importantly, the triggers—in the form of "if, then" statements. For example, if this happens, then take the trade here. Each candidate will have 2 sets of instructions for the break or pullback entry. Many times, this will also be contingent on how the overall market is trading, so you may even have to link it with an "if, then" statement regarding behavior on the SPY. For your top 2 best ideas, set an alarm at the trigger price levels in the quote table or matrix.

Once again, you will be taking the trade on 1 of 2 triggers, a confirmed breakout or breakdown, or a pullback to overlapping support and resistance levels. The first is confirmed, but more costly and needs market stability. The second may be riskier, but offers more upside and is safer in choppy markets.

As for profit targets and stops—that's what your intraday charts and training is for. Unless you are swing trading, forget predetermined stops and targets. Nothing is more irritating than when traders set a predetermined profit target that misses by pennies, and then reverses and stops out the trade. The market is not static, so your stops and targets should not be static either. As you get more experienced, it is important to use the practice of scaling into and out of a trade rather than one strict entry and exit. This allows you to spread out the risk and buy time.

> The market is not static, so your stops and targets should not be static either.

DETERMINING GALVANIZED PRICE LEVELS

When you find stock candidates to trade, pull up the daily, weekly, and monthly charts to spot the multiple overlapping support and resistance levels. Any price level with three or more overlaps is considered a significant galvanized price level.

Analyze the daily, weekly, and monthly charts and note the following levels:

- Daily 50- and 200-period moving averages

- Weekly 5-, 15-, 50-, and 200-period moving averages

- Weekly upper and lower Bollinger bands

- Monthly 5-, 15-, 50-, and 200-period moving averages

- Monthly upper and lower Bollinger bands

The wider the time frame, the more significant the price level.

Make specific notes on any of the above levels that overlap within a 0.20 range. The wider the time frame, the more significant the price level. If any price level overlaps three or more times (including sticky 2.50 and sticky 5 levels as well), that is a galvanized support and resistance level to pay extra special close attention to. These galvanized levels are where you want to pay closest attention.

If there is a mini pup or mini inverse pup on the weekly or monthly, specifically note the 5-period moving averages for that time frame, as that will be the line in the sand to preserve the mini pup.

From the above, you should have a top down list of price levels with special markings on the galvanized price levels. Your focus will be on this price list after earnings are released. The initial reactions will have a pinball effect off the significant price levels.

Say for example that stock ABC closed at 28.95 going into earnings. Your notes may look like this:

- No trend in daily or weekly, monthly has a mini pup in place.

- 32.60 = monthly upper Bollinger bands, sticky 2.50s

- 31.80 = weekly upper Bollinger bands

- 30.60*** = monthly 50-period moving average, weekly upper Bollinger bands, daily 200-period moving average, sticky 5s

- 29.50 = weekly 5- and 15-period moving averages, sticky 5s

- 27.50 = sticky 2.50s, daily lower Bollinger bands

- 26.85** = monthly 5

- 25.50*** = monthly 15-period moving average, weekly lower Bollinger bands, sticky 5s

- 23.50 = monthly lower Bollinger bands

*** Indicates galvanized price level overlapping three or more times

** Indicates a mini pup support level

CORE TRADING STOCKS

These are stocks that you are familiar with. I have also referred to them as "basket stocks" in the past. Your core stocks should be liquid, higher priced, and correlated with the noodles movements. Core stocks may or may not be traded every day, depending on how well they are correlating with the futures movements. Stocks like AAPL, RIMM, AMZN, and GS make good candidates. However, don't get too attached to trading them every day. Even the best core stocks can have nutty off days where they just trade in their tune. For this reason, it's good to have other candidates ready. When you take three straight stop losses on a core stock, use a better mouse trap—meaning, revert to other candidates to trade. When markets get into macro valley periods or bad intraday periods, core stocks tend to chop sporadically as well and can be more pain than gain.

Keep these stocks on a quote matrix or table and add new candidates from pre-market research to keep an eye on the list. The basic data should include: last trade, price change, bid, ask, volume, high, and low. This information is all you need. If there are galvanized areas on an existing pattern like a perfect storm, set an alarm to sound upon testing that level.

LINKING LAGGARDS TO YOUR CORE TRADING STOCKS

If possible, try to have a sympathy or laggard stock pinned to each of your core trading stocks. For instance, make PALM laggard to RIMM, so that if RIMM takes off too fast, you can jump on PALM as a laggard. MS is a laggard to GS. MOS is a laggard to POT, and so forth. You can find the laggards by looking up the leaders and then clicking "competitors" online at Yahoo Finance. Good, obedient laggards tend to have a smaller beta, which is what buys you the time to jump into them when the leader takes off. We'll talk more about stock beta later, but RIMM has a beta of 2.01, while PALM has a beta of 0.60. This makes for a very nice laggard trade if RIMM explodes too fast. The saying that "dogs can't move without wagging their tails" describes RIMM and PALM in a nutshell. On rare occasions, like a super strong earnings report, the tail may take off so strong that it wags the dog. In these cases, it's just a matter of reversing the tail with the dog. Most important, since you are already familiar with both, you should be able to trade the situation seamlessly.

GAUGING AND GROUPING STOCK RHYTHMS

Group the volatility by sector. In most cases, the rhythm of the stocks within a sector will pretty much indicate how thick or thin the stocks actually move. Solar stocks (FSLR, SPWRA, TSL) are thin by nature, as are fertilizers (POT, MON, MOS). From there, you can take them down the tiers and recognize the movements. Sector betas also give a good indication of the volatility. Individual stock rhythms can only truly be acclimated by watching the stock move on Level II, and watching the time of sales as well. Thinner stocks tend to have smaller floats and more slippery bid-ask spreads that thin out very quickly on volume spurts (i.e., BIDU). They are often—but not always—higher priced stocks trading in the triple digits. Thicker stocks are the opposite and take tons of volume to move (i.e., CSCO) and trade under $25 to single digits.

When you observe a stock for the first time to gauge the rhythm, note how it correlates with the 1-minute noodles fluctuations and how tight and wide the spreads get. Remember to watch the time of sales with the Level II. Note how smoothly it tends to move through round numbers and the reactions to the sticky levels at 2.50, 5, 0.30, and 0.75. When they overshoot a round number, do they tend to coil off the plus or minus 0.10 coil support and resistance levels, or overshoot past them to the 0.30 and 0.75 coil levels? When the spreads and Level II move around sporadically, does it happen from heavy volume on time of sales, or do the bid-ask spreads seem to jump around on small 100 share lots?

Many of the thinner stocks have so many peg orders that the illusion of liquidity often gets shattered by just a few small trades on time of sales. You can test the liquidity first-hand with 100 shares on the inside bid or ask. The inherent liquidity must be known so that you don't find yourself jumping head first into a pool and finding out that it's empty just before you do a face plant. This is what it feels like to take 5,000 shares long and then find out that it's virtually impossible to sell the whole lot at once without sweeping -0.30 under the inside bid. Of course, you wouldn't jump headfirst into 5,000 shares without knowing this, right?

STOCK BETA CONSIDERATIONS FOR CORE TRADING STOCKS

The beta of a stock uses regression analysis to measure a stock's volatility against the S&P 500 Index. The actual index has a beta of 1. A stock with a beta of 1 moves exactly with the market. If the market goes up 15%, then the stock goes up 15%. A stock with a beta of 0.70 implies that it moves 70% of the market move. A stock with a beta of 1.20 implies a 20% greater move than the market. Higher beta stocks carry more volatility and risk, but also more reward. Lower beta stocks are less volatile, but return less. This is not an exact science, but a general indication as to the volatility of your stock. Different data providers will have different beta numbers for the same stock. This discrepancy usually stems from the number of months or years worth of data that is used to calculate the beta, as some vendors will use anywhere from 6 months to a year, while others will use 5 years. The key is to make sure that you use the same beta figures from the one same provider.

> I like to use Yahoo Finance under "key statistics" for any particular stock and get my beta number from there.

Obviously, higher beta stocks cater more towards traders, as the greater volatility provides larger windows of opportunity and price ranges to profit off fluctuations. As of this writing, RIMM has a beta of 2.15, PALM 0.60, AAPL 1.51, AMZN 1.23, GOOG 1.1, GS 1.49, POT

1.27, MOS 1.33, AMGN 0.41, and GE has a beta of 1.62. The more volatile a stock is, the higher its beta. For core stocks, you naturally want at least a 1 or higher beta. Widely traded stocks with a beta of 1.5 to 3 make for ideal core trading candidates. Disregard the beta on stocks that explode on news, since that volatility will be short lived.

> Widely traded stocks with a beta of 1.5 to 3 make for ideal core trading candidates.

RESEARCH ROUTINE

This preparation is half the battle going into the trading day. As I mentioned, the goal is to start off with two or three solid candidates to trade for the day. Always check your core stocks' current daily, weekly, and monthly charts to note nearby galvanized price levels. When you choose candidates, it is imperative that you are familiar with the rhythm of the stock and how thin or thick the spread movements are. Always watch how a stock trades first to get acclimated.

DAILY PRE-MARKET

- **Analyze the pre-market noodles and futures.** Note any trends, formations, and galvanized support and resistance levels

- **Scan for point gainers and losers lists.** These are available on most broker platforms. Pick two or three from your list and note the galvanized support and resistance levels. Make sure the candidates have volume.

- **Scan core stocks.** Note any pup or mini pup formations on the wider time frames. Note any nearby galvanized support and resistance levels.

- **Post candidates to track on your stock table.** Data should include the last trade, point change, bid, ask, high, low, and volume. Your core trading stocks should already be on this table along with their sympathy and laggard counterparts, if there are any.

- **Set alarms as needed in your stock table.** Any decent charting or broker platform should allow you to preset audio alarms. Set these to trigger on the furthest, strongest galvanized support level and resistance level on these stocks (the goal is to alert you in case of an exceptional move). Also set alarms on converging breakout or breakdown price levels. But don't set too many alarms. You don't want to wake the neighbors or yourself!

INTRADAY SCANNING

Opportunities arise during the day, so speedy access to information is key. Scanning programs are highly recommended, but at the minimum, consider subscription based newsfeeds.

Scanning Programs

- **Sector Heatmaps.** These are graphic indications of what sectors are hot and cold throughout the day. They are a decent general visual tool to find ideas, especially for sector laggard plays. There are lots of free sites that offer these; check out NasdaqTrader.com.

- **Trade-ideas.com.** An excellent intraday scanning program that comes prepackaged with many pattern configurations.

Newsfeeds

- **Dow Jones Newswire.** This is the industry standard for immediate news releases.

- **Briefing.com.**

- **FlyOnTheWall.com.**

You can also use chat rooms for research during the day. Paid, moderated rooms are more controlled and filtered. Check out UndergroundTrader. com (shameless plug, I know). Then there's CNBC. As much as I despise this television channel, they do make an impact with their "news" stories and softball interviews. Unfortunately, you have to sit through 90% bile to get to the 10% meat. Most notably, check their guest list on their website (pre-market) for CEO appearances ahead, near, or just after an event.

POST-MARKET AND EVENING RESEARCH

Scan your core stocks' closing action, and note if the 60-minute or daily closed with a pup or mini pup. Perfect storm formation closes with 8- or 13-minute stochastics up are also viable overnight gapper candidates. Note if there was a consistently stubborn resistance or support level throughout the day, as these levels can form a line in the sand the next day.

WEEKEND RESEARCH

Analyze the SPY, DIA, and QQQQs for perfect storms on the daily, weekly, and monthly charts. Run patterns and candles scans on sector ETFs and stocks. Look for perfect storm patterns and stars or hammers on the daily, weekly, and monthly charts. Any sector ETF with a perfect storm makes it much easier to work through the tiers to find trading candidates as well as laggards. StockFetcher.com has a nice candle and pattern filtering function, and StockCharts.com has some nice free pattern and candle scanning tools.

Pick three to five candidate stocks to track. Note the galvanized support levels and Bollinger band targets. On perfect storms, note the 5-period moving averages of the mini pup time frames and Bollinger band target areas. These will provide nice food for the week, as wider time frame perfect storms give many intraday opportunities to play with the underlying trend on the shorter time frames.

Add these stocks to the core stock quote table or matrix to track during the week. Set alarms on your top two picks using the "if, then" statements.

BRING IT FULL CIRCLE: TEST YOURSELF

(1) Which of the following are stronger galvanized supports for AAPL?

a) 206.50 is the daily 5-period moving average on mini pup, weekly 50-period moving average, and monthly 5-period moving average supports.

b) 206.50 is daily upper Bollinger band, sticky 2.50s, and 60-minute 200-period moving average.

c) 206.50 is the 3-minute 5-period moving average mini pup and 13-minute 5-period moving average.

(2) A laggard stock tends to lead the sector.

a) True
b) False

(3) A stock trading at $150 will usually trade thinner than a stock trading at $12.

a) True
b) False

(4) If POT is trading up +8 points, MON is trading +3, and MOS is trading down -2 without any news, then MOS may be what type of play?

a) Momentum
b) News
c) Laggard
d) Turd

For answers, please visit the
Traders' Library Education Corner at
www.traderslibrary.com/TLEcorner.

CHAPTER 8

BASIC TRAINING

This section will apply to newbies as well as seasoned traders who are going through a slump or coming back from an involuntary hiatus. The goal is to systematically acclimate or re-acclimate the trader with the proper methods by breaking them down into chewable pieces. The first time trying to understand the methods and coordinate all the charts and nuances can be confusing and overwhelming. It shouldn't be. Even seasoned traders can get so jammed up with all the time frames and nuances that they lose grip of the basics.

This is meant to take you back to the beginning, starting from scratch.

WHICH TRAINING REGIMEN IS RIGHT FOR YOU?

REFRESHER: REMEDY FOR SLUMPS

This is like rebooting your computer system in safe mode, stripped down to bare bones, so you can assess where the problem lies. For a trader, it's a refresher. Refer to Chapter 11: The Playbook, if you are in that situation.

BOOT CAMP: FOR NEWBIES

When this trading system is taken in all at once as a whole, it's easy to get overwhelmed and choke. For traders new to the methods, the best approach is to break the system down into small, digestible pieces and chew slowly. The key to proper training is to break it down into smaller pieces to digest and add the other components slowly and thoroughly until you reach the whole.

That is how the boot camp training has been structured. Take it slow and one piece at a time as recommended.

    Report to Day 1 stripped, soldier!

RE-BOOT CAMP: REMEDY FOR EXPERIENCED TRADERS WHO CRASHED

Just like an older computer that has been bogged down with loads of programs and updates that eventually starts to run like crap due to so many corrupted files that it eventually crashes, experienced traders also need to reboot in the equivalent of safe mode.

On a side note, how ironic that my main system completely blew out the motherboard, the hard drive crashed, and my CPU completely burnt out two days before this book's deadline!

In safe mode, everything is stripped to a minimum to assess where the problem is by working backwards. A trader who blows out is the equivalent of a computer crash and more drastic measures need to be taken to rebuild the system. We are rebuilding and reinstalling the operating system—creating a clean slate—and then methodically and systematically reinstalling the necessary programs. For those who haven't been acclimated to the 5- and 1-minute full data rifle charts, this will actually be an upgrade. This is the weapon we will start with, eventually. Proceed with Day 1, sergeant.

    This ain't just a refresher, it's a complete re-install!

STARTING FROM SCRATCH: STRIPPED!

DAY 1: STRIPPED!

1. Have one sheet of paper and a pen. Make six columns, and mark them as follows: pre-market, opening hour, mid-morning, deadzone, witching hour, last hour.

2. Start up your broker or chart platform.

3. Set up a single 1-minute price chart (full market hours data) linked to Nasdaq Level II on a core stock, such as RIMM. Just watch it from 8:30 a.m. to 9:30 a.m. EST. This is known as pre-market. Just watch, and only watch. Resist the urge to trade the move. How can you? You (should) only have one chart, which is the 1-minute candlestick price chart with no stochastics or indicators. The only things to watch are the 1-minute candlestick chart, Nasdaq Level II, time of sales, and the clock. Write down RIMM's characteristics during the pre-market in your own words. Is it moving up or down? Fast or slow? How tight or wide are the spreads? How is the pace of the trades? Is it slow or fast? Can you tell where the stock is moving to? The only tool you have is the candlestick chart.

4. On your piece of paper, train your eyes to spot hammers and shooting star candles. Write down the closing price and the time of shooting stars that form only after at least three green successive candles, and hammers that form after at least three successive red candles. You will do this throughout the day. This is your only exercise. This is an exercise in solid filtering for stars and hammers. Remember, only note those stars and hammers that have subsequent candles.

5. Observe the 9:30 a.m. opening bell and how fast RIMM's stock moves out of the gates. Keep jotting down confirmed instances of stars and hammers. Note the time periods and how RIMM tends to trade fast or slow. Are heavy sizes or small 100 share sizes dominating the time of sales? Try to see if you can predict where the stock price is going for each time period.

You know what a hammer and a shooting star candle look like, right? These are reversal candles that come at the end of a progressive series of down candles for hammers, and up candles for stars. Refer to Chapter 5: The Tools for more on hammers and stars.

6. After the first hour, you should be able to almost anticipate what happens to RIMM after a hammer or star forms, especially if it's after a larger number of preceding continuation candles. The more preceding up, green candles before a star, the more likely RIMM falls, and vice versa on the hammers.

7. As you get to the mid-morning and deadzone periods, notice the effectiveness of the stars and hammers. Do they fall as much on stars? Do they bounce as crisp and sharp as the opening hour on hammers?

8. Watch through the deadzone period and note the veracity of the moves and how much follow-through they are getting compared to the opening hour. Feel the rhythm, range, and volume of trades slowing down as the market takes a pit stop.

9. Watch and note how the witching hour plays out from 1:00 p.m. to 2:00 p.m. How is the follow-through? Is RIMM getting consecutive up or down candles? Has the range tightened? How is the volatility? Compared to opening hour and deadzone?

10. Note if the pace picks up going into the last hour. Feel the flow.

11. In the last hour, try to see if you can anticipate in what direction RIMM will be going. Are the stars and hammers getting follow-through? Note the pace in the last five minutes going into the 4:00 p.m. close.

After Day 1, review your notes. Compare the pacing, velocity, follow-through direction, and stars or hammers follow-through in each of the trading periods. Most importantly, were you able to have any accuracy predicting the direction of the stock during any of those periods? What periods did RIMM tend to follow through in a direction with consecutive candles the most? What periods did RIMM tend to just chop around randomly without much direction and a tight range? Observe how the sticky 2.50s, 5s and especially the 0.70 and 0.30 levels react on heavy, moderate, and light volume.

Rate from top down, the order of trading periods (pre-market, opening hour, mid-morning, deadzone, witching hour, and last hour) where you could predict some of the follow-through and direction. Which trading periods felt the most fluid? Use any intuition or feel. Chances are likely that the opening hour is at the top of the list with deadzone or witching hour near the bottom. At the very bottom of your page, ask yourself what tools you would need to help you analyze better. Would a roadmap and a momentum oscillator help?

DAY 2: GROUNDHOG DAY—DEPRIVATION CONTINUED

Repeat the steps from Day 1. Keep notes just like yesterday. Once again, at the bottom of the page, write down what you really need to get a better handle on anticipating the price moves on RIMM.

DAY 3: ENTER THE STOCHASTICS OSCILLATOR
AND BOLLINGER BANDS

1. On the 1-minute chart, add the following studies:

    • Slow stochastics settings: 15, 3, and 1 for smoothing (CobraIQ)

    • Bollinger bands settings: 20 periods and 2 standard deviations

    • 200-period simple moving average

    • 5-period simple moving average

2. Now repeat the same observations on RIMM from Day 1 and Day 2, but this time, only mark the stars that form on a candle close under 1-minute upper Bollinger bands with an 80-band stochastics slip.

3. Only mark shooting star candles closing under the 1-minute upper Bollinger bands and 80-band cross down.

4. Only mark hammer candles closing about the 1-minute lower Bollinger bands and 20-band cross up.

Continue to observe and note which trading periods had the most follow-through into and after the stars and hammer candles. How did the Bollinger bands hold the ranges? What happened when the Bollinger bands started to constrict? And when they expanded? What about when only one of the Bollinger bands constricted while the other was expanding? How often did the candles push beyond the Bollinger bands, and what trading periods have the most instances of that? Count how many of these newly marked candles got full follow-through to the opposite Bollinger bands versus those that fell to the 1-minute 20-period moving average and reversed back.

Figure 8.1

1-Minute
Mini Pup

For a closer
look, please visit
TradersLibrary.com/
TLECorner.

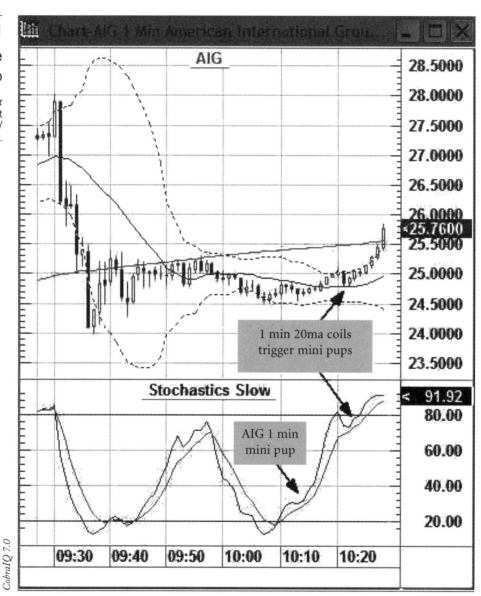

DAY 4: ENTER THE MINI PUP

1. Continue with the regimen of Day 3.

2. Mark the 1-minute star closes under the upper Bollinger bands and the 80 stochastics band cross down. Mark it "extra special" if the stochastics has a mini inverse pup.

3. Mark the 1-minute hammer closes above the lower Bollinger bands and 20-band stochastics cross up. Mark it extra special if the stochastics has a mini pup.

4. Mark stochastics mini inverse pup 80-band cross downs.

5. Mark stochastics mini pup 20-band cross ups.

6. Mark stochastics mini pups and mini inverse pups at the 1-minute 20-period moving averages.

Today we add the mini pups like the one in Figure 8.1 to the hit list. Mark down the stochastics mini pups at the 20 and 80 bands and at the 1-minute 20-period moving averages. Note carefully the trading periods during which these occur and how much follow-through they have. We are not looking at random mini pups but specifically 20- and 80-band reversals only! Usually these reversals will move to the 1-minute 20-period moving averages, at which point they will usually test and fail, or form another mini pup to continue for full oscillation to the next Bollinger band. Please note whether or not they fail at the 20 band, if they break and form a full oscillation move to the 20 band or the lower Bollinger bands, or the 80 band or upper Bollinger bands. At the end of the day, count up the full oscillations and rank the trading periods starting with the most completed full oscillations, ranking lower those trading periods that had the most failed oscillations.

DAY 5: DRILLING THE MINI PUP
Repeat the Day 4 routine, let it marinate.

Same drill. Stick to the game plan and watch like a sniper. Be meticulous. You know what you are targeting to spot. The notes are important, because we will be reviewing them next week with the historical charts. Make the notes more technical now, meaning rhythm gauging, pace, etc. should be first-hand knowledge. These characteristics will be defined by the 5-minute charts tomorrow.

DAY 6: ENTER THE 5-MINUTE CHART

1. Create a list of full data for the 5-minute chart (with pre- and post-market data included), and add the following studies:

- Slow stochastics settings: 15, 3, and 1 for smoothing (CobraIQ)

- Bollinger band settings: 20 periods and 2 standard deviations

- 5-period simple moving average

- 15-period simple moving average

- 50- and 200-period simple moving average

- Volume

2. Repeat Day 5 routine and note the same shooting stars closing below 5-minute upper Bollinger bands and hammers that close above 5-minute lower Bollinger bands.

3. Mark 5-minute trends after 3 consecutive candle closes above the 5-period moving average, trend channel, and 5- and 1-minute stochastics moving up.

   - An uptrend has rising 5- and 15-period moving averages. The reason for marking only after 3 consecutive candle closes is to filter for steady, no-chop trends. We want to build a solid frame of reference and train your eyes and mind to accept only the best patterns. Build up that ability and reinforce it. Starting off with sloppy filtering is how you end up with corrupted files that will eventually crash. We don't want that!

   - For example, if a 5-minute uptrend is in place, but the third candle closes under the 5-period moving average as the fourth closes above, then that is still filtered out.

   - Rule out flat moving averages! They must have a trading channel that is rising.

   - A downtrend has falling 5- and 15-period moving averages and 5- and 1-minute stochastics moving down. Mark only after 3 consecutive red candle closes that do not close above the 5-minute 5-period moving average.

   - Make sure stochastics cross down with the moving averages' downtrend, with channels with at least 3 consecutive closes under the 5-period moving averages.

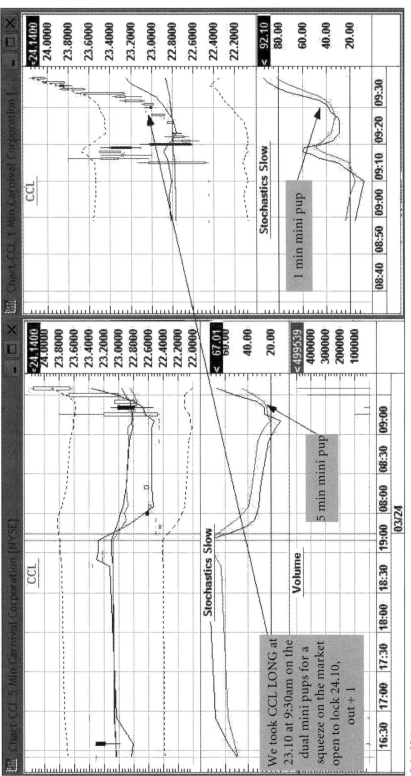

Figure 8.2
5- and 1-
Minute
Mini Pups

For a closer
look, please visit
TradersLibrary.com/
TLECorner.

While all these notes and filtering may seem like a lot, the actual occurrences that meet the specific criteria will be a handful at most. See Figure 8.2 for an example. The key is tight filtering and not wavering on what you are marking. As for rhythm and stock pacing observations, there is no need to repeat those anymore, you now should be very familiar with how the stock moves.

DAY 7: USING 5- AND 1-MINUTE PUPS AND MINI PUPS FOR BREAKOUT AND BREAKDOWN PLAYS

1. Mark 5-minute moving average pup breakouts and breakdowns. Make sure 5- and 1-minute stochastics are crossed in the direction of the pup. Ignore make-or-breaks; only confirmed pups should be marked. Put a special mark on 5- and 1-minute dual mini pups.

2. Mark 5-minute mini pups and mini inverse pups. Make sure 5-period moving averages don't get any candle closes above. Put a special mark on 5- and 1-minute dual mini inverse pups.

3. Make a special mark for combined 5-minute moving average pups that contain 5-minute mini pups and 1-minute mini pups.

4. Make another special mark for combined 5-minute moving average inverse pups that contain a mini inverse pup and 1-minute mini inverse pups.

Take a look at Figure 8.3. The 5-minute charts are your trend charts. The pups and mini pups are the dominant strength pattern. Note any pre-market 5-minute pups or mini pups using the 1-minute stochastics trigger. Observe how 5-minute mini pups tend to grind to the Bollinger bands. Note the trading periods in which they are strongest, with the most follow-through, as well as fluid consecutive candles that don't close under the 5-period moving averages.

DAY 8: USING 5- AND 1-MINUTE CHARTS FOR CHANNEL TIGHTENING PLAY

Mark channel tightenings with a 5-minute 5-period moving average sloping up with a 5-minute mini pup and a 1-minute stochastics cross up trigger. The inverse applies for a short channel tightening play; mark the 5-minute 5-period moving average sloping down with a 5-minute mini inverse pup and a 1-minute stochastics cross down trigger.

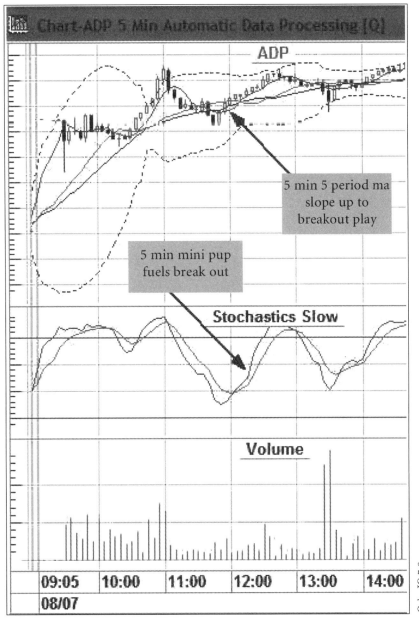

Figure 8.3
5-Minute Pup

For a closer
look, please visit
TradersLibrary.com/
TLECorner.

By this time, you should be fully immersed in the workings of the 5- and 1-minute full data charts and their synergies. You should be aware of oscillation and exhaustion trading on the 1-minute, and the 5- and 1-minute pups and mini pups for trends and channel tightening. You should be able to pull up a 5- and 1-minute chart on the fly with other stocks and immediately point out formations and potential setups and targets.

DAYS 9-14: COMBAT SIMULATION

1. Continue to mark for the various setups on the 5- and 1-minute charts.

2. Trade on simulator or light shares, and time triggers on 1-minute stochastics crosses.

3. Limit your trading to the most fertile periods: pre-market, opening hour, and last hour.

4. Filter tightly for only 5- and 1-minute pup and mini pup formations.

5. Target scalps to 1-minute 20-periods or Bollinger bands. Practice exiting into momentum ahead of exhaustions.

6. Try to time 1-minute high and low band mini pup exits.

7. Hit a 70% accuracy rate for 4 out of 5 days to proceed to the next stage of your training.

DAYS 14-19: MORE TARGETS

1. Add the rest of the daily charts: 60-, 13-, 8-, 3-, and 1-minute time frames, regular market hours, and noodles charts.

2. Add in channel tightening plays.

3. Add in stars and hammer trades.

4. Add in oscillation trades.

5. Hit a 70% accuracy rate for 4 out of 5 days to proceed to the next stage.

DAYS 20+: OFF TO THE WAR ZONE—TIME TO EARN

1. Increase share size incrementally.

2. Focus on tight filtering and pacing.

3. Maintain a 70% accuracy rate.

4. If you ever have 3 straight losing days, take a day off to regroup.

5. Consider adding more core stocks.

6. Add in the rest of The Playbook strategies from Chapter 11.

7. Incorporate research routines to find candidates.

8. Add the rest of the daily charts, including the 60-, 13-, 8-, 3-, and 1-minute time frames, regular market hours, and noodles charts.

9. Incorporate the pump and release method and the daily trading model.

At this point, you are your way, or back on track. If you find yourself getting out of control or cracking again, take a break and go through the refresher before you blow out.

 Good work soldier!

A NOTE ABOUT TRAINING MODE

If you are trading 100 shares of any stock for scalps, then you are still in training mode (unless it is a triple digit momentum mover). Don't mistake this for earning mode, where you are actually trading to make profits and earn. Training mode is one level above trading on a simulator. The purpose is to alleviate the money factor so that you can concentrate on the actual trade and let the methods play out. The goal is to be able to objectively make trades with little financial risk while implementing real time execution.

LEARN BEFORE YOU TRY TO EARN, OR YOU WILL BURN

When a trader complains about his commission costs eating into his "profits" while trading 100 shares for scalps, he is defeating the purpose. It's called training for a reason. The goal is to sharpen the skills and execute proper trade management while maintaining a comfort level, so that the trader can eventually work his way up to 1,000 shares. Once a trader is scalping 500 shares or more, that is when he enters the earning mode. He has successfully built up a foundation that will come into play on every trade, especially during disasters. He can also add the range or swing trading and paring element into his style. It's very easy to make mistakes during training mode. The other thing is that a trader can do a lot of damage by treating scalps and range setups with the same share size of 100 shares. How can someone range 100 shares that he would also scalp 100 shares with in the same stock? The risk is disproportionate to reward and this is how the old "4 winners and 1 loss" situation wipes out all the prior gains.

Commissions become irrelevant once a trader goes into earning mode. The goal is to earn the right to trade higher shares by slowly transitioning it in proportion to the consistency.

BRING IT FULL CIRCLE: TEST YOURSELF

1 Simulator training is meant to:

a) take more risks than you normally would.

b) trade exactly as if you were trading real money.

c) practice trading in deadzone and post-market.

2 A trader should start training with just the initial pieces and add on as they get aligned with each tool.

a) True

b) False

3 The Rifle Charts are:

a) the 5- and 1-minute full data (pre- and post-market data) stochastics moving averages charts

b) the 13-minute and 8-minute full data stochastics moving average charts

c) the 5- and 1-minute regular hours market data stochastics moving average charts

d) the 3-minute, 8-minute, and 13-minute regular hours market data stochastics moving average charts

4 A trader should use the Rifle Charts on:

a) every intraday trade.

b) daily swing trades.

c) every weekly swing trade.

For answers, please visit the
Traders' Library Education Corner at
www.traderslibrary.com/TLEcorner.

CHAPTER ⑨

QUICK FUNDAMENTAL ANALYSIS

CPS: CASH PER SHARE PLAYS

I'm not a big fundamentals guy, as I see a company and its stock as two separate entities. However, there are times when a stock may be considerably undervalued compared to the sector or unto itself due to a fundamental news event. While assets for a company such as backlog, inventory, patents, receivables, etc. can be subjective, there is one thing that is always king—cash.

The basic undervalued stock is one that is trading below its cash per share value. The exception is banks and financials, because these entities can fiddle with the cash position in all kinds of wicked ways. Technology companies, biotechs, pharmaceuticals, mining companies, and so forth are good candidates to filter. The cash per share figure can easily be found online at Yahoo Finance, under "key statistics." The next thing you want to factor in is the debt and the cash burn rate. If the debt is not overwhelming (that rules out REITs), and the company has a positive cash flow, then it meets the mark.

Usually I don't set out actively searching for undervalued plays, which I probably should. I will often come across them when they dump on earnings news, merger fallouts, or FDA rejections. This immediately thrusts them into the limelight on panic selling accompanied by huge volume. I love getting into dumpers that fall to, or especially under, their cash per share with a positive cash flow. If the company has a negative quarterly burn rate, that can be a little more hairy in the long run, but we are working for scalps anyway.

Use the cash per share price level as a solid support area on any dumper that trades below, but not at, book value. Book value is too subjective and is not the same thing as cash per share. In fact, this is a good scanning technique to plug into a market scanner. Scan for stocks that are trading at or below cash per share. Throw out any banks, insurance companies, REITs, mutual funds, and financials in general.

> Scan for stocks that are trading at or below cash per share.

That list of stocks will give you something to start with, and then you can pull up the daily, weekly, and monthly charts and compare them to the sector. If the stock is a laggard in a strong sector, then that is even more favorable.

SECTOR LAGGARDS

Stocks that are trading weakly compared to their respective sectors should be kept on the radar as well. These can often be laggard stocks that will soon see money flow once the leaders become overbought. The way to compare is to take the top two or three sector leader charts and see how the undervalued stock is performing in regards to trend and Bollinger bands, and how it is positioning relative to the 50- and 200-day moving averages. If the top three sector leaders are all trading in an uptrend on the weeklies, and above the monthly 15-period moving averages on the monthly, then that sets the bar. If the laggard stock is downtrending but starting to turn on the daily stochastics, this sets up a good laggard play. Keep in mind, if the leaders are all profitable and the undervalued stock in question is bleeding cash, that is key reason for it to be laggard. This goes back to cash per share. The closer it is to or below cash per share, the better the value of the stock, even if it is a pig. Couple this with a daily mini pup tightening while everyone else is in uptrends at their daily upper Bollinger bands, and you've got a good laggard play to consider before the market notices and brings it back up to value.

SEXY SECTORS

Every market has its share of sexy momentum sectors in play, even in bear and downtrending markets. In fact, the weaker the market, the more a sexy sector makes itself apparent. These can be solars, shippers, financials, biotechs (with bios, the novelty plays can branch off into a certain disease factor, like prostate issues, vaccines, Alzheimers', etc.). If the sector is white hot and squeezing higher, then actively look for the laggards even if they appear to be no good, as a sexy sector will actively reach the lowest tiers eventually. Your goal is to get in on them just before or at the very moment of the momentum surge. One thing to keep in mind, however, is that once the momentum hits these kinds of stocks, it's usually a sign of peaking in the sector. In the markets, it's not so much the cream rising to the top, but the lowliest stocks floating to the top just before the sector gets flushed like a toilet. In the end, bagholders are left. Don't be one of them.

CHAPTER ⑩

UTILIZING OPTIONS FOR LEVERAGE AND HEDGING

I often get asked about options and to recommend books on options. Unfortunately, it's usually out of desperation. A trader will usually over-trade or overleverage their account and fall under the PDT (pattern day trading) rule, which roadblocks their trading activity and buying power. The first thing they usually reach for is leveraging through options. Even more unfortunate, these traders will overleverage with options and take their account deeper into the hole because they are unprepared to react, and unaware of the limited window of opportunity to walk away with a profit before the market bites back.

> " This is another way the PDT rule undermines the smaller traders and forces them into an arena where the deck is stacked completely against them. "

First of all, any method or instrument that is arrived upon during a desperation spell is likely bound to fail. This is not because the trade doesn't play out. Very often, the trade will play out well, but the mental state of the desperate trader will inevitably guarantee a nasty loss. If the options trade goes well, traders will get greedy and hold too long, which then sets up the time and volatility premium against them, even if the intrinsic value is stabilized in-the-money. Too often, traders will get greedy when they are up and will not sell in time, letting their profits erode. Or, they may hold too long as the underlying stock exhausts and the option drops considerably in value. Most options contracts end up worthless. This fact is the reason that one can assume that most options traders end up losing their shirts.

It still bewilders me sometimes when traders start off trying to learn complicated options strategies with no methods to track the underlying stock. After all, the underlying stock is what the options contract is based on. However, that is just one component, albeit the most obvious and mistakenly, the most often focused on component.

I am not going to go into too many complex options strategies in this chapter. I just want to go over the ones I have used for profits in layman's terms. The first basic rule of options trading is to have a foundation of methods to determine how the underlying stock price should play out.

MULTIPLE FACTORS

Most people lose when playing options for a simple reason. They don't understand that the deck is stacked against them, much like a casino maintains the "house edge." Most people think of options as a cheap way of gaining leverage and limiting downside risk. It brings out the gambler in people. The simple thinking is if the stock price passes a certain strike level, the option will move incrementally higher with the underlying stock price.

Many people tend to think only of the price that the underlying stock needs to hold to make globs of money. That is what is sold to people in the infomercials and marketing packages. As I pointed out earlier, the cold reality is that most options buyers end up losing money, even if the underlying stock goes in-the-money. In fact, it's the temporary upside in the trade that keeps most suckers…err, traders… in on the trade for way too long.

This is mainly because the underlying stock price is only a third of what comprises the value of the option. The other two components are time and volatility. While the underlying stock price gets the most focus, the effect of volatility can surpass that many times over on the eve of significant events, like earnings reports or FDA panel meetings.

WHAT IS AN OPTION CONTRACT?

An option is named very accordingly to what it actually is—the option to purchase a stock at a certain strike price level up to the third Friday of the expiring month of the contract. Since options only cost a fraction of the price of the actual stock, the benefit is the added leverage and limited downside, since you can only lose your initial investment in the option contract, no matter how far the underlying instrument moves against you. However, on a percentage basis, you can lose 100% of your investment. Remember that. The exception to this is selling naked calls and puts, a very dangerous practice.

THE THREE COMPONENTS OF AN OPTION CONTRACT

Options usually price in 2.50 increments up to $50, and then move in $5 increments—most of the time. However, the very thick liquid stocks and index options can price in $1 increments. These levels are called strike prices. Equity options expire on the third Friday of every month. The options markets close a few minutes after the equities markets.

Call options expect the underlying stock price to move above the chosen strike price level and are considered bullish. Put options expect the underlying stock price to fall below the chosen strike price level and are considered bearish. When the underlying stock price is trading above the strike price for a call or below the strike price for a put, that option is considered to be in-the-money. The further beyond the strike price the underlying security is trading, the deeper the option is in-the-money. The deeper an option is in-the-money, the more the intrinsic value takes precedence over the volatility and time premium. Deep in-the-money calls should be used strictly when playing the underlying stock price movement for the purpose of leverage. By eliminating the time and volatility premiums, the house edge is severely diminished.

INTRINSIC VALUE

The intrinsic value is the value of the option based solely on the difference between the underlying stock price and the strike price. For example, if MSFT is trading at $20.05, the intrinsic value of a 20 call is 0.05 since the stock is only trading 0.05 above the strike price of that call option. If MSFT is trading at $19.90, a 20 call is technically worth zero since it is trading under the $20 strike price. However, the option may have some value depending on the two other components.

TIME PREMIUM

Knowing that options expire on the third Friday of every month with an average of 20 trading days in between expirations, you can quantify the time erosion pretty easily by subtracting the intrinsic value from the price and dividing the rest of the premium proportionately into 20 increments.

VOLATILITY PREMIUM

If a stock's average trading range expands on heavier volume, then the volatility premium will start to kick in. Usually, volatility will rise going into important events such as earnings reports and FDA decisions. Knowing this ahead of time is a key factor in playing straight calls or puts, as often times the underlying stock price movement against the direction of your option can be offset simply because of the added volatility premium. On the flipside, if you buy an option the day before or the day of the critical news release, you have to be aware that you are paying a heavy premium that will evaporate the next day. This is where newbies can get massacred.

So many times a trader will think that a company will blow out its earnings, so they will buy calls in the stock the day before. To their shock, the stock may very well be trading higher and above the strike price, but the option will have dropped in value. For example, Little Timmy thinks YHOO will blow out their earnings (ha-ha) and he buys the July 20 calls for $1.20 when YHOO is trading at $19.85. YHOO miraculously blows out earnings and gaps up to $20.90 the next morning. To Timmy's disappointment, his call options are trading at 0.90, even though the stock is a full dollar higher than it was when he bought the options. Welcome to the world of volatility premium. Premiums drop the day after the expected event in all cases. This is why it's important to make sure that if you play strictly for underlying stock movement, it's best to neutralize the volatility and time premiums by buying deep in-the-money calls. In Timmy's case, he would have been better off buying the July 15 calls priced at $4.95, which were then trading at $5.95 after earnings. Of course, as much as this makes logical sense, the gambler in Timmy figures he won't make as much money due to the lesser amount of contracts he could afford to buy. The greed overrides logic.

On the flipside, when it is known that the volatility will rise starting five days or so before a company's earnings release, astute traders tend to buy the out-of-the-money calls at this time with the sole intent of locking in profits before the earnings release. They are not gambling, but rather profiting off the gamblers.

DELTA

Delta is something to watch carefully. The delta is a number from 1 to 100 that tells you basically how much the option will move based on the underlying stock's price. If the July 80 calls on AMZN have a delta of 25, that means the option generally will move 25 cents for every $1 move that the underlying AMZN stock moves, and vice versa on negative deltas. The delta will change based on the time and volatility premium as well, since it is not based solely on price. The delta will be a key factor to consider before taking an options trade.

If you want to play strictly for the underlying stock movement, then make sure you get deep in-the-money call options with a minimum of premium. If you are looking to profit off of volatility premium, then buy the options a week before earnings (make sure the daily chart sets up in your favor first!) and make sure to sell your options the day before earnings to maximize on the volatility premiums, because they will absolutely, 100% drop in value.

OPTIONS STRATEGIES

When should you use options? First of all, options trades need to be premeditated and not done out of desperation. This is absolutely vital. You have to think through several steps and then plug in the right options. You should not use options just because your account has fallen under the pattern day trading rule balance. Keep in mind that options commissions can be pretty hefty as well, especially if you are taking a gamble trade on a whim. Don't let the cheap price of the option suck you in without figuring out your cost and the required move to break even.

There are dozens of different strategies for using options. In this chapter, I am just pointing out the two key ones that I implement without getting overly complicated. Both of these strategies are completely contingent on the underlying stock pattern. In fact, it all starts with the underlying component, as well as the market in general. As I mentioned earlier, there is no point in messing with options if you don't have a setup with the underlying stock to support the trade. To complement the setup, it helps if the market in general is also setting up in the direction of the trade—up or down.

Options trades need to be premeditated and not done out of desperation.

Then, you want to just stack any other components on top to arrive at a trading plan. Just one component alone is not enough, but a stacked combination of components is what makes options strategies appealing. The right combination allows one to plot out a very specific game plan that can be recalibrated along the way as necessary. Most important, it allows for leverage without tying up too much capital, allowing you to trade other stocks in the meantime.

For scalpers in general, options give an opportunity to expand the arsenal, often eliminating the tick sweating based on the delta. In the right situations, it allows a scalper to be a swing trader even through it conflicts with their natural style of trading.

STACKING THE FACTORS IN YOUR FAVOR

The following are the four main component factors that will significantly increase your upside probabilities. You should have at least two factors stacked in your favor. If you can get all four factors stacked in your favor, then you have a very high probability options trade.

1. **Overlapping perfect storms on the 60-minute, daily, weekly, and monthly time frames.**

   Usually a 60-minute coupled with a daily mini pup or pup pattern is good for a two-day move. If you add in a weekly or monthly pup or mini pup, that move may stretch out for up to five days with strong momentum. The wider time frames you have, the easier it will be to walk away with profits, as the window of opportunity to do so should be very wide.

2. **Laggards and intrinsic value.**

Compare the daily and weekly charts of at least two other same sector companies. A good example is when three other same sector stocks are at daily upper Bollinger bands while the stock in question is just starting to trend up with a daily mini pup. The laggard component acts as a buffer as well. Once money starts flowing into the laggard, it will often continue to move higher to reach equilibrium levels with the sector, even as leaders exhaust and sell off. This is only temporary though, so be aware that the laggard will eventually resume following the leaders.

3. **Pre-event setups and volatility premium.**

Earnings reports are the events that most commonly cause volatility premiums to spike. The key to these is to make sure the stocks are set up in your chosen direction five to seven days ahead of the earnings report. The premiums will usually peak out 48 to 24 hours prior to the reporting date. The goal is not to hold the options into the report. That is gambling, and you will lose many more times than win in those situations.

FDA decisions, panel meetings, and clinical trial results all rocket volatility premiums. Just make sure that you are getting in at least five to seven days ahead of the scheduled date, and sell one or two days before the event. The one thing to be extra careful with is biotech events, with the possibility of a stock halt ahead of the news release. This takes control completely out of your hands. This is why it is important to scale out of your positions 48 to 24 hours ahead of time. Always remember that you are not only selling the news, but selling right before the news.

> Profit off other people's greed, don't fall victim to it.

4. **Heavy options volume in favor of your position.**

If you are long calls, an explosion in call volume is always a good thing that adds to the volatility premium. If the calls outnumber puts at least three to one, that's even better. Remember, once again, this is all a façade, as you ultimately will want to lock profits into the height of optimism. Never believe the hype, especially if the hype turns out to be true. Always plan on cashing out 48 to 24 hours prior to the event.

EXAMPLE: GE JULY 13 2009 CALLS TRADE

This is a real example of one of my personal options trades. In July of 2009, I played the GE July 13 2009 calls. On July 13, 2009, I took 400 contracts at 0.02 before an earnings announcement on Thursday morning, July 17, 2009, while the stock was trading at 11.25. Friday, July 19, 2009 was an expiration Friday. The daily stochastics had a mini pup and GE was a laggard to the rest of the financials and banks. The daily upper Bollinger bands sat at 12.75 with triple resistances at 13 including a daily 200-period moving average, weekly upper Bollinger bands, and monthly resistance. The calls were technically worthless because they were almost 2 points out-of-the-money.

While a newbie will see this trade as a lottery ticket for GE earnings, the reality to me was that the daily chart was enough to expect a $1 move to the upside ahead of earnings. The delta on the calls was 10, which meant for every $1 move on GE, the calls would move 0.10. As it turned out, the markets grinded higher and GE ramped up to 12.50 before the earnings release on Thursday morning, one day before expiration Friday. I dumped out 399 contracts at an average price of 0.10 (from 0.08 up to 0.15) for a nice healthy profit, grossing around $2400 into buyers. The calls jacked up as high as 0.18! GE came out with earnings and they didn't do squat for the stock as the sell news reaction kicked in. Even though GE was trading down in the 12.30s, the calls were selling at 0.01 whereas the day before, they were trading at the same price.

In this trade, this is how I stacked my factors:

- **Laggard**: GE was a laggard, as the rest of the financials were trading at or above their daily upper Bollinger bands. BAC, WFC, JPM, and GS were trading way above their daily upper Bollinger bands. In fact, GE was the only one that actually had yet to break back into an uptrend on the daily. The SPY was in breakout mode as the weekly formed a mini pup breakout and daily stochastics were crossing back up with a close above the daily 5 at 88.30. SPY eventually ramped to 95.

- **Daily Mini Pup**: GE formed a daily mini pup. The weekly was in a make or-break, and the 11.47 level was the weekly 15-period moving average resistance that was the key break. All the aforementioned financial stocks had broken through their weekly 15-period moving averages.

- **Earnings Events**: GE earnings were scheduled for the following Thursday morning, with options expiration on the Friday. More important, the leading back stocks were coming out with earnings during the whole week, kicked off by GS on Tuesday. A lucky break was a GS upgrade out of the blue from super bear Meredith Whitney, which sent GS up +7 on Monday. These actually lifted volatility premiums on banks' stocks across the board.

- **Call Volume**: Call volume went through the roof, outnumbering put volume 3 to 1, especially in the out-of-the-money contracts.

All these stacked factors made for a pretty stress-free trade. The calls chopped around the 0.03 x 0.04 bid-ask spread until Tuesday. Then the volume skyrocketed over the next 2 days to peak out calls around 0.18 as GE peaked out near 12.70. I scaled out at 0.08, 0.10, 0.12, and the last contracts out at 0.15.

A stacked combination of components is what makes the options strategies appealing—creating leverage without tying up too much capital, and allowing you to trade other stocks in the meantime.

COVERED CALL PREMIUM PLAYS

If you happen to really like a stock for the long term and it has a daily, weekly, and monthly uptrend, you may consider writing covered calls to collect time premiums. This involves buying the stock first, then selling the contracts afterwards. Ideally, you want to enter on a perfect storm pattern and get maximum upside before selling the calls slightly out-of-the-money. It's best to do this far in advance of an event like earnings and options expiration—at least two or three weeks out—so that you can collect time premiums daily without getting screwed with volatility premium. Remember, the goal is to buy back the options cheaper as a result of time decay. If you take these immediately before earnings, the volatility will pop, causing you to possibly pay a higher price to buy back.

I used to do these covered call time premium plays with CSCO and then close out the position at the beginning of expiration week, collecting a good ten days of time premium. Make sure that the wider time frames support the upside move and have galvanized support levels above your breakeven point (total stock cost minus premium). This method ties up a good chunk of buying power, so make sure you aren't in a hurry to exit.

OPTIONS TRADE EXECUTION AND MANAGEMENT

ROUTING

This depends on your broker. CITI is the route I tend to use with the CobraIQ platform (www.cobratrading.com). Just don't use snail mail.

SPREADS

Depending on the liquidity of the underlying stock, the spreads on options trades can vary from a few pennies to several dollars. This is why it's very important that you scope out the liquidity and volume of not just the underlying stock, but the option as well. Too many newbies jump headfirst into a call option only to face sticker shock when they realize the nearest bid is $0.50 below where they just bought the call. Don't let this happen to you. Always watch how the options trade relative to the stock for at least 15 or 20 minutes—preferably during volume periods—to see how it trades. Always jot down the delta of the option, as that will be the first clue on the core movement of the contract.

A common newbie mistake is to jump headfirst into an option and then be shocked that the trade just started off with a big deficit based on the spread alone.

SCALING IN AND OUT

Very similar to stocks, options can be scaled in and out. If it's an event play, it's crucial that you do scale out as the event gets closer. If it's a pattern play, scale out every day up to the target price area and make sure to up the trail stops. Remember that pure pattern plays lose value daily in the form of time premium. A pure daily mini pup play is good for a two-day play at best. Very rarely do you want to hold into expiration.

PRE- AND POST-MARKET HEDGING

Another pitfall by options players going into an event is the inability to lock in gains during the pre- and post-market since options markets are closed. It's so frustrating to see an underlying stock make the favorable move in the pre- or post-market, only to lose those gains without being able to profit because options markets were still closed.

There is a way to lock or hedge your gains, as long you have buying power to purchase the underlying stock. This technique works best with in-the-money options. Once earnings are released, you simply take the opposite side of the option with the correctly allocated share sizing. In-the-money call options are easiest since you have a delta of at least 1, which means you just match up the actual share sizes with your contracts for a hedge that locks your gains. Out-of-the-money calls are tougher since so much of that is volatility premium, which will evaporate the next morning anyway. For this reason, you never want to go into earnings with out-of-the-money options unless you are just considering it a lottery ticket, fully anticipating that they will be worthless.

If you happen to score nicely on the out-of-the-money call, then you can hedge your gains once the call gets in-the-money, forming a 1 delta. Then short the same number of shares as your contracts (remember that one contract is 100 shares!) in the post-market to hedge your gain. Make sure you have a gain first! For example, if you bought ten July 15 calls of ABC for $0.10 to hold for a gamble trade on an earnings release, you would need to wait for ABC to get up through $15.10 before even considering a hedge ($15 is the strike price, plus your cost of $0.10). Let's say ABC pops to $16.10 post-market. You would then short 1000 shares at $16.10 while holding the July 15 calls into the market open. Regardless of what ABC does, you are locked in for a 1 point x 10 contracts (1000 shares) gain. If ABC tanks to $15, then your option would be worthless, but your stock short is worth $1 x 1000 shares. If ABC ramps to $17, your call options would be worth $2,000, while your stock short loses $1,000, still netting you the $1,000 profit. Nice trick! One more thing—when you exit the positions, try to do so simultaneously when spreads tighten and action slows down. You don't want to give back too much of your profit from slippage closing out the positions.

> Make sure your out-of-the-money options turn in-the-money before you hedge!

BRING IT FULL CIRCLE: TEST YOURSELF

1 The delta value of an option refers to:

    a) the parallel amount the option will move relative to the underlying stock.

    b) the volatility premium of the option price.

    c) the beta of the underlying stock relative to its sector.

    d) the beta of the underlying stock relative to the market.

2 When you sell a call option contract on a stock you own, it means:

    a) you will collect a premium payment.
    b) you have to pay a premium payment.
    c) you have bought more stock.
    d) you are getting margin called.

For answers, please visit the
Traders' Library Education Corner at
www.traderslibrary.com/TLEcorner.

CHAPTER 11

THE PLAYBOOK

Now that we have gone through the tools, patterns, mental preparation, allocation, and execution, it's time to get to the coveted playbook. These are the types of trades that you will be implementing contingent on market climate, your style, and setup. Although I may be repeating portions of the book here, this chapter is meant to be the go-to reference that contains all the strategies in one place. These are the raw strategies—the allocation and execution is in your hands.

"Vision without execution is hallucination…"

-Thomas Edison

 Plan wisely, young jedi.

INTRADAY PLAYS

Always gauge the trend direction of the noodles prior to taking the trade. The noodles are on a full 24-hour data feed for the 60-, 13-, 8-, 3-, and 1-minute charts, always. The noodles will lead. Pay particularly close attention when the noodles form perfect storms! In these cases, you can literally throw a dart at a sector leader stock and make money. This is the ideal case.

In trend trades, you want to be on the side of the futures—the exception being fades and exhaustions. The futures are aptly named because they move first, and the market follows. Always note if the futures are flat or trending, especially on the 60-minute chart. In a flat tight range consolidation, it's important not to overtrade because liquidity, volume, and follow-through are lacking. These are the main characteristics of an infertile market trading environment. Remember, it's about filtering and taking the higher probability setups, not curve fitting anything to force trades.

“ When in doubt, stay out. ”

Figure 11.1

Pre-Market
Breakout Play

For a closer
look, please visit
TradersLibrary.com/
TLECorner.

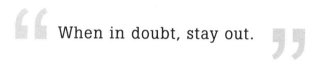

PRE-MARKET TREASURE HUNTING

BREAKOUT PLAY

Objective: To profit from an uptrend move.

Context: Uptrending stock in the pre-market with trend channel and volume. See Figure 11.1.

Main Weapon: 5- and 1-minute pre-market data charts.

Long Trade Setup: 5-minute mini pup with 1-minute cross up or mini pup trigger. Make sure there are at least 2 or 3 successive green candles that haven't violated the rising 5-period moving average. Wait for a pullback near that area on exhaustion with a 1-minute pullback. If the 1-minute stochastics crossed down, then wait for the cross back up for entry. The best trigger is a 1-minute mini pup as the stock coils off the 5-minute 5-period moving average.

Primary Targets: 1- and 5-minute upper Bollinger bands. Pivots, sticky 2.50s, and other resistance levels are natural and more immediate targets, whichever come first.

Stop Loss Trigger: Violation of the 5-minute 5-period moving average.

Notes: The volume is important and will usually come from a gap up or down based on news. If the futures are trending very strong pre-market, then tier 1 generals like AAPL or RIMM may be considered as candidates.

For Regular Market Hours: Continue to use the 5- and 1-minute charts as the primary weapon, but use the regular market charts (1-, 3-, 8-, 13-, and 60-minute, as well as daily) to expand the viewing area. Make sure to play in the direction of the 8- and 13-minute charts. Always make sure there is an existing trend on these charts, and a trading channel. As noted before, the shorter time frames may appear to be trending, but without the 8- and 13-minute charts indicating an uptrend, there will be a lack of follow-through, resulting in too many headfakes. Always confirm a trend first. The best setups will include mini pups on the 8-, 13-, and 60-minute, as well as the

Always watch the futures, including the noodles, the Nasdaq 100 e-minis and the spoos, the S&P 500 e-minis futures.

Figure 11.2

Pre-Market
Breakdown
Play

For a closer
look, please visit
TradersLibrary.com/
TLECorner.

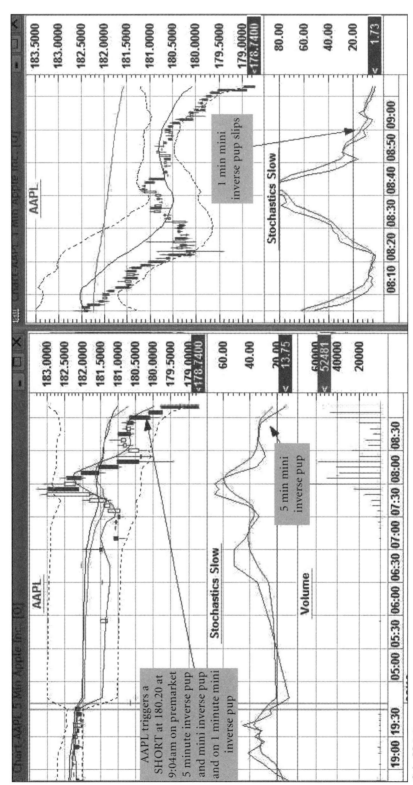

daily time frames to form the foreshadowing effect that we discussed in Chapter 5: The Tools.

BREAKDOWN PLAY

Objective: To profit from a downtrend move.

Context: Downtrending stock in the pre-market with trend channel and volume. See Figure 11.2.

Main Weapon: 5- and 1-minute pre-market data charts.

Long Trade Setup: 5-minute mini inverse pup with 1-minute cross down or mini inverse pup trigger. Make sure there are at least 2 or 3 successive red candles that haven't violated the falling 5-period moving average. Wait for a coil to the 5-period moving average to test and hold resistance. Let the 1-minute stochastics complete its oscillation and cross back down for entry. The best trigger is a 1-minute mini inverse pup as the stock rejects off the 5-minute 5-period moving average.

Primary Targets: 1- and 5-minute lower Bollinger bands. Pivots, sticky 2.50s, and other resistance levels are natural and more immediate targets, whichever come first.

Stop Loss Trigger: Violation of the 5-minute 5-period moving average with a candle close above and 5-minute stochastics cross back up. Make sure that you get out before the 20 band cross! The 20 band cross on the stochastics chart is standard area for buyers.

Notes: The volume is important and will usually come from a gap up or down based on news. If the futures are trending very strong pre-market, then tier 1 generals like AAPL or RIMM may be considered as candidates.

For Regular Market Hours: Continue to use the 5- and 1-minute charts as the primary weapon, but use the regular market charts (1-, 3-, 8-, 13-, and 60-minute, and daily) to expand the viewing area. Make sure to play in the direction of the stochastics and moving averages on the 8- and 13-minute charts. Always make sure there is an existing trend on these charts as well as a trading channel. As noted before, the shorter time frames may appear to be trending, but without the 8- and 13-minute charts indicating a downtrend, there will be a lack of follow-through resulting in too many headfakes. Always confirm a trend first. The best setups will include mini pups on the 8-, 13-, and 60-minute, and the daily time frames to form the foreshadowing effect discussed in Chapter 5: The Tools.

Figure 11.3

Perfect Storm Breakout Play

For a closer look, please visit TradersLibrary.com/ TLECorner.

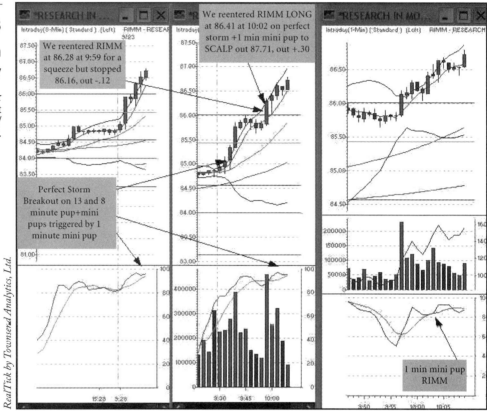

PERFECT STORM BREAKOUT PLAY

Objective: To profit from a strong uptrend move supported by 3 or more pup or mini pup time frame patterns.

Context: Perfect storms are the most powerful break patterns. The key is to spot the first 2 pups or mini pups on the wider intraday time frames such as the daily, 60-, 13-, and 8-minute charts. Once these are spotted, time the entry upon the 1-minute stochastics coil back up. Usually the third mini pup forms on the 3- and 5-minute charts upon the 1-minute trigger. In the best cases, the 1-minute stochastics will trigger with a mini pup. Make sure the futures are rising. The best case is when the noodles are simultaneously forming a perfect storm. See Figure 11.3.

Long Trade Setup: At least 2 pups or mini pups on the daily, 60-, 13-, or 8-minute charts and a 5-minute uptrend, entry upon the 1-minute mini pup trigger off 5- and 3-minute 5-period moving average support.

With an uptrend in place on the 60-, 13-, and 8-minute charts, note the overlapping support areas (the 5-period moving averages on whichever time frames have mini pups). The 5- and 3-minute charts may or may not be trending. The foreshadowing element kicks in here in the absence of 3- and 5-minute trends. If the 5-minute is trending, then prepare for entry upon pullback to the 5-period moving average support tests followed by the 1-minute cross back up, or even better, a 1-minute mini pup.

Primary Targets: For scalpers, the 1-minute upper Bollinger bands will be the primary and initial target, and then the respective upper bands on each time frame with a mini pup to scale out. As always, pivots, 50- and 200-period moving averages, sticky 2.50, 5, 0.30, and 0.75 levels should always be considered profit taking areas. The key is to lock in profits or scale out most on 1-minute high band mini pups above the 80 bands into the climax pops.

Stop Loss Trigger: The 5-period moving average support violation on 5-, 8-, or 13-minute moving averages. A shooting star candle is the first sign to locking out profit. The key is to scale out most into the initial pops at 1-minute high band thrusts to get a nice profit cushion to determine how much wiggle to absorb. If you scale out ¾ of the scalp size, then you can revert to the 13-minute, 5-period moving averages for the final profit/loss stop.

Variations: Always be aware when the noodles and futures set up a perfect storm breakout! The force of this breakout will resonate throughout the rest of the market, starting with the leader stocks and working its way down to lift the markets. When noodles form a perfect storm breakout, it's imperative to find stocks to play on the long side. Consider playing the QID short, or SPY long. Noodles perfect storms tend to stimulate perfect storms in the rest of the leader stocks.

Sometimes the 3- and 5-minute charts will be in a consolidation while the 8-, 13-, or 60-minute charts are in pups or mini pups. In these situations, the foreshadowing element will play out. Use the 1-minute mini pups for entry as the third mini pup.

Notes: Make absolutely sure that the moving averages are uptrending with a trend channel on at least 2 wider time frames. It's easy to see stochastics form mini pups while the moving averages may be flat. This will usually result in a small pop and headfake right back down. The kryptonite for perfect storms is lack of volume, which is often indicated by flat moving averages. The uptrend must be established first! These are also the rare occasions when you can enter the trade on a 1-minute high band—provided there is a mini pup—as long as you take your profits into the spike before a star forms and stochastics slip the 80 bands.

PERFECT STORM BREAKDOWN PLAY

Objective: To profit from a strong downtrend move supported by 3 or more inverse pup or mini inverse pup time frame patterns.

Context: This is the inverted version of a perfect storm breakout—just as powerful, but to the downside. The key is to spot the first 2 inverse pups or mini inverse pups on the wider intraday time frames like the daily, 60-, 13-, and 8-minute charts. Once these are spotted, then time the entry on the 1-minute stochastics cross back down. Usually the third mini pup forms on the 3- and 5-minute charts upon the 1-minute trigger. In the best cases, the 1-minute stochastics will trigger with a mini inverse pup. Make sure that the futures are falling. The best case is when the noodles are simultaneously forming a perfect storm breakdown.

Short Setup: At least 2 inverse pups or mini inverse pups on the daily, 60-, 13-, or 8-minute charts with a 5-minute downtrend, entry upon the 1-minute mini inverse pup, with trigger off the 5- and 3-minute charts, and 5-period moving average resistances.

With a downtrend in place on the 60-, 13-, or 8-minute charts, note the overlapping support areas (the 5-period moving averages on whichever time frames display mini pups). The 5- and 3-minute charts may or may not be trending. The foreshadowing element kicks in here in the absence of 3- and 5-minute trends. If the 5-minute is trending, then prepare for entry upon pullback to the 5-period moving average resistance tests, followed by a 1-minute cross back down, or even better, a 1-minute mini inverse pup.

Primary Targets: For scalpers, the 1-minute lower Bollinger bands will be the primary and initial target, then the respective lower bands on each time frame with a mini inverse pup to scale out. As always, pivots, 50- and 200-period moving averages, sticky 2.50s and 5s, along with the 0.30 and 0.75 levels should always be considered profit taking areas. The key is to lock in profits or scale out most on 1-minute low band mini inverse pups below the 20 bands into the climax panic leans.

Stop Loss Trigger: The 5-period moving average resistance violation on 5-, 8-, and 13-minute moving averages. A hammer candle is an early sign to lock out most profits. The key is to scale out most into the initial leans on the 1-minute low bands to get a nice profit cushion, which allows you to determine how much wiggle to absorb. If you scale out ¾ of the scalp size, then you can revert to the 13-minute 5-period moving averages for your final profit/loss stop.

Variations: Always be aware when the noodles or futures set up a perfect storm breakdown! The force of this breakdown will resonate throughout the rest of the market, starting with the leader stocks and working its way down to sell off the markets. When the noodles form a perfect storm breakdown, it is imperative to find stocks to play on the short side, or at least play the QID long (2 times inverted QQQQ ETF), or short the SPY ETFs. Noodles perfect storms tend to stimulate perfect storms in the rest of the leader stocks.

Sometimes the 3- and 5-minute charts will be in a consolidation while the 8-, 13-, and 60-minute charts are in inverse pups or mini inverse pups. In these situations, the foreshadowing element will play out. Use the 1-minute mini inverse pups for entry as the third mini inverse pup.

Notes: Absolutely make sure that the moving averages are downtrending with a trend channel on at least 2 wider time frames. It's easy to see stochastics form mini inverse pups, while the moving averages may be flat. This will usually result in a small drop and headfake right back up. The kryptonite for perfect storms is lack of volume, which is often indicated by flat moving averages. The downtrend must be established first! This pattern is strong enough that you can chase an entry on a 1-minute low band mini inverse pup, as long as you are quick to take profits before a hammer forms and coils the stochastics back through the 20 band.

FAILED PERFECT STORM PLAY

Objective: To profit from the panic resulting from the failure of the most powerful pattern.

Context: As strong as a perfect storm pattern setup is, the failure is twice as strong. Usually the perfect storm will hit an exhaustion resistance level that can't break. The first clue will be when it fades the noodles. Use a Fibonacci count with 3, 5, and 8 attempts without breaking the resistance. This will cause the stock to reverse very strongly upon the break of the 3-minute 5-period moving averages, and then fade the coil attempts to form a 3-minute mini inverse pup. This sets up tightening to the 3-minute 15-period moving average, and then a test of the 5-minute 5-period moving average, and so forth. It's as if every branch gets hit on the way down as each time frame's mini pup cracks and reverts to a mini inverse pup once the coils fail.

Failed perfect storms also indicate either an infertile market environment, or a strong underlying selling wave. Use this powerful pattern as a litmus test for market climate.

Short Setup: Watch for initial sell fades on noodles thrusts at a galvanized resistance level. If the resistance can't break after 3 to 5 tests, use the noodles reversals combined with a 5-minute 5-period moving average support break for a trigger. Usually the 3-minute will form a mini inverse pup. Use the 1-minute stochastics mini inverse pup though the 80 band as a trigger. Use the 5-period moving average rejections and subsequent time frame mini inverse pup with a 1-minute stochastics slip or a mini inverse pup as the trigger for entry.

Primary Targets: Target the 5-minute 15-period moving average and the 13-minute 5-period moving average for initial profit areas—but use the 1-minute stochastics oscillations through 20 bands to trim out most. The stochastics are more important than price levels. The 13-minute 5-period moving average is a key break. If that cracks, then the 13-minute 15-period moving average is the next target.

Stop Loss Trigger: Each 5-period moving average break becomes the resistance and the trail stop, just above that. If the 3-minute 5-period moving average breaks, a candle close above that 5-period moving average becomes the trail stop. It is likely that that 3-minute 5-period moving average will act as resistance and a mini inverse pup, setting up a move to the 15-period moving average. Each successive 5-period moving average time frame that breaks becomes the trail stop.

Variations: The inverted version of the above applies when a perfect storm breakdown fails. The nice part about these failures is that each time frame's mini pup takes some time to crack, allowing entry and re-entry on each successive 5-period moving average retest failure, accompanied by a mini inverse pup on that time frame—hitting every branch on the way down.

MINI PUP DOPPLER BREAKOUT PLAY

Objective: To utilize the foreshadowing effect of the 8- and 13-minute charts to enter 3- and 5-minute breakouts on the 1-minute trigger.

Context: This is just a scaled down version of a perfect storm. Many times, these setups will form first and then trigger a 3- and 5-minute mini pup further into the pattern. They can often be the precursor setup to the perfect storm.

Long Setup: Both the 8- and 13-minute charts form pups or mini pups with an uptrend and a trading channel, a 3- or 5-minute stochastics cross back up, and a 1-minute stochastics cross up or mini pup. Usually the 1-minute stochastics will cross up on the 3- or 5-minute cross. Experienced traders can step in on the 1-minute stochastics cross up, especially if the futures are set up in the same formation with 8- and 13-minute dual pups or mini pups in an existing uptrend. The safest trigger is a 1-minute mini pup entry after the 3- and 5-minute stochastics firmly cross up.

Primary Targets: For scalpers, the 1-minute upper Bollinger bands will be the primary and initial target, then the respective upper bands on each time frame with a mini pup to scale out. As always, pivots, 50- and 200-period moving averages, the sticky 2.50s and sticky 5s, as well as the 0.30 and 0.75 levels should always be considered profit taking areas. The key is to lock in profits or scale out most on 1-minute high band mini pups above the 80 bands into the climax pops.

Figure 11.4

Channel
Tightening on
5- and 1-
Minute Charts

For a closer
look, please visit
TradersLibrary.com/
TLECorner.

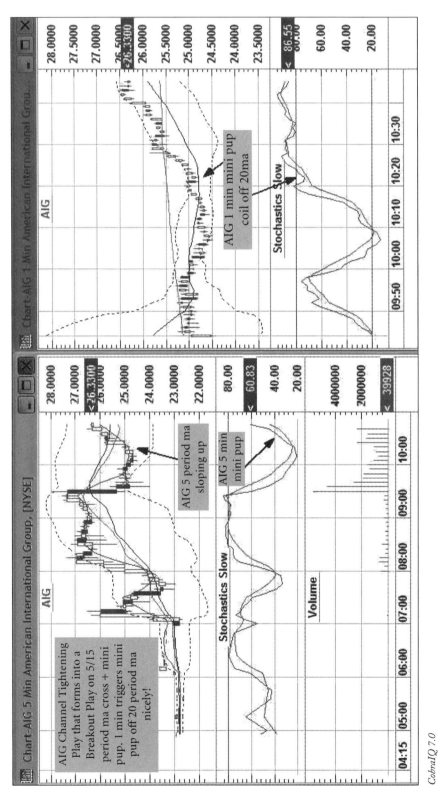

Stop Loss Trigger: The violation of the 8- and 13-minute 5-period moving averages is the final trail stop. This may be pretty far down depending on your entry. A preemptive stop can be taken if the 3- or 5-minute 15-period moving averages close below.

Variations: The inverse of the above setup is used on short trades involving 8- and 13-minute dual inverse pup or mini inverse pup setups.

Notes: Pare out shares as each successive time frame target gets hit. The wider the time frame, the less you should play.

CHANNEL TIGHTENING PLAY

Objective: This is a countertrend trade designed to profit from the tightening from the 5-period moving average to the 15-period moving average. These plays can often transition into a breakout or breakdown play on the 5- and 15-period moving average crossover trend reversal fueled by a mini pup.

Context: The downtrending stock bounces off the 5-minute lower Bollinger bands and the 1-minute stochastics cross up. Wait for the 5-minute 5-period moving average to retest and close a candle above that level. The bears will try to push it back down after the initial candle close. See Figure 11.4.

Long Setup: Watch for the 5-period moving average to slope up to form a mini pup, and then enter on the 1-minute cross, or better yet, a mini pup trigger.

Primary Targets: The 1- and 5-minute upper Bollinger bands. Pivots, sticky 2.50s and other resistance levels are natural and more immediate targets, whichever comes first.

Stop Loss Trigger: Violation of the 5-minute 5-period moving average. If that 5-period moving average breaks, get out as soon as possible.

Variations: Although the 5-minute time frame was mentioned here, you can use a 3-, 8-, 13-, or 60-minute time frame just as well. The key is to be aware of the impending resistance on the wider time frames. For example, when the 5-minute chart is forming a channel tightening with a mini pup, the 5-minute 15-period moving average may also overlap as resistance with the 13-minute 5-period moving average. This would be a double resistance area to take profits prior to testing. If the 13-minute 5-period moving average breaks, retests, and coils, then the 13-minute would trigger a mini pup for a tightening and the 5-minute would likely be in an uptrend, which can be played upon the mini pup trigger with a 1-minute cross or mini pup. The wider time frame tightenings have stronger and more critical 5-period moving average supports. The important thing here is to make sure you have the sloping up of the 5-period moving average and a stochastics mini pup in the respective time frame.

The inverted version of this play would be a 5-period moving average sloping down with a mini inverse pup on an uptrend.

Figure 11.5

Panic Bottom
Slingshot
Long Play
on 1-Minute
Charts

For a closer
look, please visit
TradersLibrary.com/
TLECorner.

HURN formed a 1 min hammer off the lower bbs and coiled with a mini pup trigger at 10.20 coil to 11.35 upper bbs

Notes: Make sure to take profits at the next resistance levels. Since these are countertrend trades, if the 15-period moving average holds support firmly enough, it can cause a reversion upon the break of the 5-period moving averages. Don't get greedy. Take profits at the resistance targets and look for re-entry if they break with a mini pup trigger for the next leg.

A nice added bonus on channel tightening plays is that they can transition into a breakout or breakdown play on the 5-period moving average crossover of a 15-period moving average and mini pup.

PANIC BOTTOM SLINGSHOT LONG PLAY

Objective: To catch a heavy volume capitulation bottom off the lower Bollinger bands to the 5-period moving average, or the hammer to the lower bands. See Figure 11.5.

Context: These are scalp trades that target the next support level depending on entry. These are earlier entries than the aforementioned channel tightening trades, which also makes them riskier, so you must make sure that you take profits ahead of trend support levels.

Main Weapons: 5- and 1-minute full data charts.

Long Setup: Hammer candle close at or above the lower Bollinger bands and a 1-minute candle close at or above the lower bands, a 1-minute stochastics cross up through the 20 band, or mini pups are even better. Stronger setups occur near galvanized support levels.

Primary Targets: The 1-minute 20-period moving average, then the 1-minute upper Bollinger bands, then the 5-period moving average and the pivots or sticky levels.

Stop Loss Trigger: The violation of the hammer body low (no need to wait for a candle close, you can always re-enter if it closes above) or the 1-minute lower Bollinger band candle close.

Variations: A hammer on the 1-minute chart at or above the lower bands is the earliest entry upon a tick above the high of the candle.

Notes: Keep stops very tight on these trades. They are panic trades, which can propel even lower if the lower Bollinger bands fail to hold support.

Do not stick around if the 1-minute stochastics cross back down or fail a mini pup.

MOMENTUM TOP SHORT PLAY

Objective: To catch a heavy volume exhaustion top off the upper Bollinger bands to the 5-period moving average, or the star to the upper Bollinger bands.

Context: These are scalp trades that target the next support level depending on entry. These are earlier entries than the aforementioned channel tightening trades, which also make them riskier, so you must make sure that you take profits ahead of trend support levels.

Main Weapons: 5- and 1-minute full data charts.

Long Setup: Shooting star candle close at or below upper Bollinger bands with a 1-minute candle close at or below upper bands. One-minute stochastics cross down through the 80 band, mini pups are even better. Stronger setups occur near galvanized resistance levels.

Primary Targets: The 1-minute 20-period moving average, the 1-minute lower bands, the 5-period moving average, and pivots or sticky levels.

Stop Loss Trigger: The violation of the shooting star body high (no need to wait for a candle close, you can always re-enter if it closes above), or the 1-minute upper Bollinger band candle close.

Variations: A shooting star on the 1-minute chart at or under the upper Bollinger bands is the earliest entry upon a tick under the low of the candle.

Notes: Keep stops very tight on these trades. They are panic trades, which can squeeze even higher if the upper bands fail to hold resistance. Do not stick around if the 1-minute stochastics cross back up or trigger a high band mini pup.

BOLLINGER BAND +0.20 SHORT SQUEEZE LONG PLAY

Objective: To catch a heavy volume high band momentum short squeeze.

Context: The 60-minute and daily upper Bollinger bands are the strongest intraday resistance levels. These levels will usually reject, even on uptrends before expanding higher. This invites in oscillation traders and shorts to assault these levels for exhaustion trades. When a stock initially overshoots these levels, shorts tend to add higher until that +0.20 price level breaks. Oscillation traders and shorts get trapped and panic out in a buying frenzy, which triggers buyers to come off the fence, causing a high-volume, often parabolic price rise. See Figure 11.6.

Main Weapons: Daily and 60-minute charts to note the upper Bollinger band resistances. Utilize the 5- and 1-minute charts for trigger.

Long Setup: +0.20 above the 60-minute or daily upper Bollinger bands is the only trigger needed. A 1-minute mini pup thrust makes it an even stronger squeeze.

Primary Targets: Since the upper Bollinger bands have been squeezed, look to take profits into sticky resistance levels, pivots, and any moving averages that apply. The key is to get out before the 1-minute stochastics peak out or slip through the 80 band.

Stop Loss Trigger: Beware of shooting star candles! Violation of the +0.20 above the upper Bollinger band price is the typical trail stop. This level becomes the momentum support. A break of that level takes the air right out of the balloon. Some wiggle room can be given to the actual upper band price level.

Variations: If applicable, weekly and monthly upper Bollinger bands make for an even stronger squeeze.

Notes: The entries will often be high bands on the 1-minute charts. For this reason, you want to try to lock most of the profits into the initial momentum thrusts before a shooting star candle forms and the stochastics cross back down.

Figure 11.6
+0.20 Short
Squeeze
Long Play
on 5- and
1-Minute
Charts

For a closer
look, please visit
TradersLibrary.com/
TLECorner.

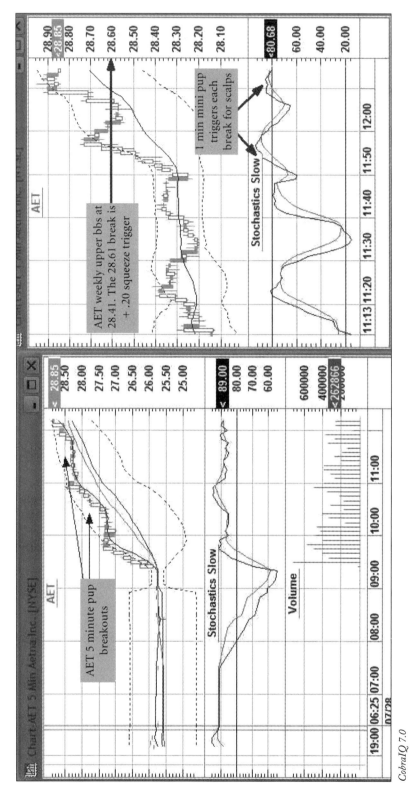

BOLLINGER BAND -0.20 TRAPDOOR SHORT PLAY

Objective: To catch a heavy volume low band panic selloff.

Context: This is the inverse version of the +0.20 upper Bollinger band short squeeze, which means shorting when the stock ticks -0.20 below the 60-minute or daily lower bands. In anticipation of exhaustion bounces off these strong lower bands, oscillation players will take low band longs. Once the Bollinger band area cracks, they will add to their positions until the -0.20 price level cracks, which is the breaking point that causes them to panic out in a frenzy before the next guy. This triggers more panic selling from sellers on the fence hoping for a bounce. The heavy volume panics allow shorts to scale out short covers on the bids. See Figure 11.7.

Primary Weapons: Use the daily and 60-minute charts to note the lower Bollinger band supports. Utilize the 5- and 1-minute charts for a trigger.

Short Setup: -0.20 below the 60-minute or daily lower Bollinger bands is the only trigger needed. A 1-minute mini inverse pup forms an even stronger panic.

Primary Targets: Look to take profits into sticky support levels, pivots, and any moving averages that apply. The key is to get out before the 1-minute stochastics bottom out or coil back up through the 20 bands.

Stop Loss Trigger: Beware of hammer candles! Violation of the -0.20 below lower Bollinger band price is the typical trail stop. This level becomes the momentum resistance. A break of that level can slingshot the price back up. Some wiggle room can be given to the actual lower price level.

Variations: If applicable, weekly and monthly upper Bollinger bands make for an even stronger squeeze.

Notes: The entries will often be low bands on the 1-minute charts. For this reason, you want to try to lock most of the profits into the initial panic leans before a hammer candle forms and the stochastics cross back up.

Figure 11.7
-0.20 Trapdoor
Short Play
on 5- and
1-Minute
Charts

For a closer
look, please visit
TradersLibrary.com/
TLECorner.

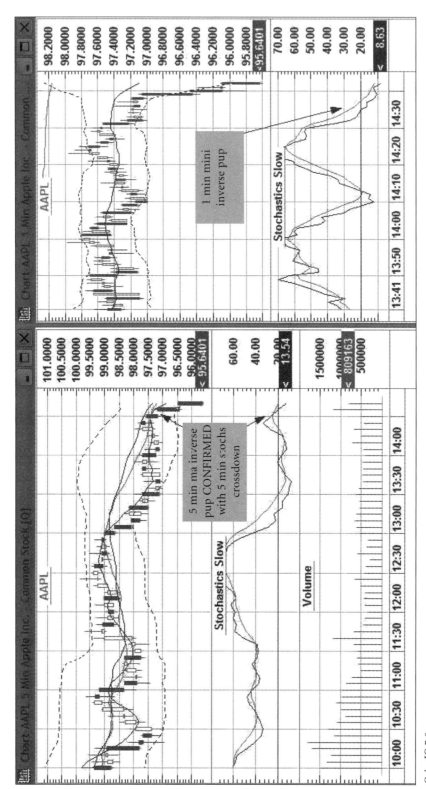

OSCILLATION RANGE SCALPING PLAY

Objective: To short overextended tops and buy overextended bottoms for fun and profit.

Context: Since stocks tend to oscillate much more than trend, oscillation traders try to capture profits by shorting the upper ranges of Bollinger band areas and taking longs off the lower band areas.

Primary Weapons: The 1-minute stochastics chart with Bollinger bands and 20-period moving average coupled with the 5-minute charts and the noodles charts (the 60-, 13-, 8-, 3-, and 1-minute time frames).

Figure 11.8

Oscillation Range Scalping Play on 1-Minute

For a closer look, please visit TradersLibrary.com/ TLECorner.

Use the wider time frame stock charts—the daily, 60-, 13-, and 8-minute charts to determine galvanized support and resistance levels ahead of time. Pivots and sticky levels apply as well.

Long Setup: Time One-minute lower band longs on bounces off the lower Bollinger bands; hammers are especially fruitful with a 20 band stochastics cross up, and mini pups are even better. The 1-minute 20-period moving average can be a good entry on a pullback with a 1-minute stochastics mini pup trigger, as in Figure 11.8. It is important to trim and let the 1-minute stochastics play out.

Short Setup: One-minute upper band shorts on slips back under the upper Bollinger bands. Shooting star candles are especially fruitful with an 80 band stochastics cross down, and mini inverse pups are the best!

Primary Targets: The 1-minute 20-period moving average, then the opposite 1-minute Bollinger bands. Sticky levels—especially the 0.30 and the 0.75 levels—or other, wider time frame resistance levels are more immediate targets, whichever come first. Note that when possible, you should let the 1-minute stochastics completely play itself out, as some of the best moves come from exhaustion attempts that mini pups back up off the 1-minute 20-period moving average.

Stop Loss Trigger: A 1-minute candle close back through the respective Bollinger bands, or a failed 1-minute stochastics cross (20 band for longs and 80 band for shorts).

Variations: Try to execute fills on the inside bid or ask to provide liquidity when possible, in order to collect ECN rebates. While entries on the bid may be tough, especially if the 1-minute stochastics exhaust, the exits are much easier, as you will be selling into the buyers on the ask or covering shorts on the bids during panics. As I pointed out earlier, the 0.002 rebate creates a 30-50% savings on commission (contingent on what your broker charges).

Notes: After a strong trending market day, oscillations tend to kick in the following day. These are the days to really focus on the oscillation scalps. Scaling into the position is usually the best way to minimize your risk. Bid out longs and inside ask out shorts. Range bound oscillations will inevitably breakout or breakdown. This is the oscillation trader's worst nightmare. For this reason, make sure that you don't go to the well too many times, and drop your size on each successive trip, especially if you notice the Bollinger bands constricting. When the range starts to tighten, that is a warning sign to slow down on the oscillation trades, because a breakout and range expansion is near. Expect the possibility of a stop on each successive trade. Stubborn oscillation players are the ones that end up getting burned hard and giving back multiples of the earlier gains.

RANGE FADE LIQUIDITY PLAY

Objective: To catch exhaustions by presetting entries just before galvanized support and resistance. This is similar to oscillation trading, but involves presetting the range levels ahead of time in order to catch a move on the inside bid or ask to attain ECN rebates.

Context: Since ARCA charges 0.04 for liquidity and rebates 0.002. Most market makers don't charge a fee.

Long Setup: Lowest galvanized support level.

Short Setup: Highest galvanized support level.

Primary Targets: Target chain.

Stop Loss Trigger: Plus or minus 0.20 above.

Variations: Sprinkle in multiple price entries to scale in, rather than take a chance at just one price level.

Notes: Make sure you set audio alarms when you get filled. With rebates and ECN fees shrinking, the rebate trading is also subsiding. The only way to really benefit is to have a broker that charges extremely cheap commissions in the 0.002 or less range. The strategy is to provide liquidity through ARCA for a 0.002 rebate and then sell back out on the ask at 0.002 for a total of 0.004 rebate.

TARGET CHAIN

To avoid having to constantly repeat the levels for targets on mini pups and tightenings, I will simply refer to the target chain. This is the order of levels in relation to the position of the stock price.

The target chain consists of 4 basic levels for the respective time frame. .

- Upper Bollinger bands

- 5-period moving average

- 15-period moving average

- Lower Bollinger bands

In uptrends, the target chain is the upper Bollinger bands, the 5-period moving average, the 15-period moving average, and the lower Bollinger bands. In downtrends, the target chain is the lower Bollinger bands, the 5-period moving averages, the 15-period moving averages, and the upper Bollinger bands.

So if you are playing a channel tightening strategy off of a 5-minute lower Bollinger band hammer and a 5-minute mini pup, the immediate target would be a tightening to the 15-period moving average. If the 15-period moving average breaks and forms a mini pup with a 5-minute moving average crossover, then the upper bands would be the next target. Naturally, the 5-period moving averages are always the support level on the trade, with a trail stop on the violation.

BRING IT FULL CIRCLE: TEST YOURSELF

(1) The +0.20 Slingshot Long Play refers to a stock that cracks through the +0.20 price level above a wider time frame upper Bollinger band. This play capitalizes on the shorts getting squeezed. After the squeeze triggers, where is the momentum support on the stock?

    a) At the +0.20 above Bollinger band price level
    b) At the lower Bollinger band
    c) At the body of the shooting star

(2) If the 8- and 13-minute stochastics are forming dual mini pups but 3-minute stochastics is still falling, then you should look for supports at:

    a) the 8- and 13-minute 15-period moving averages.
    b) the 8- and 13-minute 5-period moving averages.

(3) If a daily and 60-minute chart both show mini pups, then a trader should focus on:

    a) breakdown and downtrend plays.
    b) breakout and uptrend plays.
    c) consolidations.

(4) A trader's heaviest trading activity should be done during:

    a) post-market.
    b) deadzone.
    c) opening hour.
    d) witching hour.

5) Which of the following is not part of the target chain?

    a) Upper Bollinger band
    b) Lower Bollinger band
    c) 5-period moving average
    d) 0.719 Fibonacci price level

For answers, please visit the
Traders' Library Education Corner at
www.traderslibrary.com/TLEcorner.

CHAPTER 12

SITUATION TRADES

These trades occur when a fundamental situation presents itself, or there is some type of extreme divergence. Use the aforementioned trade plays (see Chapter 11: The Playbook) to trade these scenarios. In this chapter, details and caveats of the setups will be discussed along with the strategies to implement. Be aware that any situation where a stock immediately panics up or down without news (and sometimes with news) is prone to a stock halt. Rumor-based violent moves are the most susceptible and should only be played for quick scalps until news is released.

EARNINGS REPORT TRADING

Nothing affects a stock price more than its quarterly earnings report. These are pre-planned events. Fortunes can be made and lost in minutes trading these moves.

RECORDING GALVANIZED PRICE LEVELS

Preparation is key here. This takes no more than a few minutes. Analyze the daily, weekly, and monthly charts and note the following levels.

- Daily 50- and 200-period moving averages

- Weekly 5-, 15-, 50-, and 200-period moving averages

- Weekly upper and lower Bollinger bands

- Monthly 5-, 15-, 50-, and 200-period moving averages

- Monthly upper and lower Bollinger bands

Make specific notes on any of the above levels that overlap within a 0.20 range. The wider the time frame, the more significant the price level. If any price level overlaps 3 or more times (including the sticky 2.50s and sticky 5s), that is a galvanized support or resistance level to which you should pay extra special close attention. These galvanized levels are where you want to pay the closest attention.

> The wider the time frame, the more significant the price level.

If there is a mini pup or mini inverse pup on the weekly or monthly charts, specifically note the 5-period moving averages for that time frame, as that will be the line in the sand to preserve the mini pup.

From the above, you should have a top down list of price levels with special markings on the galvanized price levels. Your focus will be on this price list after earnings are released. The initial reactions will have a pinball effect off the significant price levels.

Here's an example.

Stock ABC closed at 28.95 going into its earnings report. Notes would look like this:

- No trend in daily or weekly, monthly has a mini pup in place.

- 32.60 = Monthly upper Bollinger bands and sticky 2.50s

- 31.80 = Weekly upper Bollinger bands

- 30.60*** = Monthly 50-period moving average, weekly upper Bollinger bands, daily 200-period moving average, and sticky 5s

- 29.50 = Weekly 5- and 15-period moving averages, and sticky 5s

- 27.50 = Sticky 2.50s and daily lower Bollinger bands

- 26.85** = Monthly 5

- 25.50*** = Monthly 15-period moving average, weekly lower Bollinger bands, and sticky 5s

- 23.50 = Monthly lower Bollinger bands

*** Indicates galvanized price level overlapping 3 or more times

** Indicates a mini pup support level

From this example, we now have a list of significant price levels to watch, and most important, galvanized areas. The galvanized areas will be the best spots to play knee jerk reactions, either from initial fades or trend re-entries. Use the plus or minus 0.20 trigger at these levels. This is for the more experienced traders if they choose to play immediately off the knee jerk reaction upon an initial earnings release.

ANATOMY OF AN EARNINGS REPORT

Just like carving up a chicken, there's primarily four meaty parts to earnings report trading. Using the analogy of the breast, drumsticks, thighs, and wings—the key is to make sure the meat is fully cooked!

Post-Market Reaction: Thigh

First of all, not every earnings report is playable in the post-market. Only the thicker, widely traded stocks should even be considered, because volume and spreads will make a big impact on liquidity. Listed stocks tend to have wider spreads by nature. In addition to the liquidity concerns, the stock must actually have a tradeable reaction. There needs to be a tradeable reaction.

Keep in mind that most domestic (U.S.-based) companies have conference calls to discuss the earnings reports, usually around 5:00 p.m., if the earnings are released post-market. Many times, stocks will actually rise about 15 minutes ahead of the conference, especially dumpers. Unless you plan on listening to the actual call, this is

Caveat: Don't trade beyond 5:00 p.m. EST post-market in most cases. At the latest, 6:00 p.m. is where even the most liquid tier 1 stocks will stall out volume and trend wise. The slippage factor after 6:00 p.m. from spreads alone is absolutely detrimental and stacked against you. This comes from way too many post-market trades.

another reason to finish your post-market trading before 5:00 p.m. Let the market digest the information and play it in the pre-market session. Conference calls can be a wild card, as they can sometimes tank gapping stocks and squeeze dumping stocks.

Use the galvanized support and resistance levels like pinball bumpers. On the most anticipated earnings report stocks, CNBC will usually chime in a few minutes after the report to talk it up or down; this adds an extra volume thrust to which you should pay attention.

The post-market reaction is not usually recommended to trade for most people, as you have to be acclimated to the movement of the underlying stock. For those qualified to play, here's the setups, if they trigger.

- **Kneejerk Reaction Fades**

  Longs will use the Panic Bottom Slingshot Play off galvanized support levels with a 1-minute hammer and a 1-minute 20-band stochastics mini pup cross up. Wait for the stock to initially bottom with a hammer, and then at least 2 green candle closes at or above the lower Bollinger bands before entry. Target the 1-minute 20-period moving average, then the 1 minute upper bands, then the 5-period moving averages. Stops trigger on 1-minute failures or Bollinger band slips.

  Shorts will use the Momentum Top Short Play off galvanized resistance levels with a 1-minute shooting star and 2 candle closes at or below the upper Bollinger bands, with a stochastics mini inverse pup down.

- **Kneejerk Reaction Squeezes and Panics**

  Longs will use the +0.20 Bollinger Band Short Squeeze Long Play upon thrusts through the monthly upper Bollinger bands, scalp sticky levels out into the momentum ahead of 1-minute shooting stars, and keep a tight stop if that +0.20 level cracks.

  Shorts will use the -0.20 Bollinger Band Trap Door Short Play upon leans through the monthly lower Bollinger bands, scalp sticky levels out into the panic, selling ahead of 1-minute hammers, and keep a tight stop if that -0.20 level cracks.

Pre-Market Gappers and Dumpers: Drumsticks

The 5- and 1-minute full data charts are used with the galvanized support and resistance levels. Look for pups and mini pups off the 5-minute charts with 1-minute triggers as in Figure 12.1. Always be aware of the direction of the noodles, as they represent the market winds. Any sharp noodles movement will likely have an effect on the stock. Make sure to align the moves with the noodles, unless there is a presence of a very strong fade. If there is a fade, then time entries right when noodles exhaust for a more forceful move.

For example, ABC stock gaps down and forms a 5-minute inverse pup pre-market. The noodles take a sharp bounce up, but ABC is sell fading the 5-minute 5-period moving average. The noodles peak at a pivot resistance as the 1-minute stochastics slip back under the 80 bands. The 1-minute stochastics form a mini inverse pup on ABC. This is the perfect trigger to step in short, as the noodles selling will magnify the effect on ABC stock since it couldn't bounce with the noodles.

If the stock is a dumper, watch to implement:

- The Channel Tightening Play long with a 5-period moving average sloping up, a 5-minute mini pup, and a 1-minute mini pup trigger.

- The Breakdown Play short on a 5-minute downtrend, playing the 5-period moving average rejections, mini inverse pups, and 1-minute mini inverse pups.

If the stock is a gapper, watch to implement:

- The Channel Tightening Play short with a 5-period moving average sloping down, 5-minute mini inverse pup, and 1-minute mini inverse pup trigger

- The Breakout Play long with a 5-minute uptrend in place with a 5-minute mini pup and 1-minute mini pup trigger.

All targets will be the respective upper Bollinger bands on mini pups.

Market Open: Breast

In most cases, you will want to lock out positions ahead of the opening bell. Even the thickest stocks can shake violently on the market open

Figure 12.1

Pre-Market 5-
and 1-Minute
Charts

For a closer
look, please visit
TradersLibrary.com/
TLECorner.

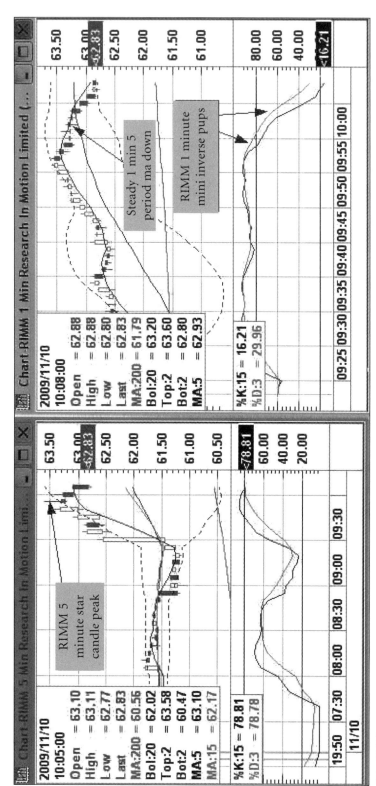

after an earnings report. The only exception is if the 5-minute chart is showing a solid mini pup-fueled trend into the open with a 1-minute mini pup. Look for a continuation move off the 9:30 a.m. opening bell, but trim down shares to a minimum.

The first 10 minutes of the open will be the most violent. Eventually, the 3-minute 5-period moving average will catch up to the stock price and either form a pup, mini pup, or a tightening. The safer trade is to wait for this to happen first. The key is to wait for this to resolve by having the market thoroughly test the 13-minute 5-period moving average with at least 2 candle closes above or below before stepping in on a mini pup for trend continuation, or mini inverse pup for tightening.

Deadzone: Marinating Process

By 11:00 a.m., gappers and dumpers tend to cool off on the volume and chop around for several hours. Don't bother playing this chop period. Consider it a marinating process that will hopefully produce something consumable for the last hour.

Last Hour Considerations: Wings

Stocks that have dramatic gaps up or down tend to take all day for the 60-minute 5-period moving averages to finally test. This is the marinating process. The last hour is usually when the final moves come into play.

If the 60-minute 5-period moving average holds support on an uptrend and coils with a mini pup, then look for a Breakout Play or Perfect Storm Play in last hour. Make sure that the shorter time frames support the direction of the 60-minute, and use the 1-minute triggers.

If the 60-minute 5-period moving average breaks with the 3:00 p.m. candle close, then revert to the Channel Tightening Play using the 60-minute 5-period moving average re-break as a trail stop. Make sure that the shorter time frames support the direction of the 60-minute, and use the 1-minute triggers.

The inverted version of this play sets up on dumpers where the 60-minute 5-period moving average held resistance going into the last hour with a mini inverse pup. Make sure that the 8- and 13-minute stochastics are crossed back down, and then take the 1-minute trigger. Often, the stock may sell fade, but the actual panic down won't get follow-through until the 8- and 13-minute stochastics cross down.

Figure 12.2

Gapper/Dumper
Trading on the
5- and 1-
Minute Charts

For a closer
look, please visit
TradersLibrary.com/
TLECorner.

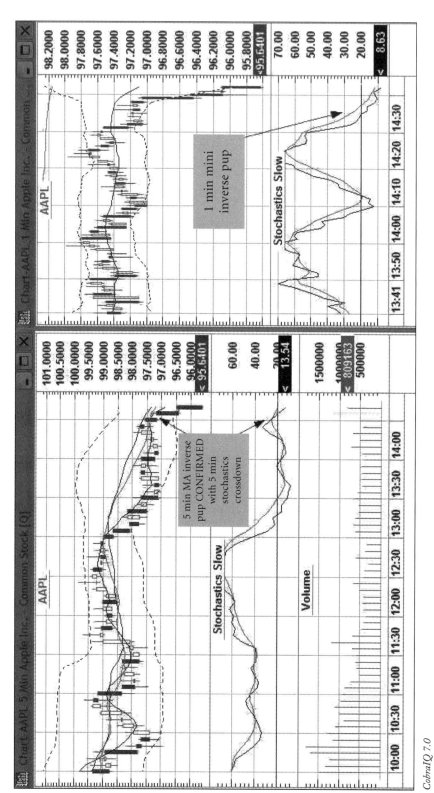

GAPPER AND DUMPER TRADING

Objective: To catch a Breakout Play long or Channel Tightening Play short on gappers, or a Breakdown Play short or Channel Tightening Play long on dumpers.

Context: Check the Nasdaq and NYSE point gainers and losers list every morning to find gapper and dumper candidates. Stock selection is important here, so make sure you pick the stocks that have liquidity trading near their galvanized support and resistance levels.

DUMPER STRATEGY

Start in the pre-market with a Channel Tightening Play long if a dumper hammers out a bottom and begins to slope the 5-minute 5-period moving average up with a mini pup. If the trend reverses back up, then make sure there is room to the 5-minute upper Bollinger bands and a mini pup for a Breakout Play long. Always note the galvanized resistance levels as critical areas to watch. A break through a galvanized resistance level can set up another leg, but expect failure at those levels first. If the dumper continues to downtrend, then wait for a 5-minute inverse pup or mini inverse pup, then use a 1-minute mini inverse pup trigger for a Breakdown Play short for a continuation move lower, as seen in Figure 12.2.

Cash Per Share Play

On extreme dumpers, make sure to quickly check the cash per share with Yahoo Finance. If the stock is trading at or under the cash per share value, then that level becomes a critical line in the sand, as well as inviting value players into the stock. This excludes any financials (banks, REITs, insurance companies, etc).

GAPPER STRATEGY

The opposite of the dumper strategy applies to gappers. This means starting out in the pre-market looking for shooting star tops that begin to slope down on the 5-minute 5-period moving average with a mini inverse pup for a Channel Tightening Play short. If the trend breaks down, then use the Breakdown Play short with a 5-minute mini inverse pup and 1-minute mini inverse pup, provided there is room to the 5-minute lower Bollinger bands and a galvanized support level. If the gapper continues to uptrend, then wait for the 5-minute 5-period moving average to form a pup or mini pup, and use a 1-minute mini pup trigger for the Breakout Play long.

LAGGARD AND SYMPATHY STOCK TRADING

Objective: To catch an impending move from correlated stocks that are lagging an exceptionally strong move by the sector leader stock(s).

Context: A stock that makes a dramatic and sustained up or down move (including gaps) will usually have an impact on the sector. The longer the move is sustained, the more interest forms by way of laggards. In these situations, you want to actively seek out two or three sympathy stocks and pick the one that has yet to be affected. The more dramatically the lead stock is moving, the deeper down the totem pole you can play.

For example, FSLR is the leader in the solar stock sector. If FSLR is exceptionally strong, then SPWRA is the sympathy or laggard to watch for if it's trading down. If both are strong, then move down the sector list to stocks like YGE, TSL, CSIQ, CSUN, or JASO. The tiers will change based on stock prices where the cheaper stocks will be placed lower down the totem pole.

Throughout the day, the stock may get analyst upgrades or downgrades. These will have initial kneejerk reactions. Often, the pattern will precede the up or down grade, so no real worries here if you are paying attention to the charts.

BUYOUT AND MERGER TRADING

Objective: To buy competitor stocks within the sector of the acquired company and profit off the near term sympathy and speculation of more buyouts within the sector. To also short the actual acquired company based on the perceived dilution effect.

Search for stocks within the sector. If you're unfamiliar, you can go to Yahoo Finance and click on the "Competitors" link for the stock to get a quick general list.

Context: Usually the company being acquired will jump so quickly in price that there is no real window of opportunity to play that stock. Often the range gets so tight that it's not worth the effort. The better alternative is to play the sympathy effect that will, at least in the near term, emanate throughout the sector of the acquired, playing upon the speculation of more buyouts to come.

MOMENTUM TRADING WITH CHEAP STOCKS

Objective: To profit off heavy volume momentum buying or selling of cheap stocks and their correlated counterparts.

Context: Similar to the laggard and sympathy trading, the focus here is on cheap stocks which tend to suck in more volume and momentum. Usually this scenario will set up in two ways. The first way is as the final money flow into a strong yet overbought sector. Note that when the lowest tier stocks in a strength sector see money flow, that is usually a sign of a top for the strength stocks.

The second scenario forms from a purely news and rumor driven event that sends a single stock parabolic on extreme volume (over ten times normal daily volume). The longer the parabolic move is sustained, the more interest will flow into sympathy stocks. The key is to get in on the early volume spikes and sell early on the lagging cheap stocks.

The momentum effect may be short lived, so make sure that you pay attention to any divergences in trading with the acquired company and cut loose quickly once momentum dissipates.

The biggest danger with this trading comes from overstaying your position to end up a bagholder—either from being stuck with too many shares, or believing the hype. These cheap stocks very often tempt traders into overleveraging the size allocation. Be aware that when the smoke clears and volume shrinks back to normal levels, not only does the price sink, but those carcasses on the ground are called bagholders… don't be one of them!

The first scenario is easier to anticipate since the big money has flowed into the top tier stocks of a hot sector, usually indicated with trading clearly above the daily upper Bollinger bands. When the best-of-breed stocks have been played out and driven up, money will look for "bargains," working its way down the totem pole to the bottom of the barrel stocks.

SHORTING CHEAP STOCKS

Taking the same approach on the long side, inevitably, most of these cheap stocks will exhaust and sell off. The question is when. The leader of these cheap stocks will be the key. What goes up will eventually come back down. Usually, the third strength day (using a fib count) is when we see the leader peak out. Daily shooting stars are best for this. With many of these stocks, it may be tough to locate short shares, which is why they tend to squeeze up, sometimes violently. So check first to see if the stock is even short-able before spending time analyzing the setup.

The third day with a gap up will be the one to watch. Use the Bollinger Band -0.20 Trap Door Short Play on slips under the 60-minute upper bands, the Channel Tightening Play short when the 60-minute 5-period gets a candle close with a mini inverse pup for tightening to 60-minute 15-period moving averages, and the Breakdown Play short on 60-minute breakdowns. Make sure to trim shares on volume leans, as coils on these stocks can be violent.

STOCK HALT TRADING

Objective: To profit off heavy volume momentum volatility upon re-open of halted stock.

Context: Earnings reports, FDA decisions, and rumor reactions cover most of the reasons for stock halts. Hopefully, you won't be caught in a stock that gets halted intraday. Stocks will usually gap up or down on halts. Have the galvanized support and resistance levels ready upon the halt re-open.

Inevitably, everyone gets stuck trading a stock that suddenly gets halted. Very heavy volume and violent price movement precedes the halt. This unexplained action should be enough of a warning to be very careful of the possibility of a halt, especially if you've been caught before. When you find yourself stuck in a stock halt, you obviously want to see if the news is in your favor or not. If the news is good, then figure out galvanized support and resistance levels and sell into the gap up, you lucky cockroach!

Since your stock is halted, there is nothing you can do until it re-opens. However, the rest of the sector stocks will likely be trading down. If the news is bad, then look to short the second in line sympathy stock. The play here is to hedge a short position in a sector sympathy stock while stuck in a long position. The share allocation is the tricky part to factor, as it involves determining a hedge ratio and beta adjusting share size equivalent to your position size. None of the hedging methods are perfect hedges. At least with the sympathy shorting, you can buffer some losses with profits on the short side.

If the news is bad, remember that it's better to lose a finger than an arm. Don't think in terms of adding to a losing position or sweating how you are going to make back losses upon reopen. The halt will at least give you a small window of time to research the galvanized support and resistance levels and assess if your stock is hedge-able.

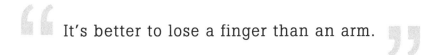

It's better to lose a finger than an arm.

Hopefully, your stock will be correlated to an ETF so that you can determine a hedge ratio and beta adjust the needed size quickly before the ETF sinks too fast. You will have to be lightning quick because the big boys are probably already doing this on the fly. I am talking inside of two minutes!

BETA ADJUSTING SHARE SIZE TO HEDGE

By taking the opposite position in another instrument as close to a -1 hedge ratio as possible, you are looking for a market neutral hedge. If your stock correlates well with an ETF, then you need to beta adjust the size to compensate for the different volatilities. The formula is:

$$\text{(Stock Purchase Price} \times \text{Number of Shares)}$$
$$\times$$
$$\text{Hedging Stock or ETF's beta}$$
$$=$$
$$\text{Dollar Value of the Hedge}$$

Then, you can take the dollar value of the hedge and divide by the share price of the hedging stock or ETF to determine how many shares to buy.

For example, let's say you are long 500 shares of POT at $100 and want to hedge it with MOS, which correlates nicely within the sector. You would apply the formula.

$$(\$96.98 \times 500) \times 1.33 = \$64,491.70$$

MOS is trading at \$53.78, which translates to shorting 1,199 shares of MOS to hedge your long 500 shares of POT.

This technique not only works on halted stocks, but any stocks that you are married to (willfully or not) for a period of time. It is a classic way to hedge a position without using options, yet you need to have enough buying power to execute the correct hedge. You will need the buying power equivalent to your position value in the stock to hedge. The benefit of a sector specific ETF is the higher amount of inherent correlation. Keep in mind this is not a perfect hedge, and it can backfire if you are either too slow to react and the move is already priced in, or the correlation is faded. This has to be played carefully, because this play can backfire and double your losses.

If you happen to get stuck in a less widely traded stock or a cheapie, then you are pretty much out of luck and will have to wait for the stock to re-open. Don't try to be a hero. You must break up the thinking into two parts. First is getting out of your position. Second is trying to chip away at the losses. Don't mix the two parts or you will likely freeze like the proverbial deer in the headlights, armed with nothing but a prayer.

TRADING STOCK HALT RE-OPEN

The best thing is to get out as soon as you can and look for opportunities using the Trading Stock Halt Re-open. This strategy is for when you are not in the halted stock, which means you need to get out first before moving forward.

Go to **www.nasdaqtrader.com/Trader.aspx?id=Tradehalts** to check on the re-opening time of the halted stock.

A stock halt re-open is made up of basically the same techniques to trade an earnings report reaction post-market (see the section on Earnings Report Trading earlier in this chapter). The only difference is that you will likely know the direction of the reaction ahead of time based on the news and opening gap.

If the stock halt re-opens on bad news with a panic gap down,

- If you are long on the initial kneejerk open, consider the Panic Bottom Slingshot Play for coils, or the Channel Tightening Play on bounces off galvanized support levels.

- If you are short on the initial kneejerk open, consider the Bollinger Band -0.20 Trap Door Short Play for continuation shorts if they lean through the weekly or monthly lower Bollinger bands.

The safest method of play after the initial reaction is to wait for a coil back to test the 3- or 5-minute 5-period moving average and either form a mini inverse pup rejection to short for trend continuation down, or base the 5-period moving average and mini pup for a Channel Tightening Play back up. Both trigger on the 1-minute stochastics chart.

It always helps to look at the reaction of sympathy stocks within the sector to see how they are reacting prior to the re-open. This can often give you an idea of how the stock may react upon the open. If the news is stock specific, then the sector may not be affected, but all too often misery loves company. The CPS (cash per share) factor may come into play if the stock trades under the cash per share value. That price level will always be a line in the sand.

FOMC RATE ANNOUNCEMENT TRADING

Objective: To profit off the kneejerk reactions from Federal Open Market Committee (FOMC) rate decisions.

Context: FOMC rate decisions are announced at 2:15 p.m. EST on a specified date. Most of the FOMC meetings are a single day, usually held on a Tuesday. Some meetings are two days long, starting on Tuesday, with a rate decision on Wednesday. There are usually three distinct reactions to these announcements—the kneejerk move, the exhaustion move, and the trend move. Make sure that you are aware of the range of the market and your stocks going into the meeting. The initial kneejerk will spike or lean extensively and usually exhaust back to the prior range ahead of the meeting before trending near 3:00 p.m. Use the momentum panic exhaustion strategy play setups for these.

Strategy: Most FOMC rate announcements are simply market speed bump events, meaning the market stalls out waiting for the news, and then resumes its path. Note the range of the market and galvanized support and resistance levels. Always use the futures as the lead indicator in these events! The futures move first and stocks follow. This is the purest event where stocks are completely pulled up or down by the futures, at least for the kneejerk and exhaustion portion.

FOMC reactions are broken into three parts.

1. **Kneejerk.** The futures spike up or down on heavy volume. Watch the pivots and daily Bollinger bands. Laggard sympathy longs or shorts trading can be incorporated for scalps in the kneejerk direction, but must be quick! Usually, you want to wait out the initial kneejerk and look for a fading opportunity on very extended kneejerks.

2. **Exhaustion.** The futures snap back to the prior range, or even the lower end of the range. Short the peaks at galvanized resistances and go long the bottoms at galvanized support levels using the Panic Bottom Slingshot Play long or Momentum Top Short Play, or the Oscillation Range Scalp Play if the reaction is not very extended.

3. **Trend.** The futures find equilibrium and resume a sustained trend move in the last hour. Use the Breakout Play long or Breakdown Play short.

Since the volume spike can be overwhelming during an FOMC rate announcement, you should always reboot your system and minimize unnecessary applications at least 15 minutes before the 2:15 p.m. announcement. The worst situation is to have your broker platform, quotes, or system lock up on you while you are in a trade. Trust me, it's no fun watching your profits turn into losses because you couldn't get out of the scalp thanks to a system lock up. A mere reboot can save you from this common and costly problem.

MULTIPLE DAY SWING TRADES

Most of these setups should seem familiar to the intraday plays since the patterns are linear, but just expanded to wider time frames. The wider time frames naturally have larger trading ranges. Allocation is a key factor. Scalpers may have a tough time with these types of trades, so make sure that you adjust the allocations according to your comfort levels. The basic rule of thumb is the longer the time frame, the smaller your share size should be.

USING OPTIONS TO LEVERAGE

Objective: To play the multiple day strategies with straight call or put options to increase leverage without tying up intraday buying power, and limiting downside risk. To capture volatility premium and price appreciation, and limit risk by exiting the position 24 to 48 hours ahead of actual earnings release.

> The longer the time frame, the smaller your share size should be.

I will note the preferred options trades with each swing play in this section. The key is determining whether to pay more for deep in-the-money options to offset time and volatility premiums, or to play the out-of-the-money options ahead of significant event dates to profit off volatility premiums. Since most of these plays are a maximum hold of four or five days, the time premiums won't be much of a factor.

HEDGING SWING TRADES

In most cases, your swing trades should simply be stopped out if they fail to produce within a day or hit stop targets. However, there may be occasions where you prefer to actually hedge the play ahead of an event. The hedge can be done with correlating ETFs, sympathy stocks, or options for better leverage and cheaper cost basis. Use the same method of determining a hedge ratio that we discussed earlier, and then beta adjust share size in the hedging instrument. With options, you will need to employ a delta-neutral strategy.

PERFECT STORM SWING LONGS

Objective: To profit off 60-minute, daily, weekly, and monthly pup and mini pup uptrend moves.

Long Setup: Intraday trigger is based on 8- and 13-minute stochastics cross up with uptrending moving averages or crossover to uptrends.

Primary Targets: The upper Bollinger bands of each time frame containing a mini pup starting with the nearest price level.

Stop Loss Trigger: Daily candle close under the nearest mini inverse pup's 5-period moving average.

Variations: These patterns allow for stronger intraday Perfect Storm Play longs since they add an additional 3 pups or mini pups to any intraday perfect storm setup. In essence, you will get 6 lanes or more on intraday triggers for explosive upside follow-through. You should trade the intraday moves and scale out profits to a small enough size to swing the rest. This provides a solid cushion of profits to offset the stop losses.

PERFECT STORM SWING SHORTS

Objective: To profit off 60-minute, daily, weekly, and monthly inverse pup and mini inverse pup downtrend moves.

Long Setup: Intraday trigger is based on 8- and 13-minute stochastics cross down with downtrending moving averages or crossover to downtrends.

Primary Targets: The lower Bollinger bands of each time frame containing a mini inverse pup starting with the nearest price level.

Stop Loss Trigger: Daily candle close above the nearest mini inverse pup's 5-period moving average.

Variations: These patterns allow for stronger intraday Perfect Storm Play shorts since they add an additional 3 inverse pups or mini inverse pups to any intraday perfect storm setup. In essence, you will get 6 lanes or more on intraday triggers for explosive downside panic follow-through. You should trade the intraday moves and scale out profits to a small enough size to swing the rest. This provides a solid cushion of profits to offset the stop losses.

The best part of both the Perfect Storm Swing setups is that the direction is set, it's just a matter of entry and re-entry, and re-entry on a scalp with the predominant downtrend. The swing trade is usually just the dessert. Sizing is important. Heavier shares can be used with a good 1-minute mini inverse pup trigger and 6 or more inverse pups or mini inverse pups. Trim out the shares on the grinds accordingly until your size is ¼ or less of a scalp size to swing the rest.

DAILY HAMMER LONGS

Objective: To profit off oversold bounces triggered by a daily hammer.

Context: This is the same setup as an intraday hammer trade. Make sure there are at least 2 to 3 consecutive red continuation candles prior to the formation of the daily hammer. There also needs to be some profit room to the next level on the target chain, usually the 5-period moving average when hammers form off daily lower Bollinger bands.

Long Setup: Intraday 60-, 13-, and 8-minute stochastics or trend moves back up trigger the entry above the daily hammer's body high price level.

Primary Targets: Use the target chain. Usually a 5-period daily moving average works well if a hammer forms at or above the daily lower Bollinger bands. If it forms way below, then target the daily lower bands.

Stop Loss Trigger: Violation of the daily hammer body low, or lower Bollinger bands.

Variations: The same setup applies to weekly and monthly hammer patterns as well.

Notes: This is a countertrend trade, so make sure that you have the intraday trends in your favor. Avoid taking longs into 60-, 13-, and 8-minute intraday downtrends! Wait for them to reverse back up before entry. Remember, when you are fighting the daily trend, you need the help of the intraday charts.

DAILY SHOOTING STAR SHORTS

Objective: To profit off shorting exhaustions off overbought price levels triggered by a daily shooting star.

Context: This is the same setup as an intraday shooting star trade. Make sure there are at least 2 to 3 consecutive green continuation candles prior to the formation of the daily shooting star. There also needs to be some profit room to next level on the target chain, usually the 5-period moving average when stars form off the daily upper Bollinger bands. See Figure 12.3.

Long Setup: Intraday 60-, 13-, and 8-minute stochastics and trend moves back up trigger the entry below the daily star's body low price level.

Primary Targets: Use the target chain. Usually a 5-period daily moving average works well if a star forms at or above daily lower Bollinger bands. If it forms way below, then target the daily lower bands.

Stop Loss Trigger: Violation of the daily star body low or upper Bollinger bands.

Figure 12.3

Daily Shooting
Star Short

For a closer
look, please visit
TradersLibrary.com/
TLECorner.

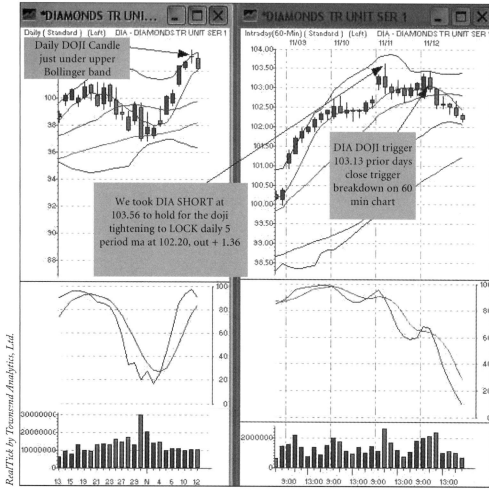

Daily DOJI Candle just under upper Bollinger band

We took DIA SHORT at 103.56 to hold for the doji tightening to LOCK daily 5 period ma at 102.20, out + 1.36

DIA DOJI trigger 103.13 prior days close trigger breakdown on 60 min chart

RealTick by Townsend Analytics, Ltd.

Variations: The same setup applies to weekly and monthly star patterns as well.

Notes: This is a countertrend trade, so make sure that you have the intraday trends in your favor. Avoid taking shorts against 60-, 13-, and 8-minute intraday uptrends! Wait for them to reverse back down before entry. Remember, when you are fighting the daily trend, you need the help of the intraday charts.

DECISION ANTICIPATION TRADING

Objective: To profit off the anticipation buying ahead of an FDA panel decision or drug decision date.

The key is to sell into the buying 24 to 48 hours ahead of the actual decision date. Do not believe the hype and hold through the actual decision. Stocks usually halt ahead of highly anticipated decisions. Don't take the risk of getting stuck in one.

Context: FDA decisions are the second most common events that drive extreme volume stock movements.

Variations: Phase III clinical results data also tend to get stocks to rise in anticipation. However, many companies will not actually pinpoint the exact release date of the information, making it very tough to time the play while avoiding the risk of getting stuck in a stock halt. If the results data do not have an exact date, then it's best to stay out. Another source of anticipation buying can be found going into the larger industry conferences like the oncology conference, whose guest presenters often release clinical trial data. Always remember, buy on the rumor and sell before the news!

PRE-EARNINGS ANTICIPATION LONGS

Objective: To profit off anticipation buying going into a company's earnings report.

The inherent optimistic nature of people will usually cause a stock to rise in anticipation of good earnings ahead of the earnings reports. The goal is to buy ahead and sell into the anticipation buying up to the day of earnings.

> Do not actually hold into the earnings report, dummy!

Context: The overall markets tend to lift about one week ahead of earnings season. Once earnings season begins, it's best to wait for a leader stock to report first with a strong positive reaction that lifts the sector. Look for the laggards in the sector to play anticipation rise.

Long Setup: Get positive earnings reaction in the sector leader stock, then look to play the laggard ahead of earnings. Try to play three to five days ahead of the actual earnings report and sell 24 to 48 hours ahead of the release, depending on target levels and stock reaction. The laggards are stocks in the sector that are at least two levels lower on the target chain. Make sure that you get at least an intraday up-

It is a wise idea to plug in "FDA" as a keyword into any streaming news feed that you have so that you can jump on these. You can also just use FDA as a keyword on Google News. Otherwise, there are a number of blogs and sites that list upcoming decisions. www.biomedreports.com has a nice FDA calendar and newsfeed.

trend going first on the 60-, 13-, and 8-minute charts prior to entry. A daily mini pup gives the stock higher probability and momentum.

Buy on the rumor, sell before the news!

For example, FSLR blows out earnings and jumps six points above its daily upper Bollinger bands. If SPWRA is still trading under its daily 5-period moving average, then the laggard factor applies since it is two levels below FSLR (the daily 5-period moving average and the upper Bollinger bands). This gives enough room for SPWRA to not only play catch-up, but continues to help fuel anticipation buying.

Primary Targets: The lagging levels of the sector leader stock and target chain if daily mini pups are present.

Stop Loss Trigger: If the pattern continues to diverge with the leader for more than two days and violates the next level down on the target chain, then keep stops. This implies that there is something more damaging to this stock that the public doesn't know. For this reason, you want to make sure that a technical reversal forms on the charts.

Variations: The weekly and monthly target chain levels can and should be used to determine additional targets as well. Mini pups on these time frames are very significant.

BRING IT FULL CIRCLE: TEST YOURSELF

(1) A trader should always take a position into an earnings report.

a) True
b) False

(2) Pre-market trading is safer than post-market trading.

a) True
b) False

(3) FOMC announcements are usually released at 2:15 p.m. EST and are composed of three reactions, the kneejerk, the exhaustion, and the _____.

a) trend
b) kickback
c) overshoot
d) backfill

(4) The best way to hedge profits on an in-the-money call option where the underlying stock explodes up post-market on news is to:

a) short the underlying stock proportionately adjusted to the number of call contracts.

b) buy the underlying stock proportionately adjusted to the number of call contracts.

c) buy put options contracts post-market.

d) sell the call option contracts pre-market.

(5) A Channel Tightening Play is a _____.

a) countertrend trade that tries to profit from a price move from the 5-period moving average to the 15-period moving average

b) continuation trend trade that tries to profit from a price move from the 15-period moving average to the 5-period moving average

c) consolidation trade that tries to get in early on a breakout

d) trend reversal trade that tries to predict a 5-period moving average crossover through the 15-period moving average

6 To prepare for a gapper play, a trader needs to research which of the following?

a) Galvanized support and resistance levels on the daily, weekly, and monthly charts

b) Gauge the pre-market rifle charts for 5- and 1-minute mini pups and hammers or stars that close at the upper or lower Bollinger bands

c) Sticky 2.50 and 5 levels

d) The noodles

e) The 3-minute 5-period moving average after the opening bell

f) All of the above

g) None of the above

7 One-minute high band mini pups are usually signals to:

a) exit a long position.
b) enter a long position.

8 What happened to the two peanuts walking across the street?

a) They got on the bus.
b) They got assalted.
c) Who cares.
d) F.U.
e) All or none of the above.

For answers, please visit the
Traders' Library Education Corner at
www.traderslibrary.com/TLEcorner.

CONCLUSION
AND PARTING GIFTS OF WISDUMB

I wish you the best with your own trader's journey. I want to leave you with a brief history of UndergroundTrader.com, some of my favorite words, and a few epiphanies I discovered along the journey.

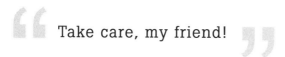 Take care, my friend!

Feel free to email me at jay@undergroundtrader.com if you have any questions or comments.

A QUICK HISTORY OF UNDERGROUNDTRADER.COM

I officially started UndergroundTrader.com in 1998 as a personal trading blog (even before "blog" was an actual term). I updated my intraday trades along with my comments. I was a member of one of the largest chat rooms at the time under the alias "Inertia." My very first mentor explained to me how the strongest force in the universe is inertia—the idea that an object in motion stays in motion. I took that to heart.

I wrote a little self-published book called *The Underground Level II Day-trader's Handbook*, which sold like crazy. The book was the first of its kind that revolutionized the use of Nasdaq Level II and time of sales reading. It also introduced the use of a 1-minute stochastics chart. Yes, that was me! It worked like a charm back then. The book was only 70 pages single-sided and printed up at Kinko's for $7 a copy. I initially wrote the little book just to keep my own notes and developments. Word got out about this project of mine and people started to ask for it. I sold it for $60, which included the $3 priority mail. The demand was so strong, I had to increase the price to deter the buying pressure. This side project was really eating into my trading day and requiring me to leave before the market close to reach the post office in time to mail it out. At $75, I sold even more books. Finally, I raised the price to $90 to squash the demand and it was at that level that I sold the most books (thousands). How ironic that the higher I priced this book, the greater the demand. Mind you, it was a very insightful book that had information not found anywhere else at the time.

In 1999, I was contacted by the senior acquisitions editor at McGraw-Hill. I had made some nice money with my first book, and Steven offered me an opportunity to publish a "real" book through McGraw-Hill. He explained the scam of vanity presses that ask for payment so they can publish you. But when he put out the royalty figures, it absolutely paled in comparison to my profits from self publishing. There was no real monetary advantage to going with a major publisher, until he asked me a simple question: "Do you want to have children some day?"

Do you know what it means to be a real published author? When you are truly published, you get an ISBN and your book is registered at the Library of Congress. Your work is immortalized in history and most importantly, you leave a legacy. When he asked me if I wanted to have children one day, he was emphasizing legacy—damn he was good. Freud mentions the two urges in life, sexual and recognition. Legacy covers the second one.

The McGraw-Hill book, *The UndergroundTrader.com Guide to Electronic Trading*, had an initial print run of 10,000 and sold out completely. I remember when the book was officially released, it climbed into the top 100 non-fiction best sellers on Amazon.com for a while. The complete run was sold out. The book received rave reviews, and I was invited to do seminars all over the place.

I remember going to the Online Traders Expo in New York in 2000 and I had to hire a bodyguard. Our booth was up to five people deep, and with over 200 people surrounding it. My bodyguard, Joe C., used to body-guard Telly Savalis (the original Kojak), Debra Winger, and Liza Minelli with Chuck Zito. He was a short man around five feet, five inches, and a spitting image of Al Pacino. I was a little taken back by his size, or lack thereof. He explained to me that his "weapon" was his mind. He was a negotiator and used words to keep the peace. However, if things got physical, help was only 30 seconds away with a call from his cell phone. Joe used to be a NYPD captain and his son was currently serving as a captain. This way, the client, me, wouldn't get sued if there was a physical altercation.

I went to work on the second book, aptly titled *Secrets of the Under-groundTrader*, which was released in 2003 with a 7,500 print run. The crazy thing was that the first book—being out of print—was being sold on Amazon zShop's auction site for as high as $200 a copy for mint condition! I don't think any signed copies were auctioned off, but they would be sold for much higher. Almost seven years later, thanks to John Boyer and Traders' Library, I have completed the trilogy and the full circle.

THE SNIPER SCOPE AX LOGO MEANING

Back in the good old days, there were dominant market makers in stocks. He made his presence known by holding levels solidly. These market makers were called the ax. The logo embodies the concept of targeting and tracking the ax to find transparency on the particular stock.

MY FAVORITE WORDS

Vibrancy	Immersion	Bliss	Fortify
Enlightenment	Acclimate	Outlier	Nurture
Reciprocity	Core	Essence	Redemption
Purity	Diffuse	Correlate	Closure
Nirvana	Clarity	Convergence	Salvation
Linearity	Galvanize	Marinate	Foresight

MORE OF MY FAVORITE WORDS

Replenish	Harvest	Scale	Culminate
Metabolize	Harness	Resonate	Resolve
Exorcise	Mongostic	Detour	Conditioned
Offset	How	By-Product	

EPIPHANIES LEARNED ALONG THE JOURNEY

0.   Life, nature, and the markets are anchored around symmetry. For every force, there is an equal and opposing force. What goes around comes around. Losing one sense will make another sense grow stronger. The more you put into something, the more you will get out of it. Reciprocity is the key. Respect is another form of reciprocity. Respect the market's means, don't be complacent or lazy. Ignorance is simply laziness. Ignorance is the deepest form of disrespect. The markets will punish that behavior. When it comes to trading, the harder you work doesn't mean trading more (usually it means trading less). It means preparing more ahead of time. It means putting in the effort to do the mundane routine of researching setups and patterns and analyzing support and resistance levels ahead of time to be prepared when the action starts. It takes effort to be aware. This effort is something that most traders will fail to consistently make. There comes a time when a trader will know they will have a good day, because they put in the time to prepare for the day—you can only "wing it" so much.

1.   Pain rewards with strength and clarity.

2.   The opposite of love and hate is apathy. (Humans are not.)

3.   Life and the universe are balanced. Every force will ultimately meet with an opposing force. This idea is known to some as karma.

4.   Enduring desire + enduring effort = destiny earned

5.   Enduring desire = starvation + deprivation + isolation + abandonment

6.   Life can not be controlled, but you can control the environment in which you place yourself.

7.   Good = know and place yourself in the right environment

8.   Great = control the environment

9.   If a tree falls in the woods and no one hears it, did it really fall?

10.   Inaction is an action.

11.   In every battle, there are two participants, the opponent and the victim. The victim is the one who thinks he's winning.

12.   Confidence = complacency

13.   Human nature is detrimental to trading.

14.   Cognitive dissonance theory = human beings' need to avoid stress through attitude or behavior change

15.   Human beings find comfort when others are in the same situation—that is how bubbles are formed.

16.   The name of the game is to find transparency before it becomes too transparent.

17.   Predicting is futile. Foreshadowing is what separates the victims from the survivors (or conquerors).

18.   Overlapping is beautiful. Need at least two to qualify, any more than that gets better with each layer.

19.   Nirvana = enlightenment, awareness, self-actualization

20.   Traders, fighters, potential, and destiny are never a given. They all have to be forged and earned. Believe in one word—marinate. There is nothing more common than wasted talent or unfulfilled potential, it is all over the place. The lack of enduring effort is what separates those who earn the destiny from those who could have. Effort is the symmetrical line in the sand. People are never born leaders. Or traders, or winners… they have to put in the effort and go through the marinating process. Talent is not intrinsic or discovered until the effort is put in. Those with talent may not have to put in as much effort, but it is a work in progress—for he who gets complacent assuming that talent is a given, earned, or uncovered once and for all is set for a reality check. He who wants it more will put in the endur-

*"He who desires
to be alone is either
insane, or has
the makings of a God."*

ing effort and by nature's laws of symmetry and harmonics, is the "chosen one" after the fact to rule the throne. Destiny is faith before and hindsight "after the fact." As they say, destiny will reveal itself. If you sit on your ass, your destiny is very clear—it's called the gutter. Believe if you earn the right to believe. It takes effort—enduring effort through struggle.

21. Guilt is something you do, shame is something you are.

22. Desperate money always loses.

23. Salvation requires sacrifice.

24. Roadblock, counteract, dilute.

25. There are three types of sight: hindsight (after the fact), insight (lesson learned), foresight (only the few make the effort).

26. Focus on the process, because the achievement is simply a by-product.

27. Last but not least, please send any feedback, questions, or comments to me at jay@undergroundtrader.com or snipertrader@erols.com.

For more information about Jea Yu,
please visit: www.traderslibrary.com/jeayu.

HARMONIC PATTERN TRADING
by Suri Duddella of Surinotes.com

Financial markets exhibit the natural ebb and flow cycles which are in sync with the growth and decline phases of the markets. These natural cycles exhibit harmonic price behavior in the financial markets. This harmonic phenomenon occurs in all walks of life and is usually determined by specific harmonic patterns. Harmonic pattern detection includes recognition of key price swings aided with Fibonacci ratios to identify key reversal points and levels.

Some of the great pioneering research in harmonic patterns, along with cycles, was done by H.M. Gartley, William Garrett, Bryce Gilmore, Larry Pesavento, and Scott Carney. To my knowledge the best work on harmonic patterns is done by Scott Carney in his two-volume text, *Harmonic Trading of the Financial Markets*.

Before I address the harmonic patterns and harmonic ratios that exist in the market, I need to address the Fibonacci series and Fibonacci ratios.

Most traders and analysts who have any exposure to technical analysis have at least heard of Fibonacci numbers, Fibonacci ratios or retracements, etc. Many analysts use a series of numbers to derive Fibonacci ratios, and common numbers are 0.382, 0.5, 0.618, and 1.618.

FIBONACCI RATIOS

Fibonacci numbers are pervasive in the universe and were originally derived by Leonardo Fibonacci. The basic Fibonacci ratio ("Fib ratio") is equal to 1.618. A Fibonacci sequence is a series of numbers where each number is the sum of the previous two numbers.

The series of "Fib Numbers" begin as follows: 1, 1, 2, 3, 5, 8, 13, 21, 34, 55, 89, 144, 233, 317, 610, and so on.

There are plenty of materials and books about the Fibonacci theory of how these numbers exist in nature and in the financial world. Fibonacci number sequences produce a great pattern between the numbers (up or down). The ratio of any number to the next higher number is 0.618, while the ratio of the next lower number is 1.618. In the mathematics world, these values are also known as phi (0.618) and Phi (1.618). The ratio 1.618 is also referred to as the "The Golden Ratio."

A list of the most important Fib ratios in the financial world which are derived by squaring, square roots, and reciprocating the actual Fibonacci numbers are depicted below:

- **Key Set of Fibonacci Derived Ratios in Trading are:**
  0.382, 0.500, .618, 0.786, 1.0, 1.272, 1.618, 2.0, 2.62, 3.62, 4.62
- **Secondary Set of Fibonacci Derived Ratios in Trading are:**
  0.236, 0.486, 0.886, 1.13, 2.236, 3.14, 4.236

Most trading software packages have Fibonacci drawing tools which can show Fib retracements, Fib extensions, and Fib projections. In addition, Fib numbers are applied to time and price in trading.

FIBONACCI RATIOS IN THE FINANCIAL MARKETS

Most technical analysts extensively use some sort of ratio analysis for potential entry and exit strategies. The application of Fibonacci numbers to this ratio analysis lead to terms like Fibonacci retracement, or Fibonacci extensions, etc. Financial markets exhibit pullbacks and extensions with enough frequency that Fibonacci retracements to ratios like 38.2%, 50%, or 61.8% have become common jargon in traders' language.

The backbone behind Fibonacci studies is made up of the price retracements and extensions. The study of these retracements and projections enables traders to identify price swings and support and resistance areas.

Markets demonstrate repetitive patterns where prices oscillate between one set of price ratios to another, making price projections possible. Market trends can be defined by geometric relationships as they exhibit harmonic relationships between the price and time swings. Markets also form cycles around the price and time levels. Many investors and traders use cycles and harmonic relationships to project future swing prices and times.

Each price swing consists of high and low prices and many bars in between them, followed by a reversal swing consisting of the same high and low prices, but in the opposite direction. If the prior swing is an up swing, then the following down swing is a reversal swing, or retracement. A high swing occurs when the current high bar has a lower-high bar before and after. A low swing occurs when the current low bar has a lower-low bar before and after.

STUDY OF RETRACEMENTS AND EXTENSIONS

Fibonacci retracements and extensions, illustrated in Figure A.1, offer key support and resistance areas. Here are some definitions of retracements and extensions.

- **Retracements:** Retracement is defined as when a price re-traces a portion of the prior swing. This portion could be defined in Fibonacci ratios like 0.38, 0.5, or 0.618.

- **Extensions:** Extensions occur when the price expands the entire prior swing (100%) and travels beyond the entire swing. The extension swing could be 127% or 162% of prior swings.

- **Projections:** Projections are defined as when the price extends away from a completed retracement swing in the same length (or more) as the first swing.

Figure A.1

Fibonnacci
Retracements
& Extensions

For a closer
look, please visit
TradersLibrary.com/
TLECorner.

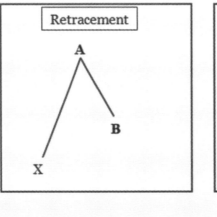

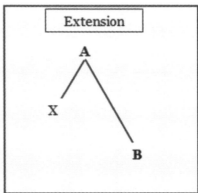

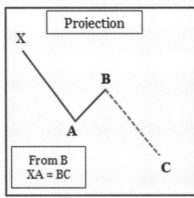

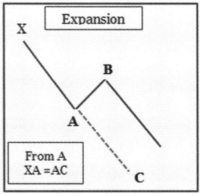

SYMMETRY AND CONFLUENCE

Gann, Fibonacci, and Elliott all studied market symmetry and found valid theories. These patterns exist in all forms in nature and certainly exist in the markets. One of the best ways to confirm symmetry in the markets is to check price and time using two or more cluster confirmations. Another key method to compute these patterns is to use percentage change of price between market highs and market lows. Symmetry is a science by itself, and traders take great advantage of knowing the potential turning points and levels using these methods.

SYMMETRY

Symmetry is visible in all markets and in all time-frames. Symmetric rallies and declines give traders an advantage to determine the key turning points. A cluster of similar extensions and similar retracements at key price ranges, or some important levels provide insights into future significant resistance and support levels. In addition to knowing key turning points, the benefits of trading symmetric price and time cluster levels include low-risk trades.

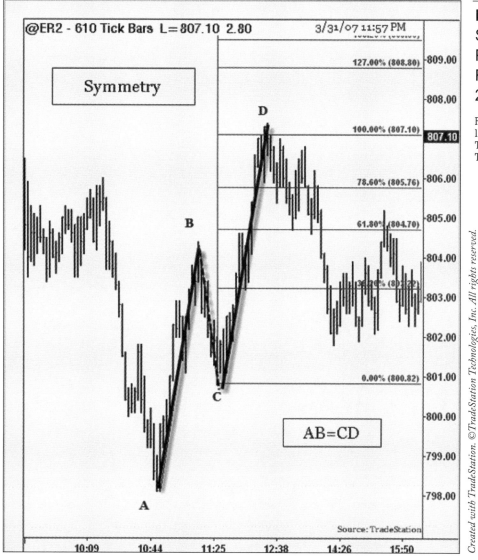

Figure A.2
Symmetry
Pattern:
Russell
2000 Futures

For a closer
look, please visit
TradersLibrary.com/
TLECorner.

Figure A.2 illustrates the symmetry pattern from the Russell 2000 futures (ER2) 610 tick chart. Symmetrical swing lengths are shown after a 50% retracement at BC swing. Market symmetry of 100% extension is expected after a retracement of less than 50% retracement levels. If the retracement exceeds 50%, the extension may be less than or equal to 100%.

FIBONACCI CONFLUENCE (FIBONACCI CLUSTERS)
Confluence of multiple Fibonacci retracement or extension levels signifies a stronger area of support and resistance. The confluence of multiple Fibonacci retracements in a fairly tight area is computed using prior swings of both retracements and extensions with certain criteria. Then each Fib retracement or extension level is grouped to

Figure A.3

Fibonacci
Confluence

For a closer
look, please visit
TradersLibrary.com/
TLECorner.

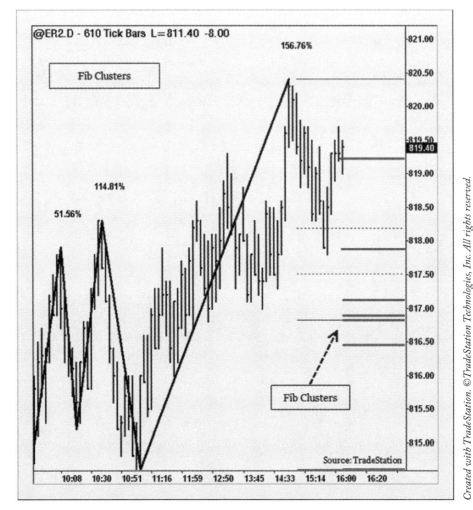

generate a confluence within some threshold to find Fibonacci clusters in an area. These cluster levels are more significant than a single Fib retracement itself. The trades are either initiated or closed at these confluence levels.

Figure A.3 shows Fibonacci confluence or clusters of various levels.

THE PATTERNS

AB = CD PATTERN FRAMEWORK

In 1935, H.M. Gartley published a book called *Profits in the Stock Market* that described the use of the AB = CD pattern along with some innovative pattern methods. Gartley described a chart pattern called "Practical Use of Trendlines," showing the AB = CD pattern. In this pattern, prices rally to an up sloping trendline in an uptrend and retrace to a parallel up sloping trendline, forming a channel. This process of "advance-retrace" continues until the price trades outside of the channel, giving a potential breakout or breakdown to terminate the AB = CD pattern.

AB = CD pattern structure forms in all markets and in all timeframes. Larry Pesavento modified and described the AB = CD pattern with Fibonacci ratios and its potential targets and reversal areas. The AB = CD patterns forecast key market turning points and profit targets for traders. AB = CD patterns pinpoint important pivot levels with high and low prices and identify key trading zones.

AB = CD pattern formation has three critical areas. The first leg (AB) is trend. The second leg (BC) is countertrend, or retracement. The last leg (CD) is resumption of trend. The retracement leg (BC) has a Fibonacci correction ratio of 0.382, 0.618, or 0.786. The resumption of the trend (CD) occurs after the correction leg and usually extends to 100% of AB from C.

Using an auto-ABC pattern algorithm, AB = CD patterns are detected by finding A, B, and C pivot points in a chart. These key pivot points are searched for various pivot strength levels and used to identify correction levels. Once the A, B, and C points are determined, a Fib level algorithm is applied to determine the level of D, which is the last leg of CD.

The trades are entered after the completion of the D level in the countertrend direction of the last leg of the pattern.

Figure A.4 shows the AB = CD patterns and its structures. The relevant ratios are shown. In AB = CD patterns, the trades are entered at D level.

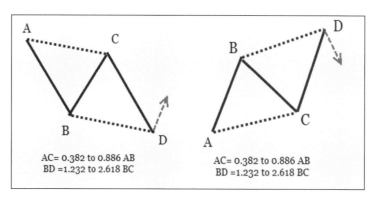

AC= 0.382 to 0.886 AB
BD =1.232 to 2.618 BC

AC= 0.382 to 0.886 AB
BD =1.232 to 2.618 BC

Figure A.4
AB = CD
Patterns

For a closer look, please visit TradersLibrary.com/ TLECorner.

Figure A.5

ABC Bullish
Pattern

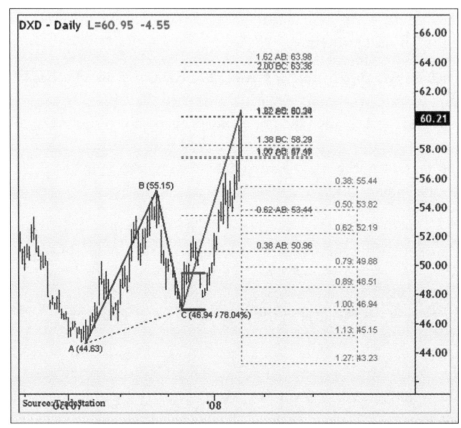

Figure A.6

ABC Bearish
Pattern

For a closer
look, please visit
TradersLibrary.com/
TLECorner.

ABC BULLISH PATTERN

Figure A.5 shows the ABC bullish pattern in a DXD daily chart. From October 2007 to December 2007, the A, B, and C pivots completed, and connecting these pivots, an ABC pattern was developed. After the completion of the C pivot at about the $46.94 price level, price traded above a two-bar high to signal a reversal in its prior trend. A long entry was triggered at about $49. A stop was placed at $46.5. The first target is placed at 0.62 AB level ($53), and second target was placed at $58.

ABC BEARISH PATTERN

Figure A.6 shows the ABC bearish pattern in Google stock. An ABC bearish pattern was developed from October 2007 to December 2007, from $745 to $616. A reversal signal was generated when the price closed below the two-bar low with a wide-range bar near $700. A short entry was placed at $700 with a stop above the C level at $725. The first target was placed at 0.62 AB level at $643, and the second target level was placed at $595 (1.0 AB).

THE 5-POINT (X5) PATTERNS

In 1932, H.M. Gartley described a 5-point "Gartley" trading pattern in his book, *Profits in the Stock Market*. Larry Pesavento improved this pattern with Fibonacci ratios and established rules on how to trade the Gartley pattern in his book, *Fibonacci Ratios with Pattern Recognition*. Larry Pesavento and Bryce Gilmore invented the butterfly patterns with Fibonacci ratios. There are many other authors who have worked on this pattern, but the best work on these 5-point patterns (Gartley, Butterfly, Crab, and Bat patterns) to my knowledge is done by Scott Carney in his two-volume text, *Harmonic Trading of the Financial Markets*. Scott Carney also was the first researcher to add specific requirements using Fibonacci ratios to validate the exact structure of the Gartley pattern. He also identified specific reversal levels using the Gartley pattern structure and coined the term "Potential Reversal Zone," or PRZ. Scott Carney is also the inventor of other 5-point patterns like the Bat and the Crab.

Gartley patterns have 5 points starting at point X, which is the lowest of all points in a bullish setup, and the highest of all points in a bearish set-up. For a bullish Gartley, from X, prices rise to form a higher swing high at "A." From A, a retracement swing low, "B," is formed within 0.382 to 0.618 of the XA range. Another swing high, "C," is formed at 0.618 of

AB. Point "D" is formed in the Potential Reversal Zone (PRZ) within 0.618 to 0.786 of the XA swing, or 1.27 to 1.62 of the BC range. D is the decision or buy trade point in a bullish Gartley setup. Point D is also a sell trade point in a bearish Gartley setup.

THE BASICS OF GARTLEY PATTERNS

The Gartley pattern (Figure A.7) has two key elements in its structure. The formation of the AB=CD pattern, and the 0.618 retracement of XA swing to the "B" level. The Gartley pattern is formed when the action-point (D) is retraced into XA swing. If D extends beyond X, the pattern becomes one of the extension patterns (Butterfly or Crab). The action point (D) is usually formed from 0.786 to 0.886 of XA swing.

Figure A.7

Gartley Patterns

For a closer look, please visit TradersLibrary.com/ TLECorner.

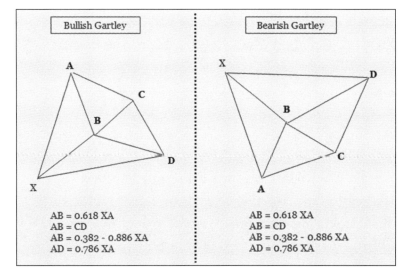

Scott Carney defined that the Potential Reversal Zone (PRZ) area is constructed by:

- AB=CD

- 0.786 XA

- 1.618 BC

Pattern completion signals for potential reversals:

- Wide range bars from PRZ

- Gap reversals

- Systematic higher highs

Potential entry signals from PRZ levels:

- Bullish: Enter a long trade one tick above the high of the confirmation bar (higher-high bar or wide range bar).

- Bearish: Enter a short trade one tick below the low of the confirmation bar (lower-low bar or wide range bar).

Stop:

- For bullish Gartley setups, the Gartley pattern fails if price closes below the "X". Place your trade a few ticks below the low of the "X".

- For bearish Gartley setups, the Gartley pattern fails if price closes above the "X". Place your trade a few ticks above the high of the "X".

Target:

- The first set of targets are the price levels of C and A.

- The second target is set at extensions of 1.27 to 1.62 of AD range from the "D" level.

Bullish Gartley Example

Figure A.8 shows a bullish Gartley formation from the daily GE stock chart. From mid-September 2006 to November 2006, GE formed a Gartley pattern. The B level retracement was 60.1% near the minimum of Gartley's requirement. The PRZ level was formed at 88.6% area at D. After the D level, the price action is closely watched for a long trade entry. GE made higher-highs from the D level, suggesting a completion of the Gartley formation. A long entry is triggered at $35.35 area with a stop below the D level at $34.30. Targets were placed first at the A level (at $36.48), and from 138% to 162% of XA range at $37.50.

Bearish Gartley Example

Figure A.9 shows a bearish Gartley pattern formation in the QID daily chart. QID formed a bearish Gartley from May 2008 to September 2008, from X level at $57.5 to D ($56.5). The center point,

Figure A.8

Bullish Gartley
Pattern

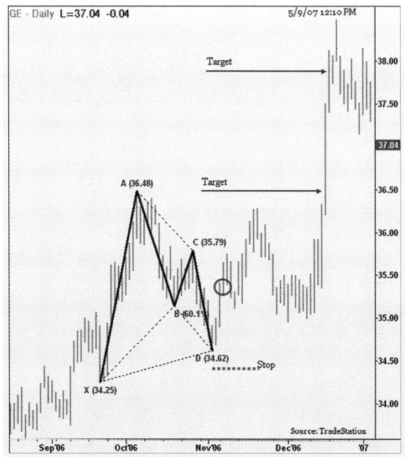

Figure A.9

Bearish Gartley
Pattern

For a closer
look, please visit
TradersLibrary.com/
TLECorner.

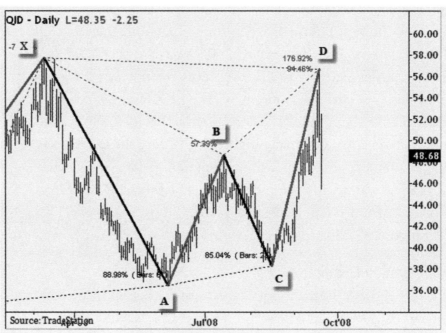

B, is formed around the $48.60 level with a 57% XA retracement. It may not be a perfect Gartley pattern but a D pivot was formed below X at $56. A trade entry is triggered at $49.60 (38% XA) level. This pattern is still in progress as of this writing.

Butterfly Pattern

The Butterfly pattern (see Figure A.10) was discovered by Bryce Gilmore and Larry Pesavento. It is one of the powerful patterns like the Gartley pattern. The Butterfly pattern has a distinct retracement level (0.786) of XA swing. In bullish and bearish 5-point swings, the pattern must have 0.786 to 0.886 of XA swing to be valid. In perfect Butterfly patterns, the AB swing will be equal to CD (AB=CD). The Butterfly pattern is an extension pattern where the action-point (D) occurs beyond "X."

Butterfly patterns usually occur at market tops and market bottoms. The pattern's success rate is much higher when the retracement and time ratios are harmonically aligned.

Two primary differences between the Butterfly and Crab patterns are:

1. The AB retracement must be 0.786 in the Butterfly pattern, whereas in the Crab pattern, it lies between the 0.382 and 0.618 levels.

2. In both patterns, the D point extends beyond the X, and the C level can be inside or outside of the XA range. The

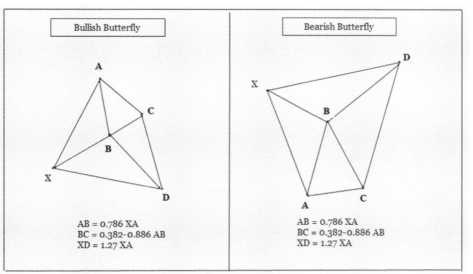

Figure A.10

Butterfly Patterns

For a closer look, please visit TradersLibrary.com/ TLECorner.

retracement of AB defines level D. In Butterfly patterns, if B is formed at 0.786, the usual retracement of D could be near 1.27 of the XA range.

The Basics of Butterfly Patterns

- Minimum AB=CD, up to CD=1.27 AB
- B occurs at 0.786 XA
- CD has at least 1.618 BC projection

Potential Reversal Zone (PRZ) area is constructed by:

- 1.27 AB
- 1.618 BC
- 1.27 XA

Potential Entry Signals from PRZ levels:

- Bullish: Enter a long trade one tick above the high of the confirmation bar (higher-high bar or wide range bar).
- Bearish: Enter a short trade one tick below the low of the confirmation bar (lower-low bar or wide range bar).

Stop:

- Butterfly patterns considered to be a failure if the price trades beyond the 2.618 XA area. But if an entry is made at 1.27 XA for bullish Butterfly patterns, place a stop a few ticks below the lowest of the pattern.
- For bearish Butterfly patterns, place a stop order above the high of the Butterfly pattern.

Targets:

- Targets are set at 100% of AD and 162% of XA from D levels.
- In bullish Butterfly patterns, beyond the A level, targets need to be protected with trailing stops.

Figure A.11

Bullish
Butterfly
Pattern

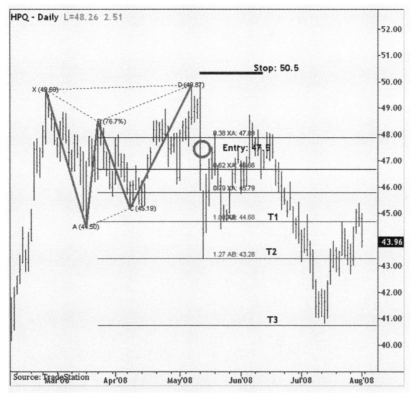

Figure A.12

Bearish
Butterfly
Pattern

For a closer
look, please visit
TradersLibrary.com/
TLECorner.

Bullish Butterfly Pattern

Figure A.11 shows a bullish Butterfly pattern formation in Amazon stock. From May 2008 to July 2008, a bullish Butterfly pattern was formed from level X at $71.56 to A at 84.88, B at 75, and C at 84.47. A first potential reversal zone (PRZ) was calculated around $68. A second potential reversal zone was calculated at 1.62 of XA, around $63. AMZN traded down to the second PRZ without any reversal bars (wide-range or two-bar high). From the second PRZ, a trade reversal was signaled as AMZN traded above the two-bar high with a wide-range bar. An entry was triggered around $70 with a stop below D level at $62.75. The first target was placed at C level to $84.

Bearish Butterfly Pattern

Figure A.12 shows the bearish Butterfly formation in HPQ stock. From March 2008 to May 2008, the bearish butterfly formed from levels X at $49.69 to A at $44.50, B at $48.50, to C at $45.19, and D at $49.87. From the D level, a wide-range bar triggered a trade entry below 38% of the XA range. A stop was placed above D level at $50.50. The first target is set at 100% of AB Level to $44.68. The second target was placed at 127% of AB at $43.28.

UTILIZING TRIGGERS AND FILTERS FOR PROFITABLE E-MINIS TRADING
by Alex Wasilewski of Puretick.com

Holy cow, I've become a guru!

For a person whose eighth grade class predicted that he would be a writer for Mad Magazine, this may come as a surprise. They were half right. My contribution to this book places me in the writer class. The topic, trading stock index futures, indicates I am somewhat mad.

I want to thank Jea Yu for the opportunity to share some of my trading ideas with you, the reader and developing trader. Indeed, Jea has taken time to provide me with trading ideas, mentoring, and follow-up coaching. His confidence was catching, and now I aspire to impart the same confidence to traders trying to reach the next level.

This chapter deals with the Puretick methodology of day trading stock index futures. We feature the Dow e-mini futures contract, so my discussion will use the term market to refer to the Dow e-mini. Good trading methods should be viable on any time frame and in any liquid market with reasonable volume and volatility. I encourage experienced traders to apply good trading methods to other markets.

Years of short term trading losses led me to despise the term "trading guru" more and more. The more I lost, the more I began to believe that perhaps anyone who taught trading or sold trading books was just an inadvertent recruiter, placed on earth to inveigle newbies to buy into the dream of trading one's own capital successfully for a living.

Each time I added to my collection of trading books, I outwardly proclaimed that I was adding to my depth of market knowledge. It really indicated that I had just disgustedly abandoned one more holy grail trading strategy.

So why should you, Mr. or Ms. Reader, decide to listen to anything I have to say, to take me on as your mentor?

For three reasons.

1. I had to make an almost unbearable transition from consistent trading loser to consistent trading winner in a process that took over four years.

2. A plethora of diverse career experiences that introduced me to the wealthiest and the most downtrodden of people.

3. The good experience of having trained with some of the most successful traders in the business.

I have worked as a police officer, stock broker, IRS auditor, Federal Reserve accountant, auto salesperson, and corporate controller. Owning businesses in the restaurant, trucking, and home improvement fields has helped me identify with all kinds of people from many areas of human endeavor. I can communicate with traders because I understand them and what makes them tick.

With all those different career backgrounds, I picked up lots of different personality attributes—some beneficial, some detrimental to trading.

I was educated as an accountant at Manhattan College. That one is probably detrimental to the gunslinger side of trading. An accountant, at least the ones not indicted for some major corporate fraud, should be able to take a set of numbers and produce the same result time after time. The stock market does not produce the same result every day. One day, a market tests support a second time, produces a classic double bottom, and decides to rally 80 points in 25 minutes. The next day, the market hesitates at another support level, starts up for 2 minutes, then collapses 100 points.

On the other hand, accounting did teach me the value of keeping good records. As a trader, if you look back at last week's trades and have no idea what made you pull the trigger to go long, how do you know if you should do it again? Markets have memories; you should too!

Accounting may not help you be a risk avoider, but at the least, you should be interested in understanding risk. And you should understand the boring but necessary skill of managing your money and the trade.

Being a professional trader and trading coach, I obviously take a great interest in understanding the backgrounds of my clients. I do want to know what they have experienced in their careers before trying to trade for a living. Traders will bring psychological baggage to trading that emanates from what skills they have needed in their past to survive. That may require "unlearning" before they can become consistent trading winners.

Engineers and pilots (I am a pilot so this one is familiar) try to deal with a pretty high percentage of success. I do not want to hear, "Good evening ladies and gentlemen. This is your co-pilot for our flight to Miami International. I am pleased to tell you that our Captain this evening has compiled a 92% success rate touching down on the runways."

An engineer should try to build a bridge that will hold 100% of the traffic passing over it. Well guess what people? Do you think that some of the previously mentioned professionals might look at a trading loss as a personal failure, necessitating an added dose of fear to that trader's outlook?

I could cite numerous other personally observed case studies. If you accept one of my beliefs that since markets are composed of individual traders, and traders bring disparate styles, thoughts, and experiences into their trades, then market behavior is really the sum of the actions of traders. Since each day brings a different set of traders to the table, the markets will always act slightly different.

It is this chaotic behavior of the markets that leads some theorists to believe that markets are completely random. Others believe just the opposite; that market behavior can be formulated in a neat, simple computer black box algorithm.

If that were true, then the equity of all traders would trace out into a pretty bell curve of profit distribution. It does not. Nearly 90% of all traders fail.

My quest to become a consistently profitable trader led me not only to buy tons of trading books but to actually contact well-known, highly profitable traders who also had the ability to teach.

In case you did not know, one of my mentors is the author of this book, Jea Yu. Jea's knowledge of stochastics and his work on prioritization of multiple time frames helped enormously in my quest for profit consistency.

You might assume that super successful traders did the one thing that assured the greatest profits. During my various personal mentorships, I found that each trader seemed to have a different style, a different method that led to the path to profits. Notwithstanding many similar psychological traits of winners—such as supreme confidence—great traders seemed to be able to create their own recipe of profitable formulas. Following that logic, one could conclude that there must be other groups of successful traders knowingly following the methods of the masters.

Since nothing I was doing seemed to work, I set out to combine the best methods of those who taught me. The problem was that every one of the best traders included large amounts of discretion into their trading methodology. It was great to hear that one mentor would say, "Trade with the trend." Why, then, would that trader not be in the market all the time, similar to a moving average crossover system? Another trader might look for a key reversal pattern, yet not take more than 30% of key reversals.

Four years seems like a lifetime to come up with a trading methodology that makes consistent profits for a trader. On the other hand, isn't trading supposed to be a profession? Looking back now, four years is a small period of time to reach any level of expertise. A medical student does not become a doctor in four years; airline pilots do not become captains in four years. So many new traders are defeated by impatience.

My conclusion and challenge was that most of the traders who mentored me made the bulk of their profits trading with the trend, yet they did not chase the market. Therefore, my methodology and moving forward, the

Puretick methodology, became a trend following method.

In short, the Puretick methodology is:

• Trade with the trend.

• Do not chase the market.

• Wait for a counter move to the trend.

• Enter a trade when the market begins to reassert its trend.

• You only make money when you can find the panic of other traders.

What is the trend? I define it as where a 5-period moving average is in relation to a 20-period simple moving average on a 15-minute chart.

Again, please don't get neurotic on me. If you want to use a 14-minute chart with a 23-period exponential moving average, knock yourself out. It doesn't matter.

After I made the transition to day trading, I began to organize the charts I followed in order of use. We use a daily, 60-minute, 15-minute, 3-minute, and an 89-tick chart on the DOW e-mini. For those traders unable to produce an 89-tick chart, a 1-minute chart will suffice.

I would like to add that beginning traders become obsessed with trying to exactly duplicate my charts, indicators, and split-second trading decisions. Trying to clone my mentors was perhaps my biggest reason for initial failure and the four years it took to build consistency.

I am aware of the daily trend but try not to let that influence the bias that I carry in to the morning preparation. If the daily charts show the stock market is in a bear market, I am aware that the trend of the market from open to close can be up on a particular day. What the daily trend will do for me is to allow a larger bet (more contracts) if the 15-minute trend that day is moving in the direction of the daily trend.

If trading with the trend is so great, then how come I have lost tons of money waiting for the market to begin to make a new high or low, then going long or short on the breakout? There are two ways to lose money trading a breakout. The first way is to guess that it is going to happen and go long (the reverse applies to short situations) a few ticks before the actual breakout happens. Of course, the high does prove to be resistance and you get out with a loss when the market rejects the resistance.

The second way to lose is to wait for the market to start breaking out, to actually make a new high or low. Of course by that time, stops are being hit by traders who actually use stops and that causes an accelerated run that can last from one to five minutes. So the new trader waits for that minute or two to prove that the market is going higher, and when the pressure of missing the big move becomes too great (greed), that trader buys. Think about what is happening. Before a market can break out, it must have been in a congestion (non-trending) period or in a previous downtrend that is sharply reversing up. The profitable traders, at least for this trade, are those who have bought lower. Human nature will compel many of these traders to realize the profits they have. They are selling just as the previously mentioned, inexperienced, greedy trader, is buying. The profit taking and lack of more substantial buying causes the market to begin declining. This turns our greedy trader into a fearful trader. Interesting how emotions change so quickly in this business.

If you have not yet had this experience, keep trading; you will. So we go back to our trading books and read that the smart money fades the first test of resistance. You feel betrayed. Seems a bit of a conflict to try to trade with the trend, yet one should not chase the market. Like me in the beginning, the confused trader keeps jumping from trading book to different trading method, adjusting the moving average periods, stochastic settings, time frames, trying to find that magic, secret setting that the "moneymakers" must know.

Years of experience have taught me that the best time to lose money is when the market is in panic mode. When you fight a losing trade to a time or price point where you can no longer stand the pain—you just dump the trade. You go into anger and blame mode.

For some of us, those with world class persistence, those who will keep losing, falling down, getting up, getting burned, but developing the scars of the potential winner, the anger and blame slowly turns inward. We begin to realize that if what we always did resulted in losses, then doing the opposite might result in profits. Perhaps instead of entering a trade when it was nice and quiet with low perceived risk (and with no clear direction) and getting out when the market exploded or tanked with us panicking on the wrong side, we begin to want to wait until we can find out when other traders might be panicking and enter a position against the weaker side.

So, looking back to the previous breakout analysis, instead of guessing that the market might break out, or trading at the first run of stops, maybe it is better to wait and put the pressure on the traders not smart enough to get stopped out quickly.

This is where the Puretick Trigger might help.

THE PURETICK TRIGGER

Before you celebrate a newfound-guru's holy-grail trading method, please realize that I am combining a bit of marketing sizzle with some truly smart, effective trading methodology that is being used by the best discretionary traders. At the same time, there is a great burden that must be placed on every trader who attempts to become a more consistent winner. World class traders have developed incredible patience, discipline, risk-averseness, confidence, and money management skills.

If you do not have the internal makeup of a professional trader you will always experience the results of the amateur. You will be the prey. Trading is not a "nice" endeavor. It is adversarial. You must think like a predator. You are entering a professional's arena. In just about any other profession, you must have some credentials before they allow you to play. Imagine trying to pick a fight with the heavyweight champion of the world—in an arena I hope—and for the chance at winning a prize. Or challenging Tiger Woods to a nationally televised winner-take-the-loser's-house match. The state boxing commission or the PGA might not let an amateur play and become much poorer or less healthy. Trading is different. Anyone with a trading platform and a few thousand dollars is allowed to try to take a payday away from successful, ruthless multi-millionaire traders.

The good news for those who survive the initial grueling, frustrating year or years of trading is that you do not have to start off trying to defeat the world champions. There are always a new crop of neophytes—newbies ready to make the same mistakes as you did. We want as our targets—sorry you macho types—the weaklings. You should build in your trading room a new paradigm statue of personal liberty to your trading account. "Bring me your overtrading, undercapitalized neophyte traders, the masses ready to get rich quick with 'holy grail' trading ideas—and I will take their money."

The Trigger is a chart-based trading method designed to help a trader enter a trade in the direction of the trend after a small retracement has occurred on a smaller time frame. It defines a probable end to a short term swing on a 3-minute chart.

The Trigger is composed of:

- Stochastics on the 3-minute chart

- Higher than average volume

- A trading bar that reverses its initial impulse

Using this method, it is important to attempt to trade with the trend on a higher time frame. We use the 15-minute chart for this purpose. If the 5-period moving average has crossed above the 20-period moving average (I use a simple moving average in this case), we say the trend is up. If the 5-period is below the 20-period, we call the trend down.

By the way, if you have been one of those traders who have strived to make your trading career notable for the magical way you can pick the high or low for each day and have traded accordingly, you might actually like this method.

Of course, we have learned that picking tops and bottoms usually only results in finding the bottom of your trading account. We have all loved and fondly remembered that one time we did it. But think of the odds. There are 130 three-minute bars that form during the normal hours of a stock index trading day. There is one high price and one low price. If you put aside the double and triple bottoms and tops, you have a .0076 chance of catching the high or low bar of the day.

The trigger bar does attempt to catch the low or high of a swing point. Since we use it mainly on a 3-minute chart, it becomes a rigorous way of trading both in the direction of a higher time frame trend, yet trading a reversal pattern of a shorter time frame.

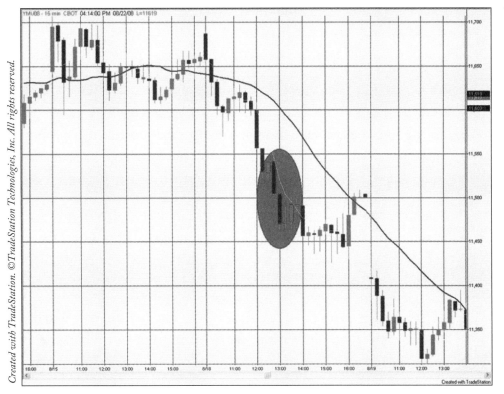

Figure B.1
15-Minute
Bars Indicating
Downtrend

For a closer
look, please visit
TradersLibrary.com/
TLECorner.

The trend as indicated in Figure B.1 (15-minute bars) at around 12:45 p.m. is down.

How many times have we watched a market continue to trend and become more and more tempted to just jump in and catch the move before it is over? We battle with ourselves because we also know that we should not chase the market. Before getting into the trade, the emotion most prevalent is greed. We are here to trade and this trend is calling to us. Of course, as the market continues to move without us, the greed wins out and we do jump in (in Figure B.1, we go short).

Amazing how the market knows when we are in and decides to move against our position immediately. It begins to rally. The reason is because as the market moves more and more in one direction, the winners are increasing their profits at the expense of those who have panicked.

Now we are the ones about to panic. Now we look for a reasonable place to put a stop and realize that a logical stop point is beyond our risk tolerance. So we set a stop most likely too small for the position, but at least it prevents disaster. As we get taken out on a stop we are reminded of the all too familiar "chasing of the trend" we swore we would avoid, yet we did it again.

This countertrend move is first caused by the successful traders who have begun to take their profits. The buying to cover the short positions pushes the market higher until it hits levels that induce panic on the too-late traders who have taken short positions. That buying propels the market higher until it runs out of buyers and attracts new short sellers, who have been patiently waiting for the retracement.

Look at Figure B.2 featuring the 3-minute bars. What appears as an uninterrupted downtrend on the 15-minute chart has now been broken down into smaller swings clearly showing 40 and 50 point Dow moves counter to the downtrend.

Better yet, the Trigger Indicator—represented by the dots above and below a few of the exhaustion bars—can point out when the price appears to complete the smaller time frame swing against the higher time frame trend and begins to get ready to continue in the direction of the higher time frame trend.

We calculate the Trigger Bar by mathematically defining what we are looking for at the end of a countertrend. We use the 14-period stochastics to identify overbought and oversold areas. When the slow stochastic line, which is nothing more than an average of the fast stochastics line of a 3-minute chart, goes below 20 for a period of time, then begins to turn up, we say that the market is oversold and ready to increase in price. That is the first part of our trigger.

Volume is the next ingredient. We will talk about time

Figure B.2
3-Minute Bars with Swings Counter to Downtrend

For a closer look, please visit TradersLibrary.com/ TLECorner.

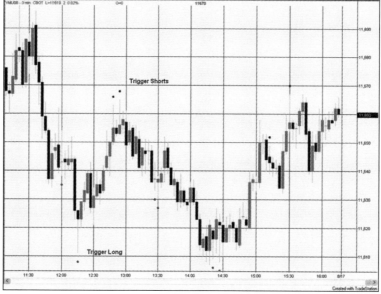

Trigger Shorts

Trigger Long

frames later, but the reason volume is important is simply because if more traders participate, there is more money in the pot for you to potentially take.

You can have the greatest setup in the world, but if you are betting correctly against one trader and that trader is willing to risk $25.00, then that is all you are going to make. This sounds strange to most traders I instruct. They are looking at their computer screen all day. They watch charts and indicators form before their eyes. They click the mouse or touch a keyboard macro and an order is placed. They may hear a sound or a digitized voice, and a price fill is reported. It does not seem like our trader had to worry about any other volume except the number of contracts placed by the trader, and there certainly was no need to see any other trader or traders.

And that may be the problem with trading from home on a computer. We believe more and more in the disembodied world of price bars, moving averages, and other mathematically based indicators that we forget that a trader can only win money when someone else loses money. If we base the reason for studying trading on the assumption that there are profitable trading methods, then we must assume that successful traders are smart enough to figure out when a good trade is about to develop.

You must further assume that if the next setup you are getting ready to trade is going to be a super winner, then there should be a nice group of patient, successful, professional traders starting to get aboard the next big trade. If so, that should create volume, right?

Looking at volume another way—let's forget the histogram for now, okay? Let's go back to a time a long time ago, to the Jurassic Park time of trading, to the time I started trading or a little further back. Groups of traders would watch a ticker tape, or, I do admit, brokerage houses had an electronic ticker board where blocks of posted trades scrolled along the dark screen.

The traders mainly looked for volume. That story was told to them in the form of large blocks of stock. When a large block of stock danced along the screen, the traders had to decide if the price was higher or lower than the last time they saw it printed. They had to decide if the block was larger or smaller. Sorry, there were no formatted blue or red numbers or little plus or minus signs. Worse, the important information was mixed in with blocks and prices of other stocks; most were not important to the trader.

Picture one successful, sophisticated market operator trying to buy a stock because of valuable insight or information. This market operator is trying to buy 300,000 shares of GM at 85.00. Remember, this was a long time ago when GM was popular. 1,000 unsophisticated traders are trying to sell 100 shares each at 85 1/8. Stocks traded in eighths then. Most of the time, 100 shares of GM go by and print at 85.00. The sophisticated trader is patient most of the time and does not chase the stock. The little guy is nervous and wants out before things go bad. The small trader is willing to bend a little just to get out and sells at 85. But every so often the trader in the know also gives in. This trader is not paying up because of fear or greed, but out of an understanding of supply and demand. The smart money doesn't want to buy 300,000 shares because he would have to pay much higher prices, but that trader can buy 1,000 shares at 85 1/8 without buying all of the supply. The specialist has enough sellers, so he allows one block of 1,000 shares to print at 85 1/8 and gives it to the sophisticated trader's floor broker.

The traders watching the tape go by might be poised to act if this kind of action had been going on for a while at ever increasing prices. They buy for two reasons. The upticks occur at much larger size than the downticks, indicating an anxious buyer or buyers with much greater financial resources than those willing to sell. And you don't get greater financial resources if you are wrong too often. This is called following the smart money. This strategy applies to shorting when volume is stronger on the downticks.

The Trigger needs increasing volume, in addition to the proper phase of the stochastics, in order to fire a signal. It is not enough to see a 3-minute chart showing an overbought or oversold condition. We need an above average volume increase in order to take action. If the setup is good, we want as many good traders on our side as possible. Put it another way— if we are going to take money from the unsuccessful traders, then the greater the power on our side, and the more likely that the enemy is going to lose. Remember that there is another person who bet against you every time you get a fill. Make sure you have an overwhelming majority of traders on your side.

The final element to a good Trigger bar is what we call reversal tape action. It literally means that you can see the beginning of the victory over your opponent even before you enter the war. It may not be brave and noble, but our war strategy is to always join the side that is winning. This is order flow analysis, or tape reading.

The Trigger has been designed to attempt to emulate the habits of a good tape reader. Tape reading, or monitoring order flow, is really an evolution of the techniques discussed earlier describing the actions of earlier traders watching the ticker tape. Today, good floor traders try to get a feel for what the institutions are doing in the trading pits and try to buy contracts before the larger institutions can complete the purchases, selling to the institutions at small but regular markups with a larger number of contracts. They attempt to sell short first when the institutions need to sell.

The last floor traders holding positions when the bigger players stop buying or selling start the market moving in the opposite direction. No one wants the inventory the trader is holding. If the floor trader is smart, a losing position is closed out quickly at a small loss before it mounts and everyone is panicking. The floor trader will take a break and come back when another opportunity presents itself.

Yes, a floor trader has a potential advantage over those of us who trade off the floor. They can see the clerks gesticulating orders to the pit. We at our home offices do not see if Merrill or Goldman is running to the pit with 3,000 contracts to dump. There has to be a reason why someone is willing to pay $500,000 up to as much as $2,000,000 for the opportunity to trade on the floor. Still there is nothing certain about trading. Institutions and top traders can place a few initial orders on one side of the market, then suddenly turn around and trade the other way. A substantial trader can begin to start buying the market while having a group of other traders selling more contracts on the initial trader's behalf, actually accumulating a net short position. If you do not think that traders do not at times think as poker players or chess players, you are making a mistake.

It is this kind of trade reversal that may create what might be called a candlestick formation hammer or shooting star. We can not go into detail on these formations, so you would need to refer to a good source on Japanese candles.

With the shooting star formation, if we are using the 3-minute bar, prices may open at the close of the previous bar and continue initially to rise, giving the bullish traders comfort in staying on the buy side. Shortly before the 3 minutes are up and another bar forms, sellers step in. It does not matter if previous buyers are getting out, or new positions are taken by traders who believe the market has gone too far to the upside. The price traces out a bar with a high "tail" and closes out near the lows. We infer from that development that the sellers are about to gain control of price movement. (See Figure B.3).

Figure B.3
Shooting Star

When the 3-minute chart forms the opposite pattern, or a hammer, it is the buyers who are said to begin to gain control from the sellers. Prices may begin to fall at the start of the 3-minute time frame, but buyers soon feel prices have fallen enough and begin to push prices to the highs reached during the 3-minute time frame. (See Figure B.4).

The previous examples given with regard to the 3-minute time frame in no way imply that there is something magic about that time. What we are doing is showing how we want to trade against the shorter time period (in this case, the 3-minute), but trade with the next higher time frame (in our study, the 15-minute).

Figure B.4
Hammer

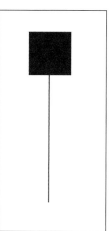

To sum up, when a Trigger bar forms, we can take a trade long or short. On its own, there is a positive expectation that a short term trend, based on the 3-minute chart, is changing direction. If we keep our profit targets conservative and our stop loss points small, and keep our position size far less than a trade with more odds in our favor, we can see profits.

For the newer trader, I do not recommend taking trades against the trend on a time frame that you are using for primary entries. The first reason is that it encourages overtrading. Overtrading implies that high probability trades occur very frequently. They do not.

Another reason to avoid the more frequent trades that Trigger only signals will induce, is that a trader becomes less concerned with the higher time frame trends, and begins to see the trading world in an ever tightening microcosm of technical indicators. I can not emphasize enough that you and I are not the only two traders placing trades today. You had better hope not, because I will take your money away. Oops, more on positive self-talk later.

Seriously, there are many different traders trading many different methods on many different time frames. You might want to jump in on that big momentum selloff after that negative report but do not want to chase the market. So you wait for 15 minutes (you might want to try for 27 minutes, but more on the 27-minute cycle later) for a little rally and determine that a 3-minute chart is overbought. Try to understand in which a trader only watching a 60-minute chart is waiting, perhaps for another 50-point rally before getting excited about taking a short.

The ideal place to take a short position would be at a price one tick below where all the other traders who are planning to go short would be placing their order. We would then only short if all of their planned selling would overwhelm all the traders planning to go long. So how do we know this? You can take a poll of all traders trading today. If you can't reach them all or some will not share that information, then the only choice you have is to try to understand the types of setups and market conditions in which a successful trader would place a trade. Since you must trade against somebody, you also must understand what would make an unsuccessful trader make a trade, what would cause action.

In an ideal situation, the short Trigger would form after the higher time frame shows a strong impulse move to the downside. After a strong, substantial move, late-coming newbies would give in to the temptation of great riches that will be theirs if they throw caution to the wind and jump in on the "obvious" down move. They will not give too much thought to the fact that lots of sharp traders who had already been short might have already accumulated substantial profits and might find it smart to cover some of their shorts.

The newbies go short just as the profitable side starts to buy and take some profits. This causes the market to begin to rebound. We may correctly assume that the sophisticated shorts have a lot more financial clout than the newbies. So prices drift up. As the market drifts upward, the hopes and dreams of the late-arriving short traders begin to unravel. Impatience leads to fear. The greater the fear, the less likely it is that a trader will stick to a plan or remain within the original plan as set by risk reward evaluations. The trader will panic.

The 27-minute cycle was briefly mentioned before. When the market is trading actively and a trend is underway, and is strong with less choppy countertrend moves, there is a regular pattern of correction—most notable on the 3-minute chart—that will last about 27 minutes. Perhaps it can be explained that 27 minutes is all that a trader positioned on the wrong side of a market move can stand before throwing in the towel and overcome by panic.

On other days, the cycle of the corrective part of the market will last longer, more toward an hour. It can not be emphasized enough that a system as complex as the stock market, composed of millions of people with different investing and trading ideas, and various hopes and fears, does not lend itself too well to discrete trading rules. The trader who places an overemphasis on a simple rule covering all market conditions and time periods will find that the market will change often enough to blow out one's trading capital. It pays to understand the reason behind the moves—the how and why of pattern development. The best way to use a setup is to combine an understanding of the patterns that develop in the markets and to attempt during the trading day to figure out what kind of setup is working as quickly as possible. If the market is making a slower transition between up and downtrends, and the 15-minute chart is showing more spiky conditions that are moving from high to low in 60-minute cycles, don't look to play 27-minute cycles.

When the 15-minute trend is down, the 3-minute stochastics are above 80 and beginning to turn down, and a 3-minute shooting star is formed on greater than average volume, my program will mark that bar as a Trigger short. At that time, a trader should consider a short entry. Stops can be placed above the Trigger bar, or a fixed dollar risk, or finally adjusted depending upon the recent volatility of the market itself.

THE PURETICK FILTERS

As I developed as a trader, making the transition from consistent loser to consistent winner, I began to look for reasons why I should not be trading. I looked for red flags that told me my setup had less of a chance of working. This is the opposite of what beginning traders or traders who have developed bad habits seem to do.

I refer to the increasing number of trades placed by a marginal trader as the "smart trader curve." In the very beginning, we learn that it is so difficult to become a profitable trader; the market is against us. We are cautious, maybe afraid to pull the trigger. We just don't want to be wrong, especially when we know we don't know.

Slowly we become educated. We buy books and learn the author's "sure fire" technique that let him or her win the "Great Trader All Star Game," and turn $10,000 into $1,000,000 in three months. When we start losing, we add the "sure fire" method to our arsenal and trade that. In three months we do not have a million, but we do have three more trading systems under our belt. We start the day, patiently watch our charts, and pretty soon one of the holy grail patterns emerges. We jump on it. We might be aware that the market action is almost showing another "magic bullet" trade that indicates a trade in the opposite direction of "sure fire," but "sure fire" fired first, so we took it. And if the trade goes against us right away, we really feel the pressure of a "magic bullet" almost telling us over our shoulder that we should be in the opposite position. Is it any wonder that as soon as the trade starts working we are quick to jump out with a little more than a surplus after covering commission costs?

The Filters are designed to trade less, not more.

The Filters are composed of:

- **Filter 1, The 15-Minute Trend:** The general direction of the market's price. Just place a simple 15-minute candlestick chart with a simple moving average. We like to use a 5-period moving average and a 20-period moving average. If the 5-period has crossed above the 20-period we conclude that the trend is up. The trend is down when the 5-period is below the 20-period. The 15-minute trend produces the largest weighting in our Filters indicator.

- **Filter 2, The Daily Pivot:** Floor trader daily pivot points are levels at which the market may change direction. They are derived by calculating the numerical average of a particular stock's high, low, and closing prices. Pivots are available in most every charting platform available today. The reason pivot points are so popular is that they are predictive as opposed to lagging. Because so many traders follow pivot points, you will often find that the market reacts at these levels. This gives you an opportunity to trade. If the current market price is below the daily pivot, then we are bearish on this filter, if above, we are bullish.

- **Filter 3, Advance/Decline Index:** A technical analysis tool that represents the total difference between the number of advancing and declining security prices. This index is considered one of the best indicators of market movements as a whole. Stock indexes such as the Dow Jones Industrial Average only tell us the strength of 30 stocks, whereas the advance/decline index can provide much more insight into the movements of the market. We look at the current advance/decline index number as well as the trend of the advances/declines to determine a bullish or bearish bias. For example, if the advance/decline was -835 and falling, our bias would be bearish. If the advance/decline was 568 and rising, our bias would be bullish. When the advance/decline is between -300 and +300, it normally means the market is in an undecided chop zone. Be careful in this range.

- **Filter 4, Stochastics:** We place a stochastics indicator on a 3-minute chart. There are times when all three of the above indicators align. If we just monitored those indicators, the strength of the Filter would many times approach 100%, and that reading would imply that a trader could just buy or short at the market and open up the cash register. We needed a way to try to help the Filter indicate that a trader might be chasing a move. The 3-minute stochastics does just that. If all the other indicators suggest a strong bullish move, then when the 3-minute stochastics rises above 50%, it begins to weigh that the percentage of success of the Filters is reduced. The percentage would increase when the reading of the 3-minute stochastics indicates an opposite move has developed on a larger time frame.

Let me comment on the weightings of the components of the filters. The exact numbers are proprietary. Before you jump up and down and finally feel that I am giving in to the notion of a holy grail, let me assure you that the only reason I have plugged numbers into the mix at all is to let a computer produce an output. Unlike humans, computers have a little problem with an instruction like "paint a blue bar if the market looks strong." The computer would answer with a snotty question similar to the movie *The Coneheads*; "Please define strong."

So we have to pick a 5-period moving average and a 20-period, just because lots of people like the 5 and 20. Yes, lots like the 3- and 50-period, so you can try that. It would be a good exercise for a trader who wants to try plugging in different combinations and criteria for weights and variables. You might want larger volume components or other indicators of trend, such as ADX.

Understand that the stock market is not an objective mathematical model—it is a giant voting machine. By that I mean the talking heads on television may tell the world that if oil supplies rise by 3%, that would be bullish for the stock market. But what if most traders at first start buying, then start to believe that increasing oil supplies indicate slowing world economic activity? Then you will see the market gap up on such an oil report, then a short time later begin to sell off and take out the low prices on the day and confuse the traders who bet heavily one way on an "obvious report."

Weak economic activity may mean some traders will bet heavily that the Federal Reserve will lower interest rates, and that will make the market go up, unless low interest rates mean more cheap money sloshing around, which brings on dreaded inflation, is bad for the market, and will kill the dollar. But wait—the declining dollar means our goods are cheaper overseas, and everyone will buy U.S. goods and help multinational companies increase earnings with stronger foreign currencies. So there you have my secret to being a guru. No matter what the stock market does, I have just predicted the outcome.

In the past, a trader with quick access to market moving news may have had a bit of an advantage over a trader who did not have access to news. But that is not the case today. We all get the news as fast as it comes out. Again, we do have to interpret it. And that, I believe, is where lots of traders get into trouble. It is still one of my personal greatest weaknesses as a trader.

We await a release of news. We have a general idea (from listening to television) of what the numbers would mean to the market. We make a decision to take a trade depending upon what the news report states. The report comes out and the market may even make an initial move in the expected direction that we anticipated. Worse yet, we place a small trade and make a few bucks in a half a minute.

This is where the problems begin. Let's say we initially planned to place a ten contract trade, yet because we have learned our lesson by betting too much, we only do one contract. We enter the trade at the market and get a "bad fill" because the market is moving too fast. We get a bit lucky because there are still a bunch of traders who have guessed the report wrong, are stuck on the wrong side of the trade, and are now panicking and have to get out.

We are worried, rightly so, that traders who have profits may soon start to take the profits, and pretty soon, the only traders who will enter the trade in our direction will be the typical group of late arrivals who have hesitated and now feel the pressure to get on board the trade, no matter how great the risk.

So we take our contract off at the market again because we are now scared of seeing our profit evaporate into a loss. We get another bad fill because apparently a few other traders thought the same thing we did and started covering their trade two seconds before we did. We still make ten points (on the Dow e-mini that is $100.00 per contract). Not bad for 30 seconds of work. Makes all that worrying worth it.

The market is not done yet. After the first wave of nervous traders take quick profits, another round of panic ensues and the market makes a new push in the initial direction. You can see the pattern here I hope. Initial momentum that is strong with much higher volume than the market had been trading for some time previously. Profit taking causing a pause; there is usually much lighter volume than with the initial thrust. Panic from those who were not ready to admit defeat on the first move now become more desperate as prices move against them.

What is happening to you, a trader who still should be celebrating a gain that made you a hell of a lot more money than a job flipping burgers, or better yet, than most trial lawyers make. That doesn't happen. You get annoyed at the potential profits you should have made. After all, you guessed correctly. You "knew" that report was going to make the market do what it is now doing before your very eyes. You even had a "plan" to do ten contracts instead of that wimpy one.

So you enter the magical world of the revenge trader. You probably pause a little to post some online messages in your trading room about how well you correctly guessed that report and the subsequent market reaction. You receive congratulations from your room buddies about what a great trader you are. Someone even makes the "absurd suggestion" that you jump back in, that trades like this are not over in a minute. If the report is as market moving as you suggest, then there is more price movement to come. You reject that idea out of hand. The original price level that you had briefly looked at to determine your loss point is very far away. You at least determined your initial risk; where the market has to go to tell you that your premise was wrong. Someone else in the room suggests that he is going to take another shot at the trade and use as a stop point the place where the market hesitated before—just so happens that's the place where you took profits. That trader suggests the risk to reward ratio is still okay. Your premise is working. That trader places the trade and the stop. The objective is the next pivot level (one of a few price levels calculated from yesterday's high, low, and close. Like a Fibonacci retracement, many technical traders use these prices as signs of support or resistance).

Ten minutes later the room trader exits at the target, for 22 points of profit and then congratulates you for coming up with the trading idea. Deep inside, that doesn't help. You did not take the second shot at this trade because the price was "too low" or "too high." You keep staring at the chart and keep replaying the mental tape that tells you what you should have done. You wish you could have that setup back; the next time will be different.

A strange phenomenon exists in the trading world. The markets usually grant a trader's wish for a second chance. Well, it always appears like a second chance. In the previous example, the market eventually calms down after the report. Guess what? The market always has another report coming up that must be evaluated. There may even be a few different ways one can analyze the previous report.

More important, the makeup of traders who took part in that last trade is constantly changing. Some who bet heavy on the correct outcome of the report may have left for the day to celebrate. Some heavy losers may have left to find a different line of work. But if you are still sitting in front of your screen seething about your previously missed opportunity you may notice one thing and not another.

For the past hour you may have interrupted your pacing in front of your mirror with your best wounded dog look to grab one or two quick trades for a profit, but mostly you are still wishing for that next great opportunity.

And there it is!

Someone in the room points out that the market price is now where it started before the report. You take a deep breath and go over a few thoughts why all the traders who made tons of money on your report premise probably can't wait to do it again. You review that last guru interview on your favorite business news network who confirms your opinion of the last report. Best of all, the market is now offering you an even better price on your "bad fill" when you entered the trade. This has to be the market's way of apologizing.

So that is all you notice. You may not notice that the weight of our filters has now changed direction. And if the report was truly responsible for the first market reaction, then what caused the initial price move to be overcome? That is not your concern now. You had a chance before. You blew it. You are getting a chance again. Your opinion of your report has not changed, it is even stronger because of the market's initial reaction. So you go in with ten contracts.

You get a great entry price and you mentally celebrate that for about ten seconds until the question of the market overcoming the initial move comes forward. You are now introduced to the first vestige of fear. But the greed is not done yet. Price moves against you by 15 points and you add ten contracts to your position.

Here is the thinking: Okay, there is an analyst (remember why that word begins with the four letters that it does) on your favorite show who is remarking about the key technical reversal despite the report that obviously calls for the market to go back in the direction it started in. You sort of agree that the market traders may have discounted that report by yesterday's action of 200 points. You are willing to get out of this trade. You just are not willing to lose anything. Not after being so right initially.

You are even willing to take a two tick loss. Not on the ten contracts you just added, but on the ten you started with. You will even be acting like the great trader you read about who is willing to take a small loss when a trade just doesn't feel right. And this trade doesn't feel right. So you desperately review the books and seminars you have studied for the answer.

The answer you want right now is a reason to wait to take a two point loss on your initial ten contracts. Of course you will take a 13 point gain on the added ten contracts. You will not tell the market that you are still in greed mode; that you want to crawl out of a bad trade, yet still make more than the $100.00 profit that started this whole mess.

You remember one seminar where they said that a Fibonacci level, only 12 more losing points away from the current price level, should act as a barrier and knock prices back from where they came from. You also remember that Puretick.com slogan, "We profit from the panic from others," and you have vowed not to be a wimpy panicker.

Sure, you may have started all this by working your premise of the "market moving report," did a couple of retracement trades using the Triggers that were in line with the Filters, and then put a greater sized trade on using the "market owes me for missing the last one" premise. Now we sort of slide into a Fibonacci Rejection premise for the hoped-for profits.

You start banging the desk or the trading screen when the market blasts through the Fibonacci level by an additional 20 points and even more to your detriment. Yes, for a brief moment your mind takes you back to the big seminar in Chicago where the head guru pointed his laser wand at the points on the chart where the 23-period moving average on the 60-minute chart almost always contained prices. You are only 17 points away from that. Hmm.

But then that part of the brain, the 962 cells still alive—they never slept during that accounting college course, nor were destroyed with their 9,038 other brain cell friends—so they scream to you, like that house in Amityville Horror:

"Get out! You are down $3,950.00. That is 15.8% on a $25,000 account." You listen. Your hand trembles as you grab the mouse for the trading platform. You no longer care about Fibonacci, moving averages, the regressive wave (I just made that term up. It doesn't exist, but I bet I can sell it as a black box trading system for $1995.00 to some newbie who does not want to work at learning the profession of trading). All you know is that if you keep up this blood bath, you will never be able to trade again.

You feel the panic.

And you exit all 20 contracts at the market. You get a good fill by two ticks and suffer a $3,750.00 loss. As you head to the refrigerator for some nervous eating, you interestingly note that the two tick better fill helped you by $200.00, twice as much as your original profit. But still a loss. I have done those kinds of trades. I will still make mistakes. The psychological advantage I believe I have is running a trading room. All I would have to do is one extremely dumb trade like the last one described and all my clients would quit. And that at least makes me a patient trader.

This situation was why the Filters and the Triggers were created. As I have said before, the mathematical models do not determine trader behavior, they only measure trader behavior in the past taking various properties into account. Being a voting machine, the market is moved by traders acting in response to the actions of other traders.

If you want a nearly perfect way to determine what the market will do five minutes from now, or 60 minutes from now, or where it will be at the close, you would need to poll the voters. Like asking every voter which candidate will be voted for, you would have to ask each trader: Where would you go long today? Where would you go short? Regardless of any report or market analysis, if every trader available Monday morning hit the buy button at 9:33 a.m. EST, the market would explode upward.

But here is another phenomenon. What price would a trader get? Think carefully. This is the critical nature of trading we all forget. Probably only a few trades would be executed, and only at a price where a few of the traders had previous limit orders to sell and forgot to cancel them when they placed the buy order. Remember the premise. All the traders want to buy. No one wants to sell. No trading can take place. No volume.

No volume on a huge up move in price is bearish right? Possibly. All I have to do is give one of those panicky buyers a place to get a trade off. So I can place a limit order to sell 1,000 points above the last trade and since everyone has a market order to buy, the tape would show one contract traded 1,000 points above the last trade. That might cause all the traders who put market orders to buy and who saw the last mother of all horrible fills to rethink their buy decision. Some might even want to be short 1,000 points higher than the last trade and may start putting market orders to sell short. Then all I have to do is put a limit order to buy 500 points below where I sold and would fill into those market sell orders.

The Filters were created to allow a trader to become more patient, by having to wait until not one variable, but at least four measures of market behavior are in line in order to indicate a higher percentage trade. This will automatically warn of choppy market conditions. The multi indicator approach is not to find some lonely setup out there that can make any given tick tradable, but to present red flags warning the trader to mostly stay out of the market until a most likely panic situation is under way.

You will notice that by using the Filters to create a personal bias, you are not predicting market behavior, you are simply identifying what the market is currently doing and using different measures, perhaps followed by a wider pool of traders, to make sure that the trend we are witnessing will be more likely to persist and not reverse like our "big report trade" example.

To avoid chasing the market—the other, higher risk which traps some traders who wait too long to identify a trend—the Trigger was designed to take advantage of the kind of trader we identified who is able to correctly find a trade, but through fear and uncertainty, takes profits too soon. The too-soon taking of profits causes the consolidation or retracement before the next wave of market momentum develops.

As the market retraces and forms the Trigger, then the Filters act as a check on the Trigger. There is always a danger that any retracement continues until it is no longer a retracement, but the start of new momentum the other way. The Filters try to tell us that the "other way" has not yet happened.

Does this work all the time? Of course not. However, I do believe the Triggers and Filters are robust enough to at least allow the trader some degree of accountability to herself. Just as I have to account to a room full of traders following my plans and actions, any trader can set up rules to only place trades in the direction of the Filters and where the percentages for success are high. The following example might point out a successful use of Triggers and Filters.

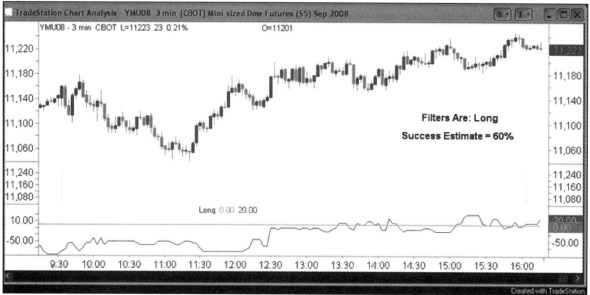

Figure B.5
3-Minute
Chart with
Filter Indicator

For a closer look, please visit TradersLibrary.com/ TLECorner.

Looking at Figure B.5, from 9:30 a.m. until 1:30 p.m., the combined filters stayed below the zero line, indicating a short bias should be established. If you waited until 11:00 a.m., you would have been guilty of chasing the market. After 11:30 a.m., the market offered good retracements but they did not turn into large winners and eventually the retracement became a new uptrend. Is there a better way to identify retracements and keep you out of the chop?

Figure B.6 shows the same chart with the Trigger indicators. If we simply look at the Triggers that formed, long and short, we see about 13 trades one could have taken. Sticking with a set of rules dramatically cuts down the trades to about two.

At about 9:45 a.m., the Filters are indicating a short bias. The market had just completed a retracement higher and a short Trigger forms. It captures the best down swing in the market with zero adverse price movement. Since the Filters were bearish, we ignore the buy Triggers. Sure, the cluster of buys around 11:00 a.m. caught the lows; the ones a half hour before did not. One ignores the setups after 11:30 a.m., as that violates the rules not to trade during lunch time, or what is affectionately called the deadzone.

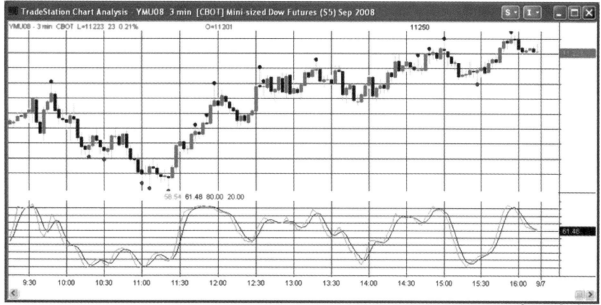

Created with TradeStation. ©TradeStation Technologies, Inc. All rights reserved.

Figure B.6
3-Minute Chart with Trigger Indicator

For a closer look, please visit TradersLibrary.com/ TLECorner.

After 1:30 p.m., we note that the Filters have indicated the probability of a rising market, so we only look for the market to retrace part of the up move; go long on an oversold stochastic reading when the volume rises and the 3-minute bar starts lower but ends at its high point—in other words, a long Trigger.

That happens right before 3:30 p.m. and catches a nice swing upward into the close on new highs for the day. By the way, this action occurred on September 5th, 2008—the day the market started going down on what experts called a horrible unemployment report. Didn't we talk about report reversals before?

For the trader loving action, this method would have only found two trades all day. A trader must ask if it is better to have action or a few reliable trades. Some professionals do not need to have great volume of business every day in order to do well. If you operate on brains, I doubt if you do 12 surgeries per day. What about the airliner sales rep at Boeing? You probably don't sell as many as the Toyota person down the road unless you offer a great deal on undercoating and pilot floor mats. So why do traders want to push the trade button 10 times more than grandma at the quarter slot machines in the casino?

One reason is the need for action. A trader makes the greatest mistakes when the focus becomes more and more narrow. In other words, when a trader begins the day, all of the indicators are more likely to be used. The trader checks whether we are gapping up or down, where the moving averages are, what the news of the day is.

After a few minutes, especially if the market is moving quickly, the first trade of the day is made. You either get a profit or a loss. The pro looks at it as the manager of a hamburger restaurant. When you walk into McDonalds the manager usually doesn't jump up and down and call a counterperson and yell out, "Wow Jack, a customer walked in."

If the customer only orders a coffee instead of a value meal with dessert and a side of beef, the manager does not start crying and wonder why Burger King gets all the good customers and is out to get this store manager.

A pro trader does not need to make money all the time; just over time. There is always another trade coming along. An amateur may apply the rules on the first trade of the day, but after that, emotions take over, good or bad.

The profitable trade leads to an educated guess on what the market might do next. Also, the amateur looks back and regrets not having done more contracts, and certainly reviews that a larger objective could have been made.

So on the next trade, instead of peeling off a few contracts at the first objective, what the Trigger Stop indicated (the Trigger Stop adjusts for volatility), the trader looks for more. Instead of trading the same three contracts as the prior trade, the newbie wants to double the size, make a profit like the "big boys." But now, instead of monitoring multiple time frames and watching for some of the Filters indicating a "no go," or avoiding dead periods of the market such as the lunch time deadzone, our gallant trader focuses on the break of a moving average that confirms the bias that the trader developed in the beginning of the trading day. Of course, that whole trade gets stopped out and not only gives back the profit made on the last one but turns the account red on the day.

Starting off with a loss impacts the amateur trader emotionally, but in the opposite direction. The trader cuts off multiple time frame analysis and other indicator red flags because of his conclusion that, "All that work is meaningless because the market is out to take my money anyway." Little by little the focus is narrowed until just raw emotions dictate trading.

At Puretick.com, we recommend a three-step process to transition from emotional trader to professional trader.

1. Begin trading three contracts or multiples of three on a simulator. In the beginning, only take Trigger trades that are confirmed by the direction of the Filters. This situation may take as long as an hour and a half to reach what we call a state of confluence. That hour and a half can be tough not trading. Keep a motivation tape nearby and listen to it. Put a hard stop in the market before you even execute the trade. That will tell you the cold fact that the trade may not work, so do not bet the ranch. At the first achievement of a profit goal, take one third of your position off at +7 points in the Dow e-mini, or an equivalent to half a point in the S&P contract. This also reinforces the fact that professional traders are always on the alert to reduce risk, not get rich on each new trade. Heck, they are already rich. The next profit level is 12 points on the Dow. Take a third off. On the final third of your position, trail your stop using many types of stop trailing techniques.

2. Move to cash. You should go to cash after a trading period of one to two months and the build up of your own track record, not a backtested one based on previous market conditions, but one where you have pulled the trigger and have produced some degree of profits and a good understanding of how many losses occurred. You should move down to one third the number of contracts you were trading in the simulator. First, the lower dollar impact on your trading equity as the market moves up and down will be less dramatic than what you got used to in the simulator. Sure it may seem boring, but a reserved detachment (apathy, as Jea Yu calls it) is necessary to running your trading business. If you wind up trading one contract, then of course it will be difficult to earn a living, and indeed one may incur a small cash drawdown during this phase of trading. That is okay. The goal is to prove to the

developing trader that one can survive and that the market is not "out to get you."

3. Increase your contract size. After one can rigorously train with fixed small stops and small first and second targets, and wind up with a net positive profit, it is time to gradually increase the contract size. You will still wind up exiting a portion of the position at small but increasing profit targets, but now you are ready for the runner. Perhaps one out of ten times the market not only lets you trade with a profit, but you experience a quick favorable move with almost zero adverse price movement. This is the time when you want to let your profit run. Obviously you can't do that trading one contract when you always have a small profit target. But at this stage you do not have a fixed target on the last third of your position. You let the market run (if it is at the top of your computer trading screen, believe it or not it can go higher). Instead of guessing where the profit run will last, you then trail the trade with an exit stop. We have found that an 89-period exponential moving average works very well in trailing a stop. If you are long, keep increasing your stop exit order two or three ticks below the 89-period exponential moving average; if short, trail about two or three ticks above.

The goal of the Triggers and Filters is to emulate the discretionary methods employed by some of the most successful traders. As one gains more favorable experience, the trader will eventually employ better and better judgment. Trade frequency and size will not simply become the ability to follow a rigid mathematical system, but the trader will be able to look back to similar market conditions and determine when the traders on the wrong side of the trade are getting financially toasted by the markets.

You will then be able to Profit from the Panic.

MADDOG TRADES
by Mark Johnson of UndergroundTrader.com

I have been an active trader employing Jea's methodology for approximately ten years, and will be giving you some examples of this in action. First, let me give you an overview of my trading process.

I tend to spend most of my trading activity looking for reversals at the extremes of range areas on "quality" stocks, both on the long and short side. In other words, I'll try to catch bounce "coils" at the bottoms of ranges, as well as playing exhaustion shorts at the extreme upper ends of ranges.

Note that when I say "quality" stock, I mean a most-likely profitable company with a favorable reputation that still trades within healthy ranges on good volume with relatively safe spreads, as opposed to what I call a "non-quality" stock, or a company that is either irrationally exuberant due to being a member of a "fad" sector at the time—like ethanol stocks in the 2006-2007 time frame—or on a healthy down slope for a good reason, either for being prosecuted, persecuted, or at minimum, exposed for a good (read: "bad") reason. It's not that I don't trade these so-called "non-quality stocks," but due to their thinly traded nature, they tend to be tougher to track predictably via traditional technical analysis constraints. So we'll use a "quality" stock for our example.

This style of trading is somewhat different than what I'll call a more "conventional" approach to trading Jea's methodology, which would normally use trend lines for support (when going long) or resistance (when going short) in order to take advantage of the prevailing trend at the time, either early in the trend, or further along in the trend's range. I have gravitated toward the "extremes" approach primarily as a function of the market changes over the last five years. When I first started trading in the late 1990s, the market was in the tail end of a long bullish phase, but was still primarily suited to creating success by following the prevailing trend—in that case, being generally long on stocks. Conversely, when the tech and internet bubble popped in 2000, a fairly extended period followed where it was generally favorable to follow the bearish trend. We've recently experienced a more dramatic example of an extended bearish trend with the onset of the financial crisis of 2008-2009.

However, I had wanted to become better at trading more range-bound market periods (both bullish and bearish), as it seemed we were entering a period of primarily range-bound activity in the mid-to-late 2000s. The beauty of Jea's methodology is that it works well in both market environments—trending as well as range-bound. Both market environments require the same disciplines of keeping stops and observing both micro and macro timelines, and the need to manage entries and exits and deploy sound account management and share allocations. This, to me, is the best of both worlds—the ability to take advantage of extended trends, as well as success trading those sometimes choppy, range-bound periods that can exist for months or even years.

In any event, let's look at an example of how the methodology works when looking for a range extreme reversal; in this case, to go short at the exhaustion of an intermediate bullish trend. I will tell you what steps I took during the process, both in terms of actual trade execution, as well as what I was thinking at the time while observing the trends play out. Due to the volatility precipitated by the financial crisis of 2008-2009, I have been trading the bank stocks a lot, especially WFC (Wells Fargo). Wells Fargo is a perfect example of what I call a "quality" stock in crisis—an otherwise profitable entity that is the proverbial "baby being thrown out with the bathwater" due to the prevailing fear. These stocks tend to recover well at some point, but tend to get knocked down a lot due to prevailing negativity, and therefore oscillate well within ranges. WFC has plenty of liquidity, making it less subject to quick and irrational moves, and it tends to follow and not "fade" the futures, in the absence of some unusual news or other external influence. I will illustrate how an initial signal on WFC may not be attractive enough on a risk/reward ratio, but may well lead to a later reversal entry with a much higher probability of working in your favor.

Chart wise, although I use all the intraday time period charts that Jea employs (1-, 3-, 5-, 8-, 13-, and 60-minute), I usually focus on the 1-, 3-, 13-, and 60-minute. This is as much a function of experience and context as anything else. At different times and with different stocks, I might use them all. Take a look at Figure C.1, which is the WFC 1-minute intraday chart illustrating a bounce coil off an extended bearish trending range. In other words, the stock has been trending down, but is currently bouncing off a temporary bottom and attempting to recover. Even though it's attempting to bounce, the stock has been on a negative downtrend, and is in the lower end of its recent trading range extreme. One could think opposing outcomes were very possible here—it could finally recover well off its lows (and being primarily an extreme-reversal player, that's what I would normally be looking for), or it could continue its downtrend after a short

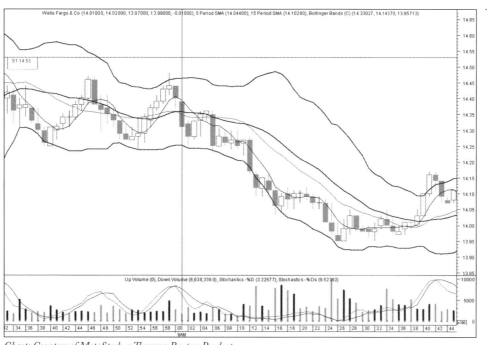

Figure C.1

WFC 1-Minute Bounce Coil off Bearish Range

For a closer look, please visit TradersLibrary.com/ TLECorner.

Charts Courtesy of MetaStock, a Thomson Reuters Product.

Figure C.2

WFC 3-Minute
Resistance

For a closer
look, please visit
TradersLibrary.com/
TLECorner.

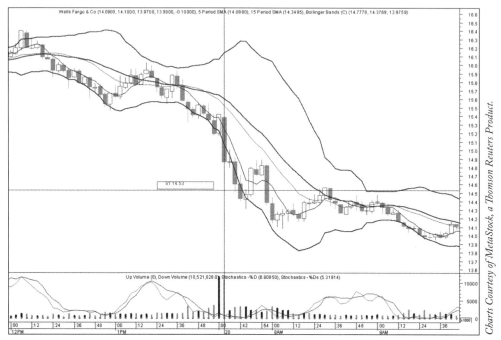

Charts Courtesy of MetaStock, a Thomson Reuters Product.

respite. I certainly wasn't convinced that this first bounce coil was the start of anything lasting, but let's see why I also didn't think it was yet ready to resume its downtrend.

As usual, we need to observe other time periods besides the 1-minute chart, as well as futures charts (both Jea and I use the e-mini futures contract) in respective time periods. WFC is 2 candlesticks into a downturn off its coil high after meeting resistance at the upper Bollinger band on the 1-minute chart. Figure C.2, the 3-minute chart, shows corresponding resistance at the 15-period simple moving average line. The futures are showing similar resistance at the upper Bollinger band on the 1-minute futures chart in Figure C.3., and the 15-period simple moving average line on the 3-minute chart in Figure C.4. Still, the stock hasn't really tested even its 5-period simple moving average resistance on the 13-minute chart (see Figure C.5). Although I don't have an example of the 13-minute futures chart for this exact moment in time, the futures weren't even close to testing even their 5-period simple moving average resistance. More on this to follow.

However, let's look forward in time a few minutes and view the 1-minute WFC and futures charts (Figures C.6 and C.7). The stock has continued to move back down with the futures. Having missed the bounce coil, have I subsequently missed a resumption of the trend back down?

Figure C.3

1-Minute
Futures
Resistance

Charts Courtesy of MetaStock, a Thomson Reuters Product.

Figure C.4

3-Minute
Futures
Resistance

Charts Courtesy of MetaStock, a Thomson Reuters Product.

Figure C.5
WFC
13-Minute
Without
Resistance

For a closer
look, please visit
TradersLibrary.com/
TLECorner.

Charts Courtesy of MetaStock, a Thomson Reuters Product.

Figure C.6

WFC 1-Minute
Down

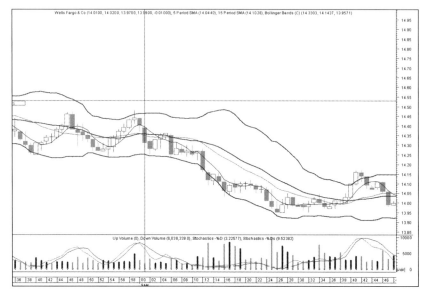

Charts Courtesy of MetaStock, a Thomson Reuters Product.

Figure C.7

1-Minute
Futures Down

Charts Courtesy of MetaStock, a Thomson Reuters Product.

Figure C.8

WFC 1-Minute
Up

For a closer
look, please visit
TradersLibrary.com/
TLECorner.

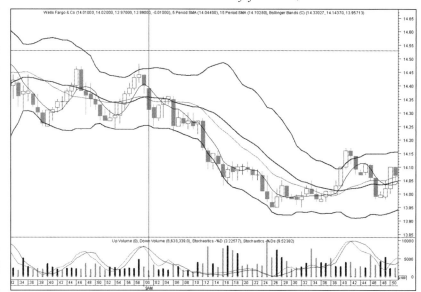

Charts Courtesy of MetaStock, a Thomson Reuters Product.

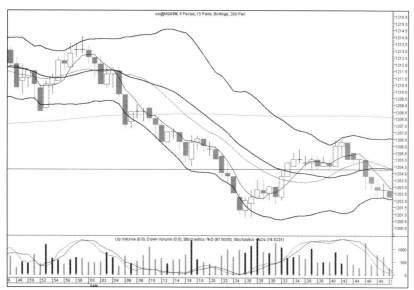

Charts Courtesy of MetaStock, a Thomson Reuters Product.

Figure C.9

1- Minute
Futures Up

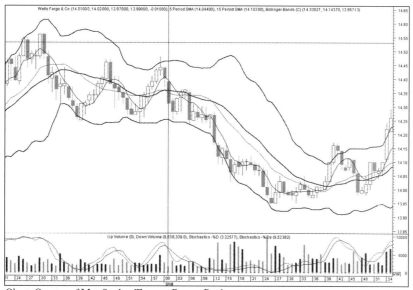

Charts Courtesy of MetaStock, a Thomson Reuters Product.

Figure C.10

WFC 1-Minute
Pop

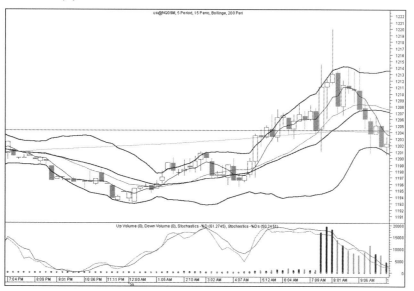

Charts Courtesy of MetaStock, a Thomson Reuters Product.

Figure C.11

13-Minute
Futures
Without
Resistance

For a closer
look, please visit
TradersLibrary.com/
TLECorner.

Weakness has continued, but there's a missing component that we haven't really paid much attention to yet that can play an important role. So let's move forward a few more minutes in time. If we now look at Figures C.8 and C.9, WFC and the futures have started to edge up.

Wait a few minutes more (Figure C.10), and WFC continues a legitimate pop upwards.

Remember our brief mention earlier of the 13-minute futures chart not even close to testing the 5-period simple moving average resistance? Look at Figure C.11 at this later moment in time—it still hasn't effectively tested its 5-period simple moving average resistance. In other words, it's logical that WFC would make an attempt to recover off its low until the futures resolved the longer-term trend. Likewise, if it does test and break above the 5-period line, WFC's bounce might have some continued legs. And Jea's trend trader would have a potential breakout to play upwards. For the reversal player like myself, I've missed the coil, so I decide to wait through this oscillation and hold out for a potential short-term peak to exhaust. If the 13-minute futures 5-period trendline confirms it, I would subsequently attempt to short WFC for a move to the downside.

The bottom line is this: although a trader could make money with quick and disciplined entries and exits in all of these stages, it's important to never lose sight of the forest for the trees. The 1-, 3-, 5-, and 8-minute charts are your trees. The 13- and 60-minute charts provide your view of the forest. Because the 13-minute futures trend hasn't yet resolved whether it wants to confirm the bounce recovery for itself, and subsequently WFC (assuming it is following and not fading the futures), you need more clarity before making a move.

Let's now move forward an hour. WFC has successfully oscillated its recovery coil upward with help from the futures. On its 1-minute chart (Figure C.12), WFC has had an initial peak on a healthy upward oscillation and has not been able to hold a secondary bounce back up. The futures are starting to ease fairly well on their 1- and 3-minute charts (Figures C.13 and C.14), and the futures 13-minute chart previously referred to in Figure C.11 is still effectively in a make-or-break situation since the most recent candle is at risk of giving up the 5-period trendline. I'm starting to see this as an upper extreme to reverse to the downside.

Charts Courtesy of MetaStock, a Thomson Reuters Product.

Figure C.12

WFC 1-Minute
Upward
Oscillation

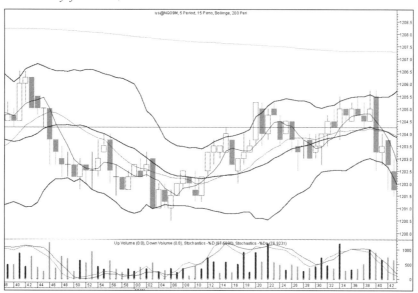

Charts Courtesy of MetaStock, a Thomson Reuters Product.

Figure C.13

1-Minute
Futures Ease

Charts Courtesy of MetaStock, a Thomson Reuters Product.

Figure C.14

3-Minute
Futures Ease

For a closer
look, please visit
TradersLibrary.com/
TLECorner.

Figure C.15

WFC 3-Minute
Support

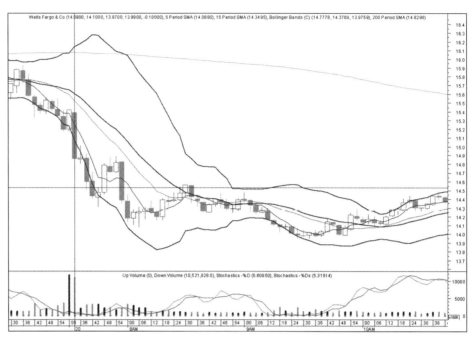

Charts Courtesy of MetaStock, a Thomson Reuters Product.

Figure C.16

WFC 1-Minute
Volume Surge

For a closer
look, please visit
TradersLibrary.com/
TLECorner.

Charts Courtesy of MetaStock, a Thomson Reuters Product.

Charts Courtesy of MetaStock, a Thomson Reuters Product.

Figure C.17

WFC 1-Minute
Drop

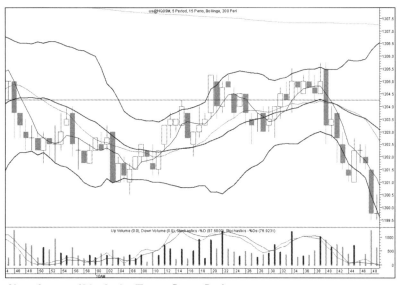

Charts Courtesy of MetaStock, a Thomson Reuters Product.

Figure C.18

1-Minute
Futures Drop

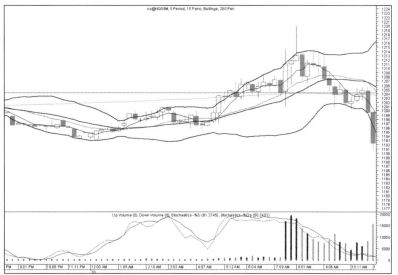

Charts Courtesy of MetaStock, a Thomson Reuters Product.

Figure C.19

13-Minute
Make-or-Break

For a closer
look, please visit
TradersLibrary.com/
TLECorner.

The only caveat is the WFC 3-minute chart (Figure C.15) is showing potential support from its 15-period trendline that could turn into a pup breakout if WFC is able to coil. I decide to short 1000 shares of WFC at $14.33 (with a $0.05 stop-loss at the ready), evenly splitting the spread between the bid and ask. WFC cooperates by immediately dropping below $14.30 (Figure C.16) on a surge in volume.

WFC and the futures continue their drop (Figures C.17 and C.18) and I pare out 200 shares, covering at $14.22.

No matter what size allocation you are playing on your trades, paring out profitable shares on both longs and shorts are your safety cushions. I'm now "playing with the house's money" and can feel comfortable attempting to get more out of the downward oscillation. If WFC suddenly bounds back up and I have to exit, I'm still positive on a failed premise.

In my mind, I have placed a mental stop on the remaining shares back at $14.28 if WFC coils back up. Note that although the most recent candle is under the 5-period line, the WFC 13-minute chart could still be considered to be in a make-or-break situation (Figure C.19), and WFC could easily reverse back up with a corresponding futures move.

Fortunately for me, WFC (and the futures) continue a strong downward move, culminating with WFC testing and breaking under the $14.00 round number level to $13.98 (Figures C.20 and C.21).

When WFC reclaims the $14.00 level on a futures coil, I close out the remaining 800 shares at $14.02 for a $0.31 gain. When including the other 200 shares pared out earlier, the total trade is profitable at $270 before commissions and fees. In retrospect, the final exit was a good one, as WFC continues up to the $14.10 level (Figure C.22) and actually beyond as the futures started to recover.

As a result, it was wise for me to accept that I had missed the original coil long at the lower extreme, and not chase the coil upwards. Likewise, if the futures had been more robust to the upside in their make-or-break situation, that could have easily changed the premise. However, waiting for an upper extreme area reinforced by longer-term futures resistance levels paid off with the best move of all, as WFC and the futures continued the prevailing trend move downwards.

Figure C.20

WFC 1-Minute Down

Charts Courtesy of MetaStock, a Thomson Reuters Product.

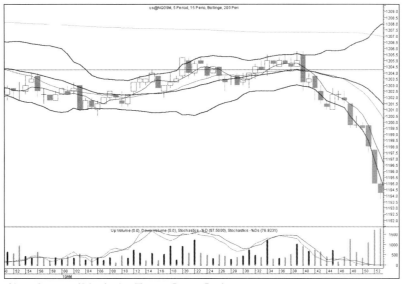

Figure C.21

1-Minute Futures Down

Charts Courtesy of MetaStock, a Thomson Reuters Product.

Figure C.22

WFC 1-Minute Up

For a closer look, please visit TradersLibrary.com/ TLECorner.

Charts Courtesy of MetaStock, a Thomson Reuters Product.

Even so, the irony is that money could be made under several scenarios. However, those in-between areas in the ranges can be very choppy, and as a result, I prefer to wait for the extreme ends of intraday ranges.

Long slow grinds in either direction are tough to read and require an especially disciplined and focused stop-loss process to keep from getting caught in a potential reversal. Stocks and the futures are normally inherently elastic, meaning that within limits, they don't usually go up or down without reversals at extreme ends of price ranges.

The bottom line: Using longer-term intraday charts in tandem with shorter-term versions can help to improve your odds for successful trading.

ABOUT JEA YU

JEA YU is president and co-founder of UndergroundTrader.com, the premiere active trader and self directed investor chat room and training site that has served over 10,000 traders, fund managers, and investors worldwide since 1999. His brainchild was voted *Forbes' Magazine's* Best of the Web for four consecutive years under the active trader category.

Mr. Yu has published two best sellers through McGraw-Hill—*Undergroundtrader.com Guide to Electronic Trading*, 2001 and *Secrets of the Undergroundtrader, 2003,* as well as two popular trading videos titled *Level II Warfare* and *Beating the Bear* published through Marketplace Books and Traders' Library.

He has been a featured speaker all over the country at various expos and seminars, enjoying a standing room-only reception in the largest convention halls from New York to Las Vegas. He is also a featured speaker for the prestigious International Speakers Bureau, demanding up to $10,000 per hour. Jea's energetic presentation style, along with his obvious mastery of the materials being covered, makes him an audience favorite. He has been quoted in *USA Today*, the *Wall Street Journal*, and the *Financial*

Times, as well as numerous articles through various trade publications. Online Investor magazine labeled Jea Yu as "an enigmatic online stock prophet." Mr. Yu is an active contributing writer for TradingMarkets.com, with over 60 articles to his credit.

With over ten years of market experience through bull mania and bear manic markets, Mr. Yu has developed a complete proprietary synergistic trading and investment methodology that incorporates multiple technical filters added to converging time frames to produce a foreshadowing element to market trends. By always having a finger on the pulse of the markets and shifting with the market paradigms, Mr. Yu has stayed on the cutting edge of strategy development. Mr. Yu's philosophy of the markets can be summed up in the following statements: "The name of the game is to find transparency before it becomes too transparent. The goal is to capture the profits before the window of opportunity shuts. When full transparency has hit the markets, the window of opportunity has closed."

Mr. Yu holds a Bachelor of Arts in Liberal Arts from of the University of Maryland.

GLOSSARY

Add/Pare: This means to add shares to a position that initially moves against your initial entry. It is very important that you are only adding shares, because the wider time frames support your trade via trend support. Add/paring means you are weathering the shorter time frames in support of the wider time frames eventually playing out. When played correctly, the added shares result in a better average cost per share, usually accumulating into a panic. It is critical to decrease the position right into the shorter time frame reversals.

Arrogance: Same thing as confidence minus the humility.

Backfill: A very short-term and limited price action that partially recovers from a quick price panic. Backfills are usually a second chance to take a stop loss on a trade, as long as the trader is aware that the backfill is temporary.

Bleed (or Pepper) Out: Means to exit a position into the momentum via small size increments as the price moves. It is the same as paring out or scaling out. Traders who do this want to maximize gains while minimizing market impact.

Buy-Fade: Refers to a stock that is moving higher against falling e-minis futures, indexes and or correlated peer stocks within their sector (for example: MS price rising as GS and S/P 500 e-minis are falling in price). Make sure that you are correctly seeing the divergence evidenced in opposing chart patterns as well. A buy-fade will usually result in a stronger price surge once the futures reverse back up.

Channels: The price trading range of a stock's trend measured between the 5-period simple moving average and the 15-period simple moving average.

Chop: Erratic price action lacking sustained price follow-through; also referred to as wiggles, head fakes, and crap.

Clip: Same as a scalp. In and out.

Cobra, Cobracharts, CobraIQ: www.cobratrading.com, the best online trading broker and platform.

Coil: A short-term reversal bounce referring to price or indicator, like a stochastics similar to a coiled spring.

Coil Resistance: The static price resistance area on peaks at sticky 2.50 and 5 upper range levels (e.g., 12.60, 45.60) as well as the .30 and .75 default price resistances on price peaks on tier 1 leaders (e.g., AAPL 188.30, 188.75). These 0.30 and 0.75 levels are support when stock is trading above, and resistance when stock is trading below.

Coil Support: The static price support area on pullbacks through the sticky 2.50 or 5 levels (e.g., 12.40, 45.40), as well as the 0.30 and 0.75 default price supports on pullbacks on tier 1 leaders. (e.g., AAPL 186.75 coil support)

Convergence: Refers to indicators and or methods that are moving in or pointing to the same direction.

Core Stock: New term for basket stock. These are stocks that are correlated with the markets and traded daily unless markets are sideways sucking.

Deadzone: The time period usually from 11:30 a.m. to 2:00 p.m. EST where the lightest volume of the day resides. This period usually has a lot of chop on light volume. While deadzone may produce some trending moves, it's much tougher to find liquidity and solid follow-through consistently during this period. Try to avoid this time period.

Divergence/Diverging: Refers to stocks, indexes, or futures that normally move in the same direction when they are actively moving in opposite directions. The divergence will revert back to normal correlation in time. Divergence is also indicated with buy or sell fades. Spotting divergences allows a trader to prepare for the reversion back to correlation.

Dual Mini Pups or Dual Mini Inverse Pups: Two different time frame charts that both have a mini pup pattern. The key is to use these as a foreshadowing tool and time the trigger for entry on the shorter time frames.

Ego: Immortal enemy to every trader, just as bad as conventional wisdom. Usually enters into the picture when trader gets overconfident or too optimistic.

Exhaustion: A price peaking point resulting in a reversal back to support levels. Countertrend scalps tend to short exhaustion peaks and buy exhaustion bottoms via shooting stars and hammer candles. Exhaustions are simply a reversion back to the mean and initially, counter trend action. Be careful not to overstay an exhaustion trade after the trend support (usually the 5-period moving average) is tested and resumes (usually resulting in a mini pup).

Flat Action/Market: Tight and light, limp, infertile, suck, same as consolidations. Describes price action that chops and wiggles a lot but can't maintain gains or losses long enough for the 5- and 15-period moving averages to form a trend. The 5- and 15-period moving averages indicate this on the chart by moving sideways with no trading channel.

Follow-through: Describes a price action that forms a direct move with minimal wiggles. Follow-through has trend, volume, liquidity, and price movement. This is what makes a market fertile to a trader. (For example, RIMM breaking out from 87 to 87.60 on a 5-minute mini pup without even testing the 5-period moving average on a single 1-minute stochastics oscillation from the 30 to the 90 band).

Grind: A slow and steady trending price movement. The shorter time frame charts tend to look choppy, as the price gains are minimal, but the wider time frames—the 8-, 13-, and 60-minute—give a better view of the overall trend. Grinds are very tough for oscillation scalpers as there is little room for exhaustion and the trend moves are short-lived as well when trying to scalp. Stocks that grind are best ranged or swung with the wider time frame charts.

Hammer: A bullish reversal candlestick that forms at the end of a final panic sell off. The tail or shadow should be two or more times the length of the body and have hit the lowest price on the downtrend. A hammer is the first sign that a downtrend has bottomed and is staging a trend reversal. Hammers should have three or more red, bearish candles prior to forming. The confirmation of a hammer usually comes on the next candle that follows the hammer, which should close above the closing price of the hammer. This is the opposite of a star or shooting star candlestick.

Head fakes: A price move that quickly reverses right through supports. These usually happen in flat channels and consolidations.

High-Band Mini Pup or Low-Band Mini Inverse Pup: These are mini pups that trigger through the 80 band for the high-band mini pups, or through the 20 band for the low-band mini inverse pups. These are most significant on the 1-minute chart stochastics, as they are indicative of a final capitulation move before exhaustion and traders absolutely need to be locking profits into the move, before the stochastics exhaust and cross back through the 80 and 20 bands.

Inside Bid/Ask: The first position price on the bid or ask. Inside bid/ asks provide liquidity. Providing liquidity by selling into the buyers on the inside ask or covering into sellers on the inside bid makes an impact on commissions through rebates if you use the ECNs (as opposed to specialists or market makers).

Leading Indicator or Stock: As the name implies, these instruments make the initial moves and pull the rest of the correlated instruments. The futures are a lead indicator for stocks. POT is usually a lead mover to MOS. The lead movers are usually the leaders in the sector as well.

Leans: A fast and hard panic sell off. Leans happen on 1-minute low band mini inverse pups for a final panic selloff. These are ideal profit-taking opportunities to cover shorts.

Make-or-Breaks: A chart setup that has the potential for a breakout pup or breakdown mini inverse pup. These are usually choppy with light volume. It is best to wait out the confirmed direction of the make-or-break and then step in for the trade.

Mini Pup: A stochastics pattern where the lead stochastics stalls as the stock price stalls and tests the 5-period moving average. If the 5-period moving average successfully holds support and reverses back in the direction of the trend, then the lead stochastics will slope in the direction of the move, triggering an explosive price move towards the Bollinger bands (upper bands on uptrends and lower bands on downtrends). The 5-period moving averages are the trail stop supports.

Momo = Momentum: Heavy volume + extended follow-through + extreme price move. Momentum hits individual stocks or flows down in specific sectors from the leaders to the turds.

Noodles: These are the Nasdaq 100 e-minis futures, used as a lead indicator for tech stocks. These are usually correlated to the markets and spoos.

Overlap Supports/Resistances: Price level where two or more indicators converge to show support or resistance depending on where the stock is trading (above means support and stock trading below means it is a resistance). The more overlaps within a 0.20 increment, the stronger that area is.

Overshoot: This is a price action where a stock will temporarily dip below a support level before bouncing back up and vice versa on downtrends where a stock will temporarily pop through a resistance before resuming back down.

Pare In, Pare Out, Add/Pare, Clip/Pare: Paring means to incrementally build or decrease your trade position by piecing it in smaller sizes and different price levels. Paring allows one to proportionately maximize gains while minimizing risk on exits. Paring also improves the average price per share when accumulating a position. Paring is best done when adding shares based on the wider time frames while utilizing the shorter time frames (the 1- and 3-minute charts) to accumulate at a discount. It is absolutely important that you are paring with the trend, not against it. You are adding on the short-term divergence to profit from the eventual convergence with the longer time frame. This is the same thing as scaling.

Peak: This is price action where a high is made and sells off, usually indicated with a shooting star candle.

Perfect Storms: This is the most powerful trade setup that forms when three or more different time frame charts produce a pup or mini pup formation. The price action results in an explosive trend move triggered by the shorter time frames converging with the direction of the perfect storm, usually the 1-minute stochastics cross in the direction.

Pup: A moving average pattern where the 5-period moving average goes flat as stock price exhausts, while the 15-period moving average continues to trend. The channel gets tighter and causes steam to build. Eventually the stochastics will cross back up, causing shorts to squeeze and buyers to come in off the fence for an explosive breakout and trend resumption on uptrends, and vice versa on downtrends (stochastics cross down and candles close under the 5-period moving averages). Breakouts on uptrends are pups, while breakdowns on downtrends are called inverse pups.

Range Trade: A position trade with smaller allocation of shares relative to a scalp, usually ½ to ¼ the size to capture a larger price movement anchored to a wider time frame trend chart like the 8-, 13-, 60-minute, or daily chart.

Rejection: This is a price action where a stock will test a support or resistance level and fail to exceed, causing it to reverse back the other way.

Reserve Order: Placing a buy or sell trade order that displays a smaller amount of shares that is trying to be traded. Reserve orders are placed so as to not dampen the momentum by displaying a large order against the move. Reserve orders are meant to deceive traders into assuming less liquidity than there really is.

Rug Pull: A rapid price fall induced by bids being pulled, resulting in an immediate panic sell-off.

Scalp/Clip: A high probability short-term trade to capture quick profits on a direct direction movement, with the goal of exiting seamlessly into maximum liquidity with minimal market impact. Scalps are allocated a larger amount of shares for the immediate and smaller price movement. Scalps have the shortest duration of hold time to offset the risk inherent when holding a position too long. Scalps target 0.04-0.25 profits (depending on the price of the stock), and the holding time is measured in minutes and focuses mostly on entry and exit based on the 1-minute chart triggers.

Sell-Fade: Refers to a stock that is moving lower against rising e-minis futures, indexes, and/or correlated peer stocks within their sector. A stock that is sell-fading will drop harder once futures reverse back down.

Short Squeeze: This is a price action where a stock makes an extreme and extended high volume price movement with very little exhaustion. Short squeezes usually tend to trigger at overbought areas as shorts get squeezed and forced to cover (buy) to cut losses. Short squeezes go parabolic on heavy volume as panic causes a buying frenzy.

Spoos: These are the S&P 500 e-minis futures, used as a lead indicator for the financials. These are usually correlated to the markets and noodles.

Star/Shooting Star: This is a bearish reversal candlestick that forms at the peak of an uptrend. A star should have three or more bullish candles prior to forming. The tail or shadow should be two or more times the length of the body and have hit the highest price point on the trend. Stars form at price peaks and indicate exhaustion as price sells off. The star is confirmed when the next candle closes below the body close of the star.

Stochastics: A momentum indicator composed of lead and laggard stochastics oscillators (%d and %dslow). The settings are 15, 3, 5 on most trading platforms.

Sympathy Stock/Play/Trade: A sympathy stock is loosely correlated to its sector. This is similar to a laggard play. The difference is that the sympathy trade only forms when the sector is extremely strong or weak and the market starts to correlate the stock. News plays are where sympathy trades tend to form. Laggards are already correlated and move with the sector regularly. Sympathy trades are detached unless there is an extreme movement where money looks for lesser known sector plays.

Three Lane Highway: This is a converging directional indicator where three different time frame stock charts are moving in the same direction both with trend and stochastics direction (e.g., 13-, 8-, and 3-minute charts uptrending with all three stochastics moving up).

Tip/Took Profits Too Early: This term is used when leaving profits on the table due to early exits. While this is may be misconstrued as selling too early, the reality is that you are selling into plenty of liquidity. Taking profits "too early" is not a sin and if done consistently, it is a blessing. Consistency revolves around being able to take profits early and if you are consistently taking those profits, then scaling is all that's left. Taking profits early is a sign of risk averseness and control—not to be mistaken for fear. If done consistently and regularly, the fear is not a factor. It's when a trader punishes himself because he is taking profits early consistently, that it becomes detrimental. Never demonize yourself for taking profits. Can you take more profits? Sure, hindsight is 20/20. But to assume afterwards that you should have held a full-scaled scalp position for a full channel move, especially if the 1-minute stochastics peaked and oscillated, is mismanagement. Just remember, it is great to leave a tip, a nice big tip. It applies in restaurants and it applies in the markets. It's karma. Ever pray for your stock to breakout? You gotta leave something in the offering tray to be heard. Taking profits early is not a problem, taking profits or losses late is. It's ironic that people don't complain about taking losses too early.

Turd: Stocks that are the bottom of the barrel of their sectors and heavily discounted by the market. Turds usually are priced under $5. These stocks may have been former high flyers (e.g., TASR, CROX) that caused a lot of bagholders. Turds tend to move at the tail end of an extreme sector move or on news.

Wiggles: A price movement that reverses quickly just as it appears that a trend may be forming. Wiggles, head fakes, and chop are all synonymous and found in consolidations, tight markets, and make-or-breaks.

Wiggle Room: This is the amount of price pullback you give your position before triggering a stop loss. Gauging wiggle room takes experience and a feel for the stock. Wiggle room can be very tricky if the market or trend is a choppy one where the 5-period moving averages are constantly being overshot but closing just above so as to maintain the trend. Wiggle room should be based on the excess amount of price movement through a support or resistance level. It also depends on the rhythm and price of a stock. Larger priced stocks tend to require more wiggle room (e.g., GOOG) while cheaper priced stocks require less (e.g., BAC). Basic rule of thumb is to give 0.10-0.20 wiggle room off a 5-period moving average support on trending stocks, depending on how thin the stock is.

INDEX

"cockroaches," 55-56

cognitive dissonance theory, 9, 33, 38, 82

containment zones

daily trading model, 69-71

overview of, 69

pump release pacing method, 71-72

convergence, defined, 91

Crab patterns, 243, 244, 247

D

deadzone

in basic training, 149, 150, 151

market activity, 15, 64-65, 70, 211

and physical activity during, 38-39, 59

Death Takes a Vacation, 7

decimalization system, vii, ix, 11, 28

demand elasticity, 19

deprivation, 16, 47-48, 82, 151

"dinosaurs," 54-55

divergence, defined, 91

DOW e-mini futures, 251, 255, 270, 279

Dow Jones Industrial Average, 10, 56, 60-61

dragonfly candles, defined, 96

Duddella, Suri, on harmonic pattern trading, 235-50

dumper stocks (*see* gapper and dumper stocks)

duplicity inflection time points, 66-67

E

earnings reports trading

deadzone and last hour considerations, 211

market open, 209-11

post-market reaction, 207-8

pre-earnings anticipation longs, 225-26

pre-market, 209

preparation by recording price levels, 205-7

and trading stock halt re-open, 218

using options to leverage, 221

ECN (*see* electronic communication networks (ECN))

the "edge," defined, 77

ego, 12-13, 19-20, 32-35, 37-38

electronic communication networks (ECN)

defined, 84

fees and rebates, 84-85, 90, 200, 201

hidden and reserve orders, 85-86

history of, ix, 12, 28